BODIES IN F

# Bodies in Pain

## *Emotion and the Cinema of Darren Aronofsky*

Tarja Laine

berghahn
NEW YORK · OXFORD
www.berghahnbooks.com

First edition published in 2015 by
Berghahn Books
www.berghahnbooks.com

**Library of Congress Cataloging-in-Publication Data**

Laine, Tarja.
  Bodies in pain : emotion and the cinema of Darren Aronofsky / Tarja Laine.
    pages cm
  Includes bibliographical references and index.
  Includes filmography.
  ISBN 978-1-78238-575-2 (hardback : alk. paper) — ISBN  978-1-78533-
      521-1 paperback — ISBN 978-1-78238-576-9 (ebook)
  1.  Aronofsky, Darren—Criticism and interpretation.   2.  Emotions in
motion pictures.   I.  Title.
  PN1998.3.A7615L36 2015
  791.4302′33092—dc23

                                                      2014029569

**British Library Cataloging in Publication Data**
A catalogue record for this book is available from the British Library

ISBN: 978-1-78238-575-2 hardback
ISBN  978-1-78533-521-1 paperback
ISBN: 978-1-78238-576-9 ebook

# Contents

# Figures

# Acknowledgements

Many friends and colleagues have contributed to this book in countless helpful ways. The idea to write a book about emotion and film aesthetics in the cinema of Darren Aronofsky was proposed to me by Mark Stanton, then senior editor at Berghahn Books. To him I extend my gratitude for having initiated the project. Many thanks also to Adam Capitanio and Elizabeth Berg at Berghahn Books, for all their support and assistance in preparing my manuscript for publication. Among all the people who have offered useful comments, my special thanks must go to Robert Sinnerbrink, not only for numerous inspiring conversations, but also for reading the original book proposal as well as parts of the manuscript. In addition, I am gratefully indebted for constructive suggestions to Laura Copier, Tim Evans, Tina Kendall, Toni Mazel, Susanna Paasonen, Patricia Pisters, Kathleen Scott and Jane Stadler. Many thanks also to all those who commented on the various stages of my project in different seminars and conferences. In particular, the editorial board of the journal *Film-Philosophy* and their annual conference have been a crucial sounding board for this project – thank you all. I am also extremely grateful to the anonymous peer reviewers of this book for providing invaluable feedback, encouragement and suggestions on how to complete the manuscript. But most personally and affectionately I want to thank Charles France, who, for some years now, has generously read, commented on and argued with the ideas presented in the pages that follow. It is to him that I am most indebted for the existence of this book, and it is therefore to him that this book is dedicated.

# Aronofsky, Auteurship, Aesthetics

After the twentieth century's predominantly ocular-centric understanding of cinema, 'cinema of the senses' and 'cinema of the body' have become new catchphrases in film studies over the last two decades. In what could be called a carnal understanding of cinema, emphasis is placed on the lived experience and sensation, while vision and cognition are often understood in terms of affect and embodiment. Tim Palmer defines this type of film as the 'cinema of brutal intimacy', characterized by 'bold stylistic experimentation' and 'a fundamental lack of compromise in its engagement with the viewer', demanding 'a viscerally engaged experiential participant' (Palmer 2006: 64, 172). Cinema of the body exploits the ability of the filmic medium to induce vivid, truculent sensations and unsettling aesthetic experiences. Thus, one cannot help but shiver in involuntary terror and pain when witnessing the feverish climax of Darren Aronofsky's *Requiem for a Dream* (2000). Here, graphic scenes of sexual abuse interweave with physical and emotional torment, accompanied by images of decaying flesh. These scenes are presented to the spectators by means of a cacophonic interplay of various dissonant aesthetic elements that directly engage the spectators' bodies in particularly disturbing fashion. Repulsive to watch, yet impossible to avert one's eyes from, this climax is perhaps the ultimate instance of cinema of the body.

The phrase *cinema of the body* is normally used to indicate the aesthetic style of such French filmmakers as Catherine Breillat, Claire Denis, Philippe Grandrieux, Gaspar Noé and Marina de Van. But it is equally relevant for understanding the cinema of, for example, Andrea Arnold, David Cronenberg, Michael Haneke, David Lynch and Lars von Trier.[1] The corporeal aesthetics of 'body cinema' are best characterized as affective, immediate and sensuous. It is a cinematic style that aims at bodily immersion and affective sharing within the cinematic event. This is not brought about by identification with the film's characters, but through the spectator's full participation in the 'life-space' of the film. As Bruce Isaacs argues, 'cinema . . . is an inherently participatory art' (Isaacs 2008: 77). The sensuous quality of body cinema triggers deeply felt physical and affective responses, both on the pre-reflective and the (self-)

reflective levels of consciousness (Laine 2011). For the purposes of this book, the cinema of the body is defined as a sensuous bodily event that offers the spectator the chance to participate in it by means of its affective-aesthetic system. I shall focus on the cinema of Darren Aronofsky and on how his films engage the spectator's lived body by means of their sheer corporeal film style. Aronofsky as a filmmaker could be also considered 'cerebral', insofar as his films often explore such topics as mathematics, madness, hallucinations, obsessions, social anxiety, addiction, psychosis, schizophrenia and neuroscience. Yet this interest in intelligence and mental processes in Aronofsky's films is deeply embedded in the affective operations of the body, shared with the spectator by means of cinematic gestures and postures. As Jennifer Barker explains, this process of sharing is based on the spectator's close bodily connection with cinema in 'texture, spatial orientation, comportment, rhythm and vitality' (Barker 2009: 2).

As far as the body is concerned, Aronofsky is a very special filmmaker. His films are full of tension-filled conflicts between body and mind, bodily (self-) injuries and cognitive disorders. There are combinations of bodily experience and technology as 'extensions of man' involving computers, televisions and microscopes, but also conflicts between psychological expression and bodily performance (wrestling, ballet). He is fond of cinematic techniques that aim at sensorial and bodily engagement. There are hip-hop montages with accompanying sound effects (scratching, sampling). He often uses extremely tight framing, lengthy follow shots and SnorriCam. He also alternates between extreme close-ups and extreme long shots to create a sense of isolation. He favours alternative special effects, such as the macro photography combined with fluid dynamics used in *The Fountain* (2006). For his biblical tale *Noah* – which is in production at the time of writing – Aronofsky had a full-scale ark constructed in order to avoid computer-generated imagery. But others of his films boast abundant visual effects. In *Black Swan* (2010), painted, photorealistic images of a baby bird's skin and quills had to be tracked digitally to an actress's arm, while a camera vividly rotated around her body during the climax of the film.[2]

Four of Aronofsky's actors have received Oscar nominations for best performance – Ellen Burstyn, Mickey Rourke, Marisa Tomei and Natalie Portman, who also won the award. In cinema in general, and perhaps in Aronofsky's films in particular, it is the physical performance of the actors that enables the spectator to grasp the attributes and affects of specific characters. As Vivian Sobchack puts it, it is the actor's lived body that makes the character intelligible, because the character's 'inner' experience is only manifest through the actor's 'outer' performance (Sobchack 2012: 434). As the same time, such performance is inextricably intertwined with the aesthetic specificity of the film. In other words, the performance of the actors is incorporated into the film's performance. This means that there is reciprocity among their bodily energy, affect, rhythm, valence and the very same attributes of the film's aesthetic system. Thus Rourke's physical on-screen performance in *The Wrestler* (2009) becomes the vehicle for the protagonist's masochistic exposure and self-deception in and through interaction with the cinematic aesthetics, e.g. the setting, the close-ups. In *Black Swan*, Portman's performance embodies a doubling rather than an enactment of character, reciprocated by the film's digital aesthetics, in which a human being is doubled by an animal. This is enhanced by 'actorly transformation', a self-imposed alteration of the body, which not only lends greater fidelity to Portman's performance (Esch 2006), but also draws an analogy between Portman and the self-mutilating dancer Nina in the film. Another example is found in *Requiem for a Dream*, in which Burstyn inhabits Sara's corporeal rhythm, which is punctuated by specific editing and sound. These augment the spectator's awareness of Sara's bodily pace and cadence as they change in response to her growing addiction to amphetamines. It would, however, require a separate research project altogether to concentrate fully on the performance of screen actors in Aronofsky's films – and in my view, performance is not restricted to what film actors do to create characters. Suffice it to say that while this book concentrates on the performance of cinematic aesthetics, this by no means aims at diminishing the importance of actors' performances. Without their spectacular renditions, the films would be hollow and fleshless.

Acting and performance apart, it is this particular 'hybrid' quality of his films that has made Aronofsky famous. He blurs the line between fantasy and reality, and employs the signature styles of various genres, such as science fiction, psychological thriller, melodrama, fantasy and body horror. His films often create uncomfortable viewing positions, something already evident in his early works, which have not been released commercially. These are student films entitled *Supermarket Sweep* (1991), *Fortune Cookie* (1991), *Protozoa* (1993) – also the name of Aronofsky's production company – and *No Time* (1994). Unfortunately, despite my best efforts, I have not been able to track down any of these titles, but extracts of *Fortune Cookie* and *No Time* can be found on YouTube.[3] *No Time* depicts two fishermen, framed in a two-shot with a wide-angle lens, attracting fish with one continually repeated, silly line: 'Come on, fish'. *Fortune Cookie* is based on a short story by Hubert Selby Jr., who is also the author of *Requiem for a Dream*, on which Aronofsky based his second commercial film. It features a salesman being harassed by a 'pervert', who fires obscenities at him. These are not merely amusing, but also embarrassing, scenes to watch, because they violate the 'contract of looking' by appearing too strange and unfamiliar to relate to. In 2011 Aronofsky directed the music video for the song 'The View' by Lou Reed and Metallica, which is strongly reminiscent of the aesthetic style of his first feature film, *Pi* (1998). The 'migraine aesthetics' of this black-and-white video are characterized by shaky camerawork, blurry, distorted images, double superimpositions and flashes of engulfing white frames.

Michel Foucault (1977) maintains that an author functions as a classifying principle that serves to constrain, but not to determine the interpretation given to a text by the reader. In this line of thought, the author is not a particular individual, but a discursive function that unifies the reader's perception of the artistic whole of the text. Within film studies, Daniel Frampton has recently proposed that the concept of author should be rejected on the grounds that it denies any film's own 'meaning creativeness', the way in which cinema can be considered its own 'mindscreen' (Frampton 2006: 29–30). Although this is an interesting approach, it fails to take into account the process of *making*, by which things visible in the world are rendered what Mikel Dufrenne terms the sensuous in cinema. The sensuous is the internal organization of the aesthetic object, with affective qualities that enable expressive resonance between the work of art and its perceiver (Dufrenne 1987).[4] It is the very element in a work of art that enables fundamental, affective reciprocity between the aesthetic object and the spectator: 'the sensuous is an act common to both the person who feels and to what is felt' (Dufrenne 1973: 48). The sensuous enables the spectator to respond to the work's 'desire-to-be' in a way that corresponds to the author's engagement with it; both are 'called upon by the work to be done'. In other words, for Dufrenne, the process of making is embedded in the work as the author's 'gesture', in which the spectator takes part by means of 'carnal familiarity' (Dufrenne 1987: 148–49). Therefore I argue that 'author' is still a relevant concept or construct within the affective-aesthetic system that invites co-creative engagement from the spectator. This process is linked to valuing cinema. Aesthetic appreciation of a film seems to be at its most intense when one is somehow able to 'compare' one's own sensory perception and intelligent deliberation with those of the film's 'author' in the very event of cinematic experience. In this context, Paul Crowther writes that we each embody a unique being-in-the-world. This becomes manifest in the quality of an artwork, as it is borne out by the artist in reaction to and while forming the sensuous. It is this particular quality to which we seek to relate in an aesthetic experience by means of engaged reciprocity with the artist 'inscribed' in the work of art (Crowther 1993: 57–59).

In the same vein, I propose that the author be considered an integral part of the process that makes a film what it desires to be, and in which the spectator can participate by engaging with the film as an affective bodily event. This notion understands the author to be a plural and hybrid phenomenon that contains both aesthetic and signifying elements embodied in the film – and nowhere else. Furthermore, this has methodological consequences in that it requires us to reverberate with the embedded 'authorial' gestures of the film. These gestures guide us to think about the affective significance of the film, which prevents us from attempting to master its formal system only. Such 'mastering' is described in Aronofsky's *Pi*, when the protagonist aims to reduce the natural world to the purely intelligible (mathematics) in order to exert control over it. In the process, he loses his sensuous relationship with the world, which has devastating consequences. As Dufrenne writes, 'if [something] becomes an object of knowledge, it is on condition that it be welcomed initially by the body, and perhaps in order to be more intensely savoured by it' (Dufrenne 1987: xi).

My own response to sensuous qualities in the cinema of Aronofsky has brought me to the conclusion that his films are independent of any definable genre or unique signature style. Nevertheless, throughout his oeuvre a certain aesthetic and thematic continuity can be observed. On a stylistic level, there is for instance the specific '"on-location" aesthetics', inspired by places such as Aronofsky's childhood neighbourhood on Coney Island in southern Brooklyn, New York City (*Pi, Requiem for a Dream, The Wrestler*), the NYC subway (*Pi, Requiem for a Dream, Black Swan*), and run-down supermarkets (*Pi, Requiem for a Dream, The Wrestler*). There are also recurring characters such as 'Uncle Hank' (*Fortune Cookie, Pi, Requiem for a Dream, Black Swan*) and the interest in religious elements (*Pi, The Fountain, The Wrestler, Noah*). Furthermore, Aronofsky is known for his extensive use of SnorriCam (*Pi, Requiem for a Dream*), or chestcam, a camera rigged to the actor's body, facing the actor directly. It creates a hyper-subjective effect, 'freezing' the character at the centre of the frame while the background is in constant 'movement'. Aronofsky's famous use of hip-hop montage (*Pi, Requiem for a Dream*) is also a recurring technique that attempts to apply the principles of music sampling to the affective-aesthetic system of film.

On a thematic level, Aronofsky's films are also marked by his constant interest in severely obsessive characters. Their obsessions often lead to a sensuous and affective shutdown that disturbs the relationship between the 'inner' and 'outer' worlds of these characters. This is not merely an issue on the level of cinematic content; it also plays a part in the spectator's emotional engagement with the film as an experiential aesthetic event. As will be re-emphasized throughout this book, Aronofsky's films engage the spectator in an affective form of viewing that involves all the senses. The book can therefore be seen as a contribution to the ever-increasing interest among film scholars in the senses. This interest is driven by the rejection of what is felt to be an unjustified privileging of some of them over others. In Cartesian thinking, it is said, for example, that vision is the sense most in congruence with reason, because it renders us separate from objects in the world. By contrast, the more physical senses of smell, taste, and touch rupture distinct boundaries between the self and the world. In the philosophy of embodiment, a different perception of vision has developed. Starting from the assumption that sight involves more than locating an object of look in space separate from one's viewing position, the emphasis is now on the meaningful, affective relationship between the embodied vision and the material world. Vision is a matter of seeing the objects 'out there' with the whole body as a sense organ entangled with the world 'in here'. Similarly, cinematic experience is simultaneously a matter of distance and proximity (Burnett 2005: 7). True, the spectator has to sit far enough away from the cinema screen in order to see the film's content. But viewing is essentially about affective participation in the cinematic event. As cinema addresses the spectator's imagination through all the senses in ways that are immediately felt in the body, it evokes a mode of vision that is best described as *seeing feelingly*.

In Aronofsky's films, this state of seeing feelingly originates from the spectator's direct engagement with cinematic aesthetics, instead of from, for instance, character identification. It is an interesting paradox in his cinema that all his films plunge deeply into the subjectivity of their characters, but that they do not necessarily invite identification. Perhaps this is because Aronofsky's characters are often damaged, emotionally isolated and psychologically disturbed, which complicates identification. Needless to say, my privileging the aesthetic system when it comes to affective experience in cinema does not entirely justify dismissing character identification as inessential. Such a dismissal would come down to what John Dewey calls the fallacy of selective emphasis (Dewey 1981: 31–32). In this case it would mean drawing the conclusion that the aesthetic system is *all* that is distinctively important in the spectator's affective engagement with cinema. This book tries to avoid the trap of this fallacy, but still shift the focus from character-affinity to aesthetic elements that are less character-bound, and hopes to complement rather than challenge earlier views of affective engagement in cinema.

It would be equally misleading to pay attention only to pure cinematic elements beyond the narrative. As stories are fundamentally organized by emotions (Hogan 2011), writing about the affective functioning of cinema without paying attention to the way in which emotions orient the narrative would be methodologically unwise. On the director's commentary track of *Requiem for a Dream*, Aronofsky explains that as a filmmaker he is 'trying to come up with a visual style that is born out of the narrative . . . trying to figure out what the movie is about and then creating a visual language out of this'. In this particular film, it is the rhythm of visual and auditory cinematic elements in particular that brings the spectator into contact with the subjective state of the characters. He or she observes them in a descending narrative trajectory, in which emotions run from hope through despair to pain and devastation.

I feel that scholarly film practice and methodology should point in the same direction. The scholar's task is less to force (theoretical) interpretations onto films than to understand how their affective dynamics resonate directly. As a result, scholars hopefully become able to grasp the affective significance of a film as it emerges from their bodily experience of the cinematic event. Cognitive theories focus on the structure of film as a formal system of elements that activate the spectator's understanding of the cinematic event as emotionally relevant. In contrast, body-centred approaches, such as the one adopted in this book, regularly emphasize the *experience* of emotional reactions to film. The methodological premise of this book is therefore best described as film-phenomenological. Even though this approach has often been criticized as too impressionistic or overtly subjective, film-phenomenology has especially been useful providing descriptions of our affective and embodied engagement with cinema that can recognizably be shared with others. This is because film-phenomenology is not merely interested in what one sees on screen, but in how films direct one's attention towards what *cannot* be seen. As Julian Hanich explains: 'Phenomenology tries to uncover what is buried in habituation and institutionalization, what is taken for granted and accepted as given, or what we have never been fully aware of in the first place' (Hanich 2010: 15). Furthermore, in film-phenomenology the lived experience and reciprocity between the film and the spectator are an essential part of research. Film-phenomenology differs significantly from those approaches that aim at an impersonal understanding of cinema located 'out there', observed from a position somewhere 'in here'. Instead, film-phenomenology explores the dynamic and reciprocal interaction of the embodied spectator and the cinematic body.

Uncovering this dynamic interaction can only take place by means of 'careful looking' (Ihde 1979), and can only be articulated in terms of direct emotional response to cinema. Combining careful looking with detailed description of their emotional experience, scholars should be able to communicate their views of the film convincingly enough to others, who might accept these views even when they do not share the same interpretation. It must always be kept in mind, though, that any film-phenomenological account of emotional experience must start and end with engagement with a film's aesthetic organization as observed and validated by a wide range of film scholars. In other words, while experiencing aesthetic emotions, one must perceive how this experience emerges from participation in the film's aesthetic organization. A film's aesthetic organization exists objectively and can be analysed systematically, after which meaning can be attributed to it – a process that can be shared and substantiated with others.

Furthermore, I understand the relationship between the spectator and the film as a reciprocal and co-creative process. In order to define emotional engagement with cinema, one needs to examine this reciprocal relationship between the spectator and the film. In this relationship both parties must be considered agents, brought together through the sensuous. This renders cinema a bodily event that activates the spectator's affective and cognitive sensitivities. In other words, neither the formal-stylistic system of film nor the spectator's pre-existing biographical and cultural dispositions alone can sufficiently define cinematic engagement. I understand this engagement to be very much embedded in the body. On the one hand, the affective quality of a film consists of the meaning it embodies. Not only on the level of content, but also on the level of its aesthetic form and audiovisual style, a film is embodied, affective meaning. On the other hand, this affective quality is intentionally present for the spectators in the way the film directs itself towards their own sentient bodies. By this I do not mean to anthropomorphize cinema, i.e. to interpret cinematic *dispositif* in terms of human characteristics, such as the ability to feel emotions; rather, I propose to think of cinema in terms of 'resonant aesthetics', a notion similar to what Jane Bennett (2010) calls 'vibrant matter'. Cinema is vibrant matter insofar as it has agency, efficacy and vitality. Films can do things, produce effects and affects, as well as alter experience. Cinematic matter vibrates and resonates with human matter, and the cinematic event is an energy field in which 'effect and cause alternate positions and redound on each other' nonlinearly (Bennett 2010: 33). Thus, cinema as vibrant matter refers to the affective efficacy of cinema that enables the spectators both to feel and think about the film at the same time, as active, (co-)creative, sensuous agents.

According to Dufrenne, this is the role of our bodies in general. The body is not so much a physical 'apparatus' intended to react to the world in a causal fashion, as it is a sensuous 'instrument' of reciprocity through which the individual encounters the world. This reciprocity is an 'attunement with the world as two musical instruments are in attunement with one another' (Dufrenne 1987: 8). Similarly, Dewey (1958) speaks of art as experience that is inscribed in the sensuous state of the body and registered in and through emotion. Emotions are continuous, intentional and sentient processes that prompt us to synthesize and reorganize our experiences actively in the world. In an aesthetic experience, the spectator's intentional attitude gets entangled with the affective attitude that is embodied in the work of art. This entanglement enables emotional response, which in turn facilitates philosophical reflection – although not necessarily in a linear fashion. This reflection is simultaneously a matter of feeling and thinking, of 'thinking-feelingly' and 'feeling-thoughtfully'. Steven Connor writes that all thinking is a form of affective feeling through the body, the affective body literally caught up in thought: 'Expressing a state of mind or a feeling means formulating an attitude, and in the process forming a relation to that attitude. All feeling involves some element of comportment towards the world and the self, which is to say some measure of taking thought' (Connor 2004: 99).

Furthermore, to think-feelingly is an *active* process of intervention, a matter of *doing* instead of merely knowing. In this context, Karen Barad argues that thinking 'must be understood as an embodied practice, rather than a spectator sport matching . . . representations to pre-existing things' (Barad 2007: 54). Similarly, aesthetic experience is the active embodied entanglement of the spectator with the work of art and vice versa, which involves processes of thinking and feeling. Perhaps it could be said that aesthetic experience is a cyclical process in which our sensuous, bodily, affective and reflective states are inextricably intertwined.[5] Furthermore, this process occurs beyond 'pre-emptive empathy' (Armstrong 2000: 166) towards fictional characters, in the spectator's direct relationship with the work of art. Methodologically, this means that in order to study the sensuous relationship between film and spectator, one needs to ask the following questions:

1.  What is the affective quality that is embodied in the aesthetic system of the film?
2.  What narrative meaning is embedded in that quality?
3.  How is the spectator invited to participate in the sensuous event that is cinema?[6]

The importance of these questions is evident from the quotation below, in which William James describes the centrality of the body in our lived experience

– including the cinematic experience – as opposed to the Cartesian mind/body dualism: 'The body is the storm centre, the origin of coordinates, the constant place of stress in [our] experience-train. Everything circles around it, and is felt from its point of view. The world experienced comes at all times with our body as its centre, centre of vision, centre of action, centre of interest' (James 1976: 86, originally published in 1912). Similarly, for phenomenological philosophers such as Maurice Merleau-Ponty and Simone de Beauvoir, the body is one's 'anchorage in a world' (Merleau-Ponty 2002: 167) or one's 'grasp of the world' (de Beauvoir 2003: 36). For them, the body is central in the dynamic way in which the 'interiority' of the subject entangles with his or her 'exteriority', thus emerging as an active participant in the world's becoming. The here and now of our bodies is the locus of our intentionality, our sentient consciousness, and our emotional and (self-)reflective orientation towards the world. This centrality of the body emphasizes the fundamental unity of body and mind as a cohesive wholeness interacting with the world. Pain is concrete proof of this, as it is a physical sensation, inextricably tied to our emotional experience of it, and as such cancelling out any dualistic assumptions about body and mind (Van Dijkhuizen and Enenkel 2009: 1). Throughout this book I shall use the term *lived-body* to indicate this 'transactional whole of body-mind' (Schusterman 2008: 184) engaging with the world. In film studies, Vivian Sobchack has argued that this notion of lived-body also applies to the relationship between cinema and spectator. In this concept, the film is considered an expression of experience *by* experience. For Sobchack, film is a significant and signifying intentional subject in its own right, engaging the spectators from within their own embodied presence. This means that films make themselves affectively felt and (self-)reflectively known through a reciprocal ground upon which the cinematic expression and the spectator encounter each other as lived bodies:

> Reciprocating the figurally literal representations of bodies and worldly things in the cinema, the spectator's lived body in the film experience engages in the form of sensual catachresis. That is, it fills in the gap in its sensual grasp of the figural world onscreen by turning back on itself to reciprocally (albeit not sufficiently) 'flesh it out' into literal physicalized sense. It is this same reciprocal relationship between the figural and literal that emerges also in our linguistic descriptions of the film experience. (Sobchack 2004: 82)

But one does not even need such 'figurally literal representations of bodies' on screen in order to understand how one reciprocally encounters cinema as a lived-body. Jennifer Barker has recently argued that the corporeal aesthetics of cinema itself addresses the spectator through bodily intimacy and reciprocity, 'through movement, comportment and gesture, in the way [the spectators] carry themselves through the world' (Barker 2009: 69). She stresses that this process is more complex than, for instance, mere bodily mimicry of the characters. The bodily responses of the spectators might be a form of mimicry or – even better – *resonance* between the expressive body of film itself and their own sensate bodies. It is through this fleshy resonance (or dissonance) between cinema and the spectator that thoughts and affects emerge. Susanna Paasonen explains the notion of resonance as follows:

> [Resonance] refers to moments and expressions of being moved, touched, and affected by what is tuned to 'the right frequency'. . . . To resonate with one another, objects and people do not need to be similar, but they need to relate and connect to one another. Resonance encompasses the emotional and cognitive as well as the sensory and affective, and it points to the considerable effort involved in separating the two. (Paasonen 2011: 16)

As already suggested, an obvious objection to this line of argument is the apparent fact that cinema is a technology that comports itself in ways fundamentally different from those of humans. But according to Barker, the similarity can be detected in the way in which

> we and the film both present ourselves to the world by moving through it, carrying ourselves and arranging our bodies a certain way in relation to space and things . . . The film's body and spectator's body exist in a relationship of analogy and reciprocity. Though neither identical, nor completely divergent, the film's body and the viewer's body are irrevocably related to one another. The film's body models itself on human styles of bodily comportment, and the viewer's body in turn might mirror the muscular behaviour of the film's body. (Barker 2009: 77)

I broadly agree with this view, although I think that the word 'mirror' is inappropriately used, for this assumes an intersubjective relationship between cinema and spectator based on distance. In contrast, the term *resonance* suggests an affective relationship between film and spectator that is based on bodily reciprocity. Furthermore, the term *mirror* connotes a transitional relation between the subject and the object in the Lacanian mirror stage, while cinematic experiences are often different from those that arise out of such psychodynamic interplay. Indeed, in the cinematic experience sensuous interplay occurs in various embodied, affective encounters. First, cinema moves us directly within a gamut of emotions, ranging from fear and disgust through adrenaline thrills to laughter and sexual excitement, in ways that are immediately felt by the body. Secondly, as Barker argues, cinema can be described in terms of skin, musculature, and viscera, as if it had a body itself. Different cinematic elements correspond with distinctive bodily characteristics, such as sound (vibration), cinematography (movement), and editing (rhythm). These elements together form an affective-aesthetic whole, which offers itself for the participation of the spectator as an intentional lived-body.[7]

According to Barad, intentionality might better be understood as ascribable to a complex entanglement of human (spectator) and nonhuman (cinematic) agents (Barad 2007: 23). In the context of cinema, this means that the relationship between cinema and spectator can no longer be understood through the model of cinematic apparatus. In this model, the film is enclosed within the frame, while the passive spectator is seated in front of it, in a state of willing suspension of disbelief. With the approach of reciprocal intentionality adopted in this book, cinema and spectator are not separated by the frame; on the contrary, cinema and spectator are both intentional agents, united in an entangled state. As intentional agents, films both embody emotions and possess an emotional attitude towards the spectator. This in turn sensitizes the spectator as an intentional agent with the dual capacity to read the emotions that films embody and react to them.

The aim of this book, then, is to understand the way in which embodied, affective intentionality in the cinema of Aronofsky engages the spectator directly by means of reciprocal attunement. What interests me in Aronofsky's films is that they often disrupt or even shut down this process with important affective consequences for the spectator. For me, one of the most important themes in his work is the notion of 'bodies in pain' as theorized by Elaine Scarry (1985). Therefore, one of the goals of this book is to investigate how such pain is directly 'transmitted' to the spectator, as a phenomenon that is simultaneously a sensation and an emotion (Jackson 1994: 201). For many philosophers of pain, the state of pain disrupts the intentionality of the body; even more keenly, pain disrupts the relationship between the lived-body and the world. In pain, one may experience one's body as an 'alien presence' (Leder 1990: 73) because it appears as strange, or 'other', to one, becoming an object instead of a subject of experience. While in normal circumstances the body is the locus from which one directs one's attention to the world, in pain the body becomes an object to which one attends. This effect of disrupted intentionality may result in the disembodied experience that 'I have a body', instead of an embodied experience that 'I am my body' (Zeiler 2010: 337). Furthermore, in the most extreme situations, such as under torture, one cannot concentrate on anything else other than pain. For Emmanuel Levinas, severe pain subjugates the self so completely that the individual is 'held fast' in pain (Levinas 1981: 52). And for Scarry, in extreme pain the self becomes pain itself, so that the individual experiences the contents of his or her consciousness as 'obliterated' and 'absent', while this pain 'swells to fill the entire universe' (Scarry 1985: 4). In such cases, the individual's whole consciousness is nothing but pain – physical, emotional, psychosomatic – while both the self and the world 'disappear'.

In contrast, for Sobchack pain is a way to bring people 'back to their senses'. Pain can function as a reminder of one's immanence, and of one's physical necessity and inherent 'response-ability'. Referring to Jean Baudrillard's tech-noerotic reading of J.G. Ballard's novel *Crash* (1973), Sobchack wishes that the philosopher had experienced some pain

> to remind him that he doesn't just have a body but that he is his body and it is on this material fact of existence that affect, and anything that we might call an ethical stance, is grounded. [This ethical stance] is based on the lived sense and feeling of the human body not merely as a material object one possesses ... but as a material subject that experiences and feels its own objectivity, that has the capacity to bleed and

suffer and hurt for others because it can sense its own possibilities for suffering and pain. (Sobchack 2004: 178)[8]

Thus two potential insights follow from these differing descriptions of pain. One is the possibility that pain renders the body an object of experience. Another possibility is that pain functions to ground the body in the world as an embodied subject. This contradiction is present in Aronofsky's *The Fountain*, which is about a couple, Izzi (Rachel Weisz) and Tommy (Hugh Jackman), who try to deal with physical and emotional pain in different ways. Izzi, who suffers from a brain tumour, experiences her pain as heightened awareness of her lived-body, which is still embedded in the world, but doomed to an approaching absence from it. This enables her to accept her impending death. Tommy's pain is (pathological) grief borne out by his refusal to accept fundamental vulnerability in the face of natural forces beyond his control. His is the existential (and irrational) struggle against absolute loss, an attempt to prevent Izzi's death retroactively. Yet it is not through these characters that pain is transmitted to the spectator, for pain is inherent in the whole affective-aesthetic system of *The Fountain*. As such, the film addresses the spectator directly with its affective quality, prompting a lived, sentient awareness of material conditions of subjectivity. The film achieves this through its rich, visual (visceral?) symbolism that creates a conflict between the denial and the reality of emotional pain, which stimulates the affective sensitivities of the spectator.

I do not wish to suggest that there is some common denominator of pain that functions as a vehicle between the cinematic and the authentic lived experience. As Scarry points out: '[W]hatever pain achieves, it achieves in part through its unsharability, and it ensures this unsharability through its resistance to language. . . . Physical pain [brings] about an immediate reversion to a state anterior to language, to the sounds and cries a human being makes before language is learned' (Scarry 1985: 4).[9] But this does not necessarily mean that pain cannot be represented, or that one cannot understand its effects, if not the experience, when not physically in pain. In pain the body 'speaks' through affect, not through language. Furthermore, this does not mean that communication through affect is void of semantic meaning altogether. In this context, Janet Wolff (2008) speaks about 'aniconic' works of art, which invite spectators to an active form of viewing, enabling them to engage with painful subject matters on their own terms. Jill Bennett writes that pain-related artworks engage the spectator directly by means of the sensation that is registered in the work itself. This transactive process touches the spectator without necessarily communicating the 'secret' of painful experience (Bennett 2005: 7). In this book I shall argue that in the cinema of Aronofsky, pain is not merely registered or expressed, but is part of the active, emotional intentionality of the films. This results in the spectator being confronted by particularly strong sensations, or, in Scarry's terms, by a 'feeling of being acted upon' (Scarry 1985: 16) by means of sheer film style. I understand pain as one affective quality of Aronofsky's cinema that entirely saturates the spectator's embodied engagement with the film. In other words, pain fulfils a central role in the experience of Aronofsky's films, which renders their affective dynamics particularly complex. Scarry writes:

> Contemporary philosophers have habituated us to the recognition that our interior states of consciousness are regularly accompanied by objects in the external world, that we do not simply 'have feelings' but have feelings for somebody or something, that love is love of x, fear is fear of y, ambivalence is ambivalence about z. . . . This list and its implicit affirmation would, however, be suddenly interrupted when . . . one at last reached physical pain, for physical pain – unlike any other state of consciousness – has no referential content. It is not of or for anything. It is precisely because it takes no object that it . . . resists objectification in language. (Scarry 1985: 5)

Normally the threat of imminent pain would evoke our basic defence of fight or flight, but in extreme cases this defence can be blocked, inhibited, and arrested, which increases the sensation of being entrapped in pain. In Aronofsky's *The Wrestler*, the protagonist Randy 'The Ram' Robinson is entrapped in pain both internally as experienced in his lived-body, and externally in his life's circumstances. This is enhanced by his inability to accept change or to grasp emerging opportunities. In turn, this feeling of entrapment is relayed to spectators, with the result that their engagement with the film assumes a clogged-up, paralysed form. They become immersed in negative emotion, triggered by the inability to stop watching the bloodshed, brutality, and self-destruction of the protagonist's ever-sharper trajectory towards Sartrean 'bad faith'. The corporeal aesthetics of the film itself becomes the source of pain that 'takes no object', while the spectator's interior state of consciousness is thoroughly 'contaminated' by this spectacle of pain, even if its source is in the external world of cinema. Enlarging on the Scarry quotation above, one could say that this is brought about because even though pain may not be *of* or *for* anything, it is still '*because* [of] something', as Lucy Bending suggests (Bending 2000: 86). Furthermore, the spectator's pain experience is not totally void of reflection, as it involves a constant shift in focus from 'my pain' (pre-reflective) to 'not my pain' (reflective).

Yet another element of Scarry's philosophy of pain is the 'pure experience of negation'. In the experience of pain there is often the immediate feeling that something external is directed against one, even though this something is located within oneself. It is identified as 'not oneself', as something so alien that it must immediately be disposed of. Simultaneously that same something is internalized in such a way that the person in pain may be dominated by a sense of 'internal agency'. Thus when a knife enters the body, for instance, one will feel one's own body, rather than the knife, hurting one (Scarry 1985: 52–53). In the film *Black Swan*, both 'modalities of pain' – external and internal – seem to be operating simultaneously. In this film, protagonist Nina mutilates herself in order to replace her feelings of insecurity with a sense of external control. Rather than being an uncontrollable, pure experience of negation, Nina's pain is experientially localized and specified at first. As a result, her pain 'exists here and now, not everywhere and always' (McLane 1996: 112) – that is, at least until the situation spins out of control and Nina's body takes over her agency, acting against and annihilating her both within and without. At this point, Nina's body no longer belongs to her, which paradoxically is also a precondition for fulfilling her true vocation as a dancer. The film seems to function by means of affective engulfing, inviting the spectator to give in to a sort of 'bodily disintegration'. This experience is painful and pleasurable at the same time, and the film is best characterized as uncannily sublime, as it stages a confrontation between bodily materiality and psychic breakdown by means of aesthetic excess and estrangement.

The argument made in this book operates on two planes. On the first plane, I analyse the spectator's direct emotional engagement with the affective-aesthetic system of Aronofsky's films. This affective encounter is best described as a bodily event, in which the 'corporeal style' of the film entangles with the lived-body of the spectator. This process is central in the film-phenomenological tradition. Within this event, I consider film an intentional agent, with affective energy, valence, and rhythm that correspond to the human emotional system, although they are not identical to it. I do not wish to suggest that all spectators react or should react to Aronofsky's films in the way I describe, or that my reading of his films is the only accurate one, so a disclaimer would seem in order. The analyses developed in this book draw on the viewing positions inherently present in the film, which I have inhabited as a film scholar and a film spectator. It is these positions to which the term 'spectator' refers throughout this book. On the one hand, my understanding of Aronofsky's films is connected to my experience and my emotions, moving outward from within. On the other hand, it is connected to the cinematic specificity of these films, moving inward from without. With reference to the subjective method of analysis applied in this book, Jean-Paul Sartre writes that 'I may ... interrogate myself and on the basis of this interrogation lead an analysis of the 'human reality' to a successful conclusion which can be used as a foundation for *an* anthropology (Sartre 1993: 13, italics added). It is impossible to conduct a phenomenological inquiry into the significance of cinematic emotions without turning one's attention to one's own emotional and embodied experience. Yet this type of inquiry is more than 'sloppy liberal humanism' (Sobchack 1992: xiv), since personal emotions and private experiences can be set in motion, put in context, and shared by others across different cultures.

On the second plane, I analyse how Aronofsky's cinema invites the spectator to engage with his films conceptually, in terms of film-philosophy. At that stage, my methodological approach could be characterized by what Robert Sinnerbrink (2011a) has termed 'romantic film-philosophy', insofar as it presupposes Aronofsky's work to be eliciting philosophical experiences and aesthetic judgments, which are sensory, emotional, and intellectual all at once. More precisely, Aronofsky's films will be considered philosophically dialogical, as they engage the spectator in the experience of (self-)reflection through their emotional dynamics. This is not a matter of matching preconceived philosophical ideas with his films, but of thinking through the emotions evoked by their cinematic aesthetics, considering both distinctive features and emerging patterns of salience. In Aronofsky's work, such distinctive aesthetic features include noisy (*Pi*), rhythmic (*Requiem for a Dream*), repetitive (*The Fountain*), fleshy (*The Wrestler*) and haptic elements (*Black Swan*).

To summarize: this book explores both how Aronofsky's cinema functions affectively, and how philosophical significance can be attached to this. Cinematic experience is a matter of affective participation in the filmic event, based on mutual resonance felt in the body and reflected in thought. It is an experience that is simultaneously aesthetic and reflective – or better, an experience in which aesthetic and reflective practices are inextricably intertwined. As Sinnerbrink argues, cinema always provokes spectators to think in response to what film enables them to feel and experience (Sinnerbrink 2011b: 137). This involves (critical) assessment of ideas embodied in the film, in an attempt to gain insight into their ethical and/or aesthetic significance. Similarly, Crowther argues that all works of art are charged with sensuous and conceptual energy in ways that reach beyond philosophical thought. Works of art embody and transcend human experiences, but they also return to them. This is the reason they cause reflective awareness of the human condition in a unique way (Crowther 1993: 46). Similarly, cinema is an event in which the sensuous and the conceptual constantly and reciprocally modify each other by folding over in negotiation. As an aesthetic form, cinema addresses our affects and senses, while as a conceptual practice it engages our thinking and imagination. It must be strictly kept in mind, though, that the sensuous and the conceptual are not distinctive elements, but rather two sides of one phenomenological event that can be reflected upon philosophically. Thus film-philosophy is both a measure of the aesthetic potentiality of cinema, and a way of approaching film. Films embody ideas, as likewise they embody experiences and emotions, but these ideas and emotions can only emerge through interaction with the spectator who thinks and feels with the film. My goal in the following chapters is to explain how affective responses to Aronofsky's films may be a basis for conceptual insights regarding knowledge (*Pi*), addiction (*Requiem for a Dream*), loss (*The Fountain*), self-deception (*The Wrestler*) and bodily materiality (*Black Swan*).

The order of chapters follows the chronological order of Aronofsky's work. I start with *Pi* and the way in which its affective-aesthetic system enables the spectator to participate in the main character's physical pain and mental anxiety. I shall argue that this pain is embodied in the corporeal aesthetics of the film itself and that it is experienced by the spectator as a sensed inability to gain control in the multiplicity of the world. On the conceptual level, I understand the film to epitomize what Michel Serres calls the (non)logic of clinamen, which manifests itself as noise that is void of any pre-existing orderly structure. In chapter two I move from noise to the notion of rhythm, which gives structure to the affective functioning of *Requiem for a Dream*. I shall argue that the film evokes an experience of affective dissonance by addressing and disturbing the corporeal rhythm of the spectator by means of its audiovisual style. The film lends itself exceptionally well to Henri Lefebvre's method of 'rhythmanalysis'. This allows us to understand affective transmission through a rhythmic relationship between the body of the spectator and the cinematic body 'in pain'. In *Requiem for a Dream*, this relationship is linked to loss of agency, which an individual can often experience as a result of mental and physical humiliation.

While pain is connected to humiliation in *Requiem for a Dream*, it is pathological grief and its painful features that lie at the core of *The Fountain*, the film that is discussed in chapter three. Martha Nussbaum has defined such grief as repeatedly experienced affective frustration, thoroughly intertwined with the grieving person's bodily and cognitive fabric. It is this reverberating, repetitive logic of grief that is embedded in the visual style of *The Fountain*, providing the film with an affective quality that directly affects the spectator. A similar direct cinematic address takes place in *The Wrestler*, which I shall explore in chapter four. The film takes the spectator disturbingly close to bleeding, hurting flesh, in ways that are immediately felt in the body and experienced as displeasure. The film celebrates a character whose defining trait is his masochism – his ability to endure, and even take pleasure in, absurd amounts of physical pain. But as Sartre has argued, masochism must first and foremost be understood as a form of bad faith. In my reading of the film, not only does *The Wrestler* depict masochism, but it also calls for acknowledgement of an affective discrepancy between 'spectatorial pain' and 'performative pain'. This in turn requires acknowledgement of one's own responsibility as a spectator – one's own bad faith – in the process of watching the pain of the other.

In chapter five, the focus is on coexistence of the uncanny and the sublime in *Black Swan*. The protagonist in this film displays a split personality: there is the embodied, material self, which is threatened by the possibility of pain and death, and the disembodied, eternal self, free from any such threat. Such division of the self lies at the core of experiencing the sublime, but in *Black Swan* the sublime is inseparable from the experience of the uncanny. Here the 'eternal self' actually appears as the ghostly double of the protagonist. There is an obvious connection with the paradox of ballet, which is to deny the materiality of the body for the sake of the ethereal quality of the dance. Hence the film carries a meaningful commentary on the tangibility of the dancer's body and the ethereality of the ballet's ideal, suggesting that totally sacrificing the former for the sake of the latter is ethically unworthy. The film achieves this by addressing the spectator as a sentient, sensual, and sensible being, with awareness of bodily materiality, which potentially leads to further reflection on the profound connection among the body, mind, and soul.

In the cinematic experience in general, and with regard to Aronofsky's films in particular, intellectual and emotional desire often seem to go hand-in-hand. As Isobel Armstrong argues, the reason for this is that the affective-aesthetic 'energizes us by demanding not judgment, but a desire of explanation, an ever more adequate understanding of its possibilities, a repeated pursuit of the meanings surrounding it' (Armstrong 2000: 168). It could therefore be claimed that cinema makes spectators reflect – with varying degrees of success – because its corporeal style of being corresponds with their sensual experience. This could prompt direct intellectual appraisal as well, for instance by attaining to philosophical insights through pain. These insights do not lead to explicit philosophical statements; rather, they pertain to the way in which films invite direct experience of a cinematic event, rendered vivid by the film's affective-aesthetic system.

## Notes

Many thanks to Kathleen Scott for her helpful comments on the earlier version of this introduction.

1.  An editorial in the journal *Senses of Cinema* describes this trend as a 'critical discourse that downplays dramatic naturalism and character psychology in favour of attention to body, gesture, "presence", physical energy and intensity' (Martin, Mousoulis and Villella 2002). However, it would be a mistake to assume that

cinema of the body is a contemporary trend only. From its very beginning, cinema has always had a profound bodily quality. Thus Tom Gunning (1990) defines the 'cinema of attractions' in terms of bodily immediacy, arguing that it evokes in the spectator an embodied response to the screen. The relationship between the cinematic body and the body of the spectator was also understood by people like Sergei Eisenstein, who aimed to sensitize spectators to new sensorial perceptions (Eisenstein 1967: 71). In his essay 'Synchronization of the Senses', Eisenstein elaborates his ideas of cinematic techniques that create a primal, visceral unity of the senses, moving the spectator to a form of bodily ecstasy comparable to religious fervour (Eisenstein 1969: 89).

2. The process is described here: *Imagineer Systems,* 2012, 'Look FX: Visual Effects on *Black Swan.* Retrieved 12 August 2012 from http://www.imagineersystems.com/case-studies-folder/look-fx-visual-effects-on-black-swan.

3. YouTube poster My Fnord. 2011, excerpt from Aronofsky's *No Time* ('Come on Fish'), *YouTube,* uploaded 29 September. Retrieved 22 November 2012 from http://www.youtube.com/watch?v=eGMzvMbH8a8; YouTube poster degitz, 2011, Excerpt from Aronofsky's *Fortune Cookie* ('Stanley B. Herman edit'), *YouTube,* uploaded 11 March. Retrieved 22 November 2012 from http://www.youtube.com/watch?v=tk2VGzcngEg&feature=related.

4. In fact, this expressive resonance renders the work of art what Dufrenne calls a quasi-subject, but a more appropriate term might be Michel Serres's notion of quasi-object. Dufrenne does not make clear whether he means that a work of art is an analogy to a real subject, or is literally a special sort of subject (Funt 1968: 124). In contrast, Serres explains in *The Parasite* that 'the quasi-object is not an object, but it is one nevertheless, since it is not a subject, since it is in the world; it is also a quasi-subject, since it marks or designates a subject who, without it, would not be a subject' (Serres 20077: 225). Cinema can be considered a quasi-object because it designates a resonant relation between itself and its spectator, without which the spectator would not be a spectator, and through which both parties participate in each other's life world – the presence of the sensuous.

5. In this context, a distinction can be made between the definitions of affect and emotion, although not necessarily on the experiential level. Affect can be seen as the pre-reflective bodily mechanism that underlies all emotion and that gives pre-semantic meaning to information that originates from our bodily systems, and, more particularly, from our senses. Emotion is the semantic account of the affective appraisal that can be narrated and remembered. Through this, we experience our being-in-the-world as subjectively, historically and culturally particular individuals. But I understand affects and emotions as unified states or processes, in which affect is an implicit quality of emotion and vice versa, since affects are not devoid of semantic meaning (Laine 2011).

6. In addition, one might consider how our affective-aesthetic experiences are shaped by learned predispositions, since there are different types of discursively shaped and determined bodies. Thus Nina's suffering in *Black Swan* is partly structured by her gender, as argued in chapter five, which is to a certain extent fundamentally different from the emotional and physical pain undergone by Randy in *The Wrestler*, explored in chapter four. In a similar vein, one might ask in what way the spectators' experiences of Aronofsky's films are socially, politically, or culturally determined by gender or some other ideological construct; that, however, is beyond the scope of this particular study.

7. I borrow this idea from Deniz Peters and his discussion on electronic music in Peters 2012.

8. Drew Leder suggests that the reason why pain involves such 'return' to the body is that normally the body is 'absent' in the sense that we are not positionally conscious of its functioning; our reflective attention is not directed to our bodily states: 'Insofar as the body tends to disappear when functioning unproblematically, it often seizes our attention most strongly at times of dysfunction' (Leder 1990: 4). But, echoing Scarry, he also suggests that pain can often lead to a body that turns in on itself (Leder 1990: 74).

9. Scarry's view has been challenged by, for instance, Lucy Bending, who argues that people not only have an overwhelming need to make sense of their pain, but they also have a large reservoir of cultural significations that enable processes of meaning-giving to experiences of pain (Bending 2000: 86).

CHAPTER ONE
# Noise
## *Pi*

Darren Aronofsky's first feature film, *Pi* (1998), is a character-centred story that does not actually invite identification with or inspire empathy for its troubled main character. Instead, it is the aesthetics of noise in this film that binds the spectator to the life-space of mathematician Maximillian Cohen (Sean Gullette). Although the film communicates the experience of its protagonist, it is primarily the film's noisy, visceral quality that is responsible for its powerful impact. *Pi* is best described as a psychological thriller, in which the character's subjective state is central, a process Aronofsky refers to as 'subjective filmmaking'. But Max's psychological disposition and his being-in-the-world are vastly different from those of most people, which complicates matters of empathy and identification. This renders the experience of the film particularly complex, the spectator remaining neither fully 'inside' nor 'outside' the character. This is mitigated to some extent by the fact that Max's inner thoughts and emotions can literally change his physical environment, allowing the viewer to be drawn into Max's worldview with a certain immediacy.

Max believes that everything in the world, including the stock market, can be understood and explained in terms of numbers, and this mathematical premise becomes the driving force of the film. The idea of mathematics as organizing principle is reflected even in the duration of the film, which is exactly 1 hour, 23 minutes and 45 seconds long (1, 2, 3, 4, 5). Max becomes involved with a Wall Street investment bank as well as with a Hasidic cabbalistic sect that is in search of a numerical encoding of Torah. Shot in 'guerrilla style', with grainy and overexposed black-and-white stock,[1] and with a minimal budget of $60,000, the film regularly cuts to mathematical formulas, numerical series and Fibonacci patterns, which are depicted as spirals, fir cones, fractals and seashells. It also frequently refers to the aesthetic principle of the golden ratio that can be found, for example, in Leonardo da Vinci's famous drawing *Vitruvian Man* (1487). Aronofsky himself has declared that he believes that patterns underlie the constitution of the whole universe:

You look at DNA and you look at the Milky Way. That's kind of weird that they have a similar form, similar shape. We're built from it, while living in a giant spiral. What does that mean? Maybe there are a lot of spirals that we're not quite seeing. We can see the big one. We can see the small one. What's in between? . . . You start to see spirals in nautilus shells, ram's horns, in the way a plant grows – they grow in spirals, in our bones we have spirals. Our fingertips, if you look really closely there's spirals. (Aronofsky 1998: 42)

The world, however, also contains chaos as a pure multiplicity that refuses to fit into pre-existing mathematical patterns. As Yvette Biro reminds us, today scientists distinguish between two different types of chaos that are not mutually exclusive: there is 'chaos' that tends towards order, and chaos that is characterized by an increasing disorder – and without the latter, there would be no dynamism in the world (Biro 2008: 12). It is this juxtaposition of 'chaos' and chaos that structures the film *Pi*, epitomized in the film's tagline 'faith in chaos', which can be understood in two ways: on one hand, to have *faith* in chaos could mean faith in the deterministic dynamics of chaos; on the other, to have faith *in chaos* could mean faith in chaos's disorderly flow without any organizing principle. As Max seeks to approach the mathematical explanation for all existence, the paradoxical coexistence of these different types of chaos causes his migraine headaches, as well as his paranoia, to become more and more violent, while the visual style of the film swerves towards total disorder. The film ends with Max trepanning himself in his right temple with a power drill, thus destroying his mathematical talent.

This chapter tracks the affective-aesthetic process of the film, which enables the spectator to sense the effects of the pain Max experiences, originating from his pursuit of mathematical unity and symptomized by his migraines and his paranoia. The spectator feels with particular acuteness the anxiety that stems from the disturbed relationship between Max's lived-body and the world, which arises from this impossible pursuit. As George Steiner once wrote: 'Analytic thought has in it a strange violence. To know analytically is to reduce the object of knowledge, however complex, however vital it may be, to just this: an object' (quoted in Csikszentmihalyi 1975: 11). The way in which Max attempts to know the whole world mathematically could be seen as a desire to objectify the world, to view it in a strictly analytical, numerical way. This signals a refusal to accept that the world is not entirely calculable, that there is always something that escapes universal quantification, mathematical prediction and scientific control. Max does not view the world as one of 'incessant and unforeseeable change and possibility, a world always about to be' (Quirk 1990: 1–2). Max's mathematical strategy also isolates him, separating him from the material reality of the world, and he internalizes the violence of his analytic thinking, as manifested in his migraines and his anxiety.

These effects, as well as their significance, are transmitted to the spectator by means of the affective noise embedded within the film. These elements are not organized according to the logic of some mathematical equation, but according to the non-logic of clinamen, based on accident and chance. 'Clinamen' is Lucretius's term for the way in which atoms spontaneously relate to each other. Michel Serres has made extensive use of this notion in order to deconstruct the dichotomy between chaos and order. The non-logic of clinamen is that of noise as pure multiplicity without pre-existing order or organization. In Serres's thinking, the concept of noise insinuates that everything in the universe is connected. This multiplicity, however, should not be understood as diversity unified by some common principle; rather, it is a turbulent field in which various elements flow together, scatter and collide. This chapter discusses *Pi* as a force field between organized and unorganized noise that manifests itself in painful physical and mental states of migraine, paranoia and anxiety. These states function as three interrelated aspects of one phenomenological experience, which is embodied in the cinematic style of the film. These painful effects are also sensed by the spectator as an inability to assume control in the manically spinning, disorderly world of the film, a situation that poses ethical questions about the nature of knowing the world in general. The film shows us what happens when knowledge is sought from a single, organizing principle removed from direct, meaningful, affective and bodily engagement with the world.

## Migraine

*Pi* unfolds around Max's frantic obsession with finding order in chaos, and the term 'chaotic' best characterizes the film's style as well. Even the film's title sequence evokes chaos. An ever-increasing number of digits representing $\pi$ runs in the background, with mathematical diagrams, algebraic equations, cerebral cross-sections, neural network models and stock market data randomly imposed over top in quick succession. This effect is enhanced by Clint Mansell's energetic, hypnotizing and intensely electric score. In the audio commentary, which appears as a separate track on the DVD release, Aronofsky states that the title sequence is Max's headache depicted in graphic form. Intensifying the effect, the graininess and high contrast of the images make it hard for the eye to discern exactly what is being depicted. As well, the editing style is discontinuous – the handheld camera frequently imitates the movements in Max's field of vision, rapidly scrutinizing his surroundings, and the use of SnorriCam creates an unusual vertigo effect for the viewer. In their textbook on film analysis, David Bordwell and Kristin Thompson advise film scholars to trace patterns of salient techniques within a film (Bordwell and Thompson 2001: 330), but the pattern in *Pi* is that there is no pattern. And this is exactly what Max's mentor Sol (Mark Margolis) tries to convince Max of – that 'there is no pattern'. This is highlighted by the fact that there is no pattern in $\pi$, the mathematical constant.

Yet while there is no pattern, the film is still characterized by some prominent and consistent aesthetic elements. These include recurring techniques such as Max's voice-overs enunciating his diary entries, and the abundant use of point-of-view shots, shaky images, whip pans, jump cuts, high and low camera angles, (extreme) close ups, mathematical inserts and frequent use of a wide-angle lens. There is a multilevel rhythmic structure with a vigorous techno-kinetic drive inspired by hip-hop music, which led one *Variety* film critic to define the film's viscerality as 'kinetically insane'.[2] This techno-kinetic structure organizes the rhythm of camera movement, editing and sound in the film, as Danielja Kulezic-Wilson points out (Kulezic-Wilson 2008a: 19). Yet, *Pi* blends together such filmic elements in a noticeably random and unpredictable fashion, in ways that seemingly avoid any narrative motivation. And this is precisely the point, for it is this blatant unpredictability and randomness that becomes a narrative motivation in itself.

*Pi* revolves largely around Max, who is present in every scene. In fact, the spectator is frequently positioned inside his head by means of point-of-view shots, sharing his actual or hallucinatory perceptions. Similarly, a particularly harassing sound enacts for the spectator the effects of his painful migraine attacks. In this way, it is the film itself that engages us on an affective-aesthetic level that strikes us as computerized, with a retro flavour to it relayed by the presence of pixel aesthetics and floppy disks. In his apartment Max has built an enormous computer called Euclid that Aronofsky defines as a 'home-made brain' in the director's commentary. Max lives in a close symbiosis with his computer, almost like a cybernetic organism – a hybrid of machine and organism like Donna Haraway defines this in her 'Cyborg Manifesto' (1991). The film's computerized setting is inspired by Terry Gilliam's *Brazil* (1985), in which – like in *Pi* – the computer appears to be a fleshy, slimy organism. In *Pi*, the computer's fleshiness is established in a shot through Max's microscope that shows something resembling brain cells, showing the computer as an organism that attracts both literal and figurative 'bugs'. It seems no accident that these literal bugs crawling in Euclid's structures are ants, insects that are famous for their highly organized colonies. When Euclid crashes after having become 'conscious' of itself, Max 'crashes' with it. He is shown walking like a somnambulist around in his apartment, which by now has become a shadowy chamber, lit only by computer screens flashing panic messages and filled with a pulsating, electric noise with the rhythm of a heartbeat – which is abruptly brought to an end. Eventually Max destroys Euclid and then proceeds to commit intellectual suicide by drilling a hole in his head. Max's relationship with his computer Euclid takes another turn when he projects onto it his repressed desire for his next-door neighbour Devi (Samia Shoaib). He frequently experiences auditory hallucinations, in which he hears Euclid moaning with sexual pleasure in a voice resembling Devi's, accompanied by a quick dissolve to a close-up of her sensuous mouth. For Max, Euclid represents both the despised self and the desired other, and thus this autoerotic symbiosis with his computer represents an extreme form of closing in on oneself.

The relationship between Max and Euclid can be characterized as prosthetic, which Marshall McLuhan defined as a physical extension of the self by means of media: the car as a biomechanical extension of the human body, the computer as a neural extension of the human central nervous system, etc. For McLuhan, the extension of the central nervous system by media is bearable 'only through numbness or blocking of perception' (McLuhan 2005: 43). Any extension by media is accompanied by 'autoamputation'. Thus Max 'autoamputates' both physically and psychologically when entering into a symbiotic relationship with Euclid, which is so consummate that it alienates him from other people and ultimately from himself as well. As Jacob Mey points out, a prosthetic relationship with the computer can only be successful if that relationship is 'embodied, not only in the person using the prosthesis, but also in the world surrounding him or her' (Mey 2000: 29). *Pi* might be seen to contain a warning against what happens when computer-as-prosthesis replaces the lived-body and its intimate material contact with the physical world. Max's pain is there to remind him of the fact that his corporeal and intersubjective existence as a 'self' has degenerated.

Max's obsession with finding numerical patterns everywhere in nature, such as fractals, spirals and golden ratios, all based on the mathematical constant $\pi$, is equivalent to chaos theory's quest to find underlying order in apparently random disorder. Kulezic-Wilson defines the audiovisual style of *Pi* as an 'unpredictable stream' that nevertheless is brought into equilibrium due to the anchoring presence of hip-hop patterns and repetitions in the film's internal rhythm (Kulezic-Wilson 2008a: 27). However, I maintain that the cinematic style of *Pi* is not conclusively established by means of comparison to the repetitive logic of hip-hop or to Fibonaccian patterns. In my view, it is more appropriately compared to the complex and chaotic non-logic of clinamen, wherein the universe is organized by means of accident and chance. In other words, the internal rhythm of *Pi* collapses into chaos, as order is overrun by the excessive stylistic complexity of the film, in accordance with clinamenian non-logic.

The Latin term *clinamen* was first coined by the Roman philosopher Lucretius to indicate the unpredictable swerve of atoms, the way in which atoms spontaneously and randomly relate to each other at an indeterminate moment and in an indeterminate place. Building on this, Michel Serres invents a logic of nonlinear dynamics in which chance is more important than order, and the world of clinamen is a complex and chaotic field of force. In his philosophy, Serres seeks to deconstruct the dichotomy between chaos and order through such concepts as clinamen, noise, parasite and the multiple. In a similar manner, Jacques Derrida attempts to subvert the order of hierarchical binary oppositions by means of his concept of *différance*. In *The Birth of Physics*, Serres distinguishes two modes of chaos: a turbulent, pure chaos and a deterministic, ordered chaos. These incessantly collide with each other, so that disorder emerges from order and vice versa. The double dynamic of these two modes of chaos is 'unstable and stable, fluctuating and in equilibrium . . . order and disorder at once' (Serres 2000: 30). Unlike Max, Serres prefers chaos to order, and defines disorder as 'the end of systems, and their beginning. Everything always goes towards chaos, and, sometimes, everything comes from it' (Girard 2005: 13). Later in his book *Genesis,* Serres replaces the concept of disorder, a negative phrase, with the positive concept of noise, or the multiple. Traditionally, noise has been understood as disturbance, destructive of significance, as opposed to organized modes of sonic expression such as language and music (Goddard, Halligan and Hegarty 2012: 2). As a sonic event, sound becomes noise when it is unpredictable, unfamiliar and uncontrollable, or when it annoys, disturbs or causes harmful psychological and physiological effects in listeners (White 2012: 236). But Serres uses noise as a positive term to describe the state of possibility and creativity: 'Everything is founded in the possible, all representations originate in the *belle noiseuse,* all states come to us from chaos' (Serres 1995: 24).[3] The distinction between disorder and noise seems relevant for *Pi* as well, since Max seems to be trapped in the former, unable to listen to the noise of multiplicity.[4] For the spectator, however, this possibility is definitely there, embodied in the film's epistemological insight that reveals itself in its 'noise', inciting philosophical reflection.

In *Pi,* it is the collision of Max's mind as an ordered chaos with the pure chaos of the world that allows random islands of order to emerge from the multiple – indeed, these are the moments in which the world makes sense to him mathematically, albeit very briefly and never in a definite form. These moments are organized by juxtaposing Max's orderly voice-over when reading diary entries with the simultaneous visual disarray of extremely mobile frames, unfocused imagery and discontinuous editing. In one curious scene, Max is on a subway train, jotting an estimation of π on top of the stock market data in a newspaper. From time to time he suspiciously eyes an elderly man in the same compartment, who then bursts into singing 'I only have eyes for you' and finally disappears.[5] Unable to maintain the orderliness he demands from the world, Max is preyed upon by noise, and he suffers from intolerable migraine attacks as a result. The scene in which Max runs through the streets to Sol's house after having been abducted by the Hasidic sect is a rapidly edited sequence of highly mobile shots of urban street life taken from different angles, combined with mathematical inserts and accompanied by cacophonic sound effects. Max himself is shot from behind by a SnorriCam, and his voice-over is vastly layered and confused. This depicted chaos represents the way in which he attempts to put order into the constant stream of data hurtling through his brain. However, just as his computer Euclid could not take the information Max was feeding it, Max himself cannot handle this dangerous and vast undertaking. He suffers one last, horrible headache, which nevertheless allows him to 'see the light', after which the scene is emptied and all we see is Max bathed in white light. But the film does not resolve the issue of whether he sees order or chaos in all this brightness.

Max's excruciating migraine attacks stem from his childhood, when, by way of experiment, he stared directly into the sun without blinking for such a long time that he permanently damaged his eyes.[6] In *Pi* these attacks are very powerfully conveyed to us in a style that parallels Max's own painful experience. This is a case of corporeal 'tuning in' to the film's affective frequency, which convincingly 'induces migraine' in the spectator. Spaces such as Max's bathroom, which is a very photophobic space in itself, contribute to this affect. The bathroom is decked out with wallpaper that resembles the kind of aluminium foil with which Andy Warhol decorated his famous Factory. But the most important filmic element to convey migraine to the spectator affectively is the use of sound. Max's first migraine attack starts with a distant noise of random radio signals, which quickly develops into the pulsating rhythm of a synthesizer. On top of this throb other sounds are layered, such as an industrial, chirping noise and the sudden, piercing sound of a drill, until the whole soundscape becomes cacophonic and nerve-rattling. Such unsuspected, asynchronous rhythms illustrate the way in which the synchronicity of one's lived-body becomes disoriented during a migraine attack. But Max experiences visual hallucinations as well. These are shared with the spectator through close-ups of his doorknob turning while the safety locks are rattling, until the door bursts open and lets in bright, engulfing white light, which Aronofsky defines as a 'white void'.

Max's second migraine attack in the subway, which is even more severe, is accompanied by a similar soundscape. The camera is focused on his agonized face and shakes around in synchrony with Max quivering in pain on the bench.

Even more pointedly, in the subway scene it is the world itself that starts to vibrate and shake, transforming from the orderly world to what Serres calls the 'grey sea'. The grey sea is the chaotic 'ground of the world' [in which] noises loom up . . . appear and withdraw, take form and dissolve, grow and disappear' (Serres 1995: 62). Max sees a vision of himself in traditional Hasidic dress, dripping blood on the subway floor. This is supported by the strongly amplified sound of blood drops hitting the ground, actually the beginning of Banco de Gaia's track 'Drippy' (1997). The use of SnorriCam combined with shaky point-of-view shots conveys the sense of Max's subjective experience as he follows his own trail of blood and finds that his own brain is lying on the subway floor (figure 1.1). This is a truly nauseating image, further enhanced by an extreme close-up of Max's pen poking the brain, supported by the sound effect of an approaching train blowing a warning whistle. And when the pen actually penetrates the brain tissue, a hallucination of a real, fast-approaching train appears on screen, its headlights engulfing the image in white light once more.

As the film progresses, the migraine attacks get more severe. At some point Max shaves his head and draws a square around a bulging vein in his scalp, the spot at which he has located the source of his migraine attacks after consulting a medieval book on brain anatomy. Then he imagines that he is armed with a drill and brutally attacks his brain, which, covered with ants, is lying in a washbasin. This particularly unsettling scene might be read as a premonition of Max's forthcoming self-destruction, and it also demonstrates the violence of his physical and emotional pain.

All the physical elements of migraine are represented in the film, such as throbbing pulsation, nausea, increased sensitivity to light and sound, visual disturbances, vertigo, ringing in the ears and delirium. However, it would be a mistake to reduce the operational logic of the film to its mere functional ability to convey Max's perceptual and mental subjectivity. Rather, the film's painful effect actually exists independent of the protagonists, insofar as the 'filmind' itself can be considered migraine-ridden here. The 'filmind' is one of Daniel Frampton's concepts, which he introduces to support his argument that cinema cannot *show* the spectator human mental states. Cinema *is* a state of mind in itself, incorporating intentions, affects, emotions and other concepts, which are transmitted to the spectator during the cinematic experience by means of the film's style (Frampton 2006: 6–7). Similarly, in

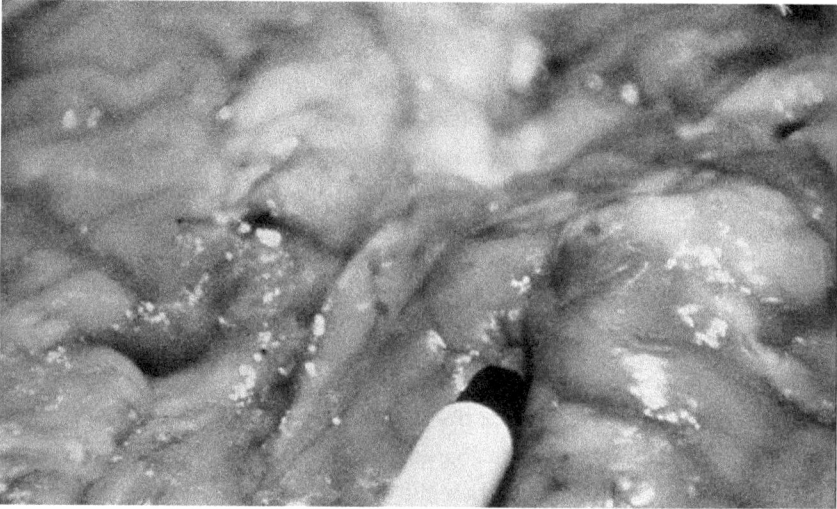

**Figure 1.1.** Migrainous nausea. Screen capture, *Pi* (1998).

*Pi*, just as the protagonist undergoes migraine attacks, so does the film itself, metaphorically speaking. *Pi*'s complex filmic style could not be accounted for merely on the basis of Frampton's concept of 'filmind', though. *Pi* constitutes corporeal aesthetics ruled by a unified, transactional wholeness of operative logic, embodying a gestural and postural similarity to Max's lived-body in pain. Furthermore, the spectator feels the effects of this pain by experiencing its significance organically from the inside, as the film's disorderly – or should I say noisy – condition violently wrecks the spectator's embodied and mindful engagement with it.

## Paranoia

Max's physical condition is accompanied by another disturbed state of the lived-body, namely paranoia, epitomized in the recurring event of Max staring through a peephole. This is shot from his point of view, followed by a series of close-ups of his hand opening the many security locks on his door. The graphic match and the quick succession of these shots almost create a jump cut effect, indicating how deeply this routine is embedded in Max's entire be-ing. Enhanced by an over-amplified clacking sound, the effect itself has as its source of inspiration the repetitive sampling technique used in hip-hop mu-sic. This is a technique that Aronofsky employs to perfection in *Requiem for a Dream*, but already in *Pi* it illustrates the protagonist's compulsive behaviour, as well as his psychological and physiological decline, beyond the strictly nar-rative function, as Kulezic-Wilson points out (Kulezic-Wilson 2008b: 129–30). The film regularly combines point-of-view shots of Max with reaction shots of his own face and its suspicious expression, closely observing his environment and especially the people in it. These shots are filmed with a ratio of only eigh-teen or even twelve frames per second, which further enhances the manic na-ture of Max's situation. Except for the scenes in which Max plays the Japanese game of Go with Sol, the film is characterized by a rapid tempo throughout. This epitomizes the stress Max feels in trying to remain safe by keeping other people out of his life-space. Interpersonal relationships would make things even more disorderly for him; Sol is the only exception.

This overall paranoid feeling in *Pi* is also transferred to the spectator, with the result that the spectator starts doubting the film's reliability altogether. Pa-tricia Pisters has made a similar claim about the film's ambiguity, in the sense of uncertainty about what actually happens in the film, such as whether Max re-ally drills a hole in his own brain (Pisters 2010: 241). In one scene, Max borrows a newspaper from a fellow passenger on a subway train. Is this co-passenger the same (imaginary) man who had burst out singing in an earlier scene? Max becomes suspicious, leaves the compartment, and then steps off the train, while the man appears to follow him. A sequence of quickly alternating point-of-view and reaction shots follows, accompanied by nervous drumming. Max finally leaves the man behind, only to find all the people in the street looking at him, knowingly and with sinister intentions. Yet the spectator is left wonder-ing whether there was any man in the first place, or if everything took place in Max's paranoid mind only.

Paranoia is typically characterized as a mental state heavily saturated by fear and anxiety, often to the point of delusion. There are irrationally per-ceived but concretely felt threats and acts of malice by others towards oneself. As with migraine, its physical effects may include increased heart rate, nausea, tension and feelings of dread as the body prepares to deal with the apparent danger. In *Pi*, these affects are clearly embodied in the nervous editing rhythm of sound and image, in the shaky camera technique and in the darkness of images that suffocate everything in the frame, such as in the scene in which Max flees the Wall Street executives and then gets abducted by the Hasidim. There is a scene with a 'surveillant' who disappears the second Marcy says 'done' in response to Max's demand to call the surveillant off. And there is a scene in which Max believes that someone is taking pictures of him on a subway train, the very person he then chases through the subway tunnels into the street, with a quick succession of clashing whip pans epitomizing his panic. The panicky motion of the camera and the nervous rhythm of editing in these scenes embody the paranoid affective quality of *Pi* that emerges when the spectator encounters the film as a sensuous, bodily event. Yet at the same time, the paranoid style of the film makes the spectators suspicious too, prompting them to doubt whether the Hasidim or the Wall Street executives truly exist outside Max's paranoid world.

## Anxiety

Another disturbed, lived-body state that combines with Max's pain is anxiety, an affective disorder that can be characterized as concern about lack of control over one's life. Max's suffering from migraine is just such an uncontrollable 'entity' in his life-world, and that is the reason why he prefers his enclosed, isolated apartment to crowded, open locations. When he happens to be outside, he tries to 'shrink' the outside world to make it fit into his mathematical vision, which he believes he can control. From the very beginning of the film, sequences of chaotically organized exterior shots are 'brought under control' by Max's voice-over addressing mathematics as the language of nature. A point-of-view shot from Max's perspective showing a treetop shaken randomly by the wind dissolves into an image that at first looks like a cloud formation, but then turns out to be stock market data running on a screen in his apartment. This emphasizes Max's recognition that the patterns found in the natural world are governed by the same mathematical principles as things like stock market fluctuations. And when his world refuses to fit into mathematical patterns, Max is stricken by paranoia and anxiety, as represented in the scene in which he is inquisitively stared at by random passers-by. It is as if Max were an object of active scrutiny by other people and not vice versa, a situation that he absolutely does not control.

When Max finally seems to gain control over the 'patterns' of the world, he is overwhelmed by the experience, for the 'order' of the world manifests itself as unmanageable. The scene in which Max runs through the streets combines chaotic, shaky, fast-motion point-of-view shots with uncanny SnorriCam shots. These shots cut to, and at other moments dissolve into, inserts of algebraic equations, Talmudic phrases, statistical curves, Go boards and overlaid spirals, accompanied by a multilayered voice-over that melds into one incomprehensible buzz. It is at this point that the visual style of the film becomes even more 'noisy' in Serres's sense: 'Noise . . . is a turbulence . . . order and disorder at the same time, order revolving on itself through repetition and redundancy, disorder through chance occurrences, through the drawing of lots at the crossroads and through the global meandering, unpredictable and crazy. An arborescent and turbulent rumour' (Serres 1995: 59). But Max, who is still striving for pure reason and uncontaminated mathematical abstraction, has not learnt to understand noise in that sense, which keeps him trapped in emotional and intellectual disorder. In this disorderly state, emotion no longer supports, but rather disturbs his continuous and dynamic exchange with the world. Normally, emotions are evaluative strategies that in a given situation direct our attention to salient features in a mass of unstructured detail. As Ronald de Sousa puts it, emotions function as 'determinate patterns of salience among objects of attention, lines of inquiry and inferential strategies' (de Sousa 1980: 137). Therefore, rather than symptomizing a given situation, emotions, grounded in the body acting in the world, 'can *reveal evaluative information* that must be taken seriously' (Stocker 1996: 64, italics added). Even though emotions can be inaccurate and misleading, more often than not they are 'even more appropriate and insightful than the calm deliberations we call "reason"' (Calhoun and Solomon 1984: 3). Thus: '[H]aving certain emotions is often systematically connected with being epistemologically well placed to make good evaluative judgments; and more strongly . . . not having certain emotions is often systematically connected with being epistemologically ill placed to make good judgments' (Stocker 1996: 105). For instance, fear is an imperative 'emergency emotion' that directs our attention to relevant details of a dangerous or fearful situation, and alerts us to be on the lookout for more relevant details that are crucial for our assessment of the situation; it also encourages us to form expectations about how we should respond to the possible evolution of the circumstances – in other words, fight or flight.

In contrast, anxiety is a disturbed, disorderly and dysfunctional emotion that is characterized by a lack of control and sense of helplessness towards future threats, danger or other impending negative events. According to David Barlow, at the heart of anxiety lies a felt inability to predict and take control of emotionally salient incidents that matter to the individual personally. This is why anxiety is characterized by 'a state of preparation [designed] to counteract helplessness' (Barlow 2000: 1247) instead of by the ability to react directly to the situation itself, as happens with fear. This means that anxiety is a future-oriented, anticipatory emotion combined with a heightened awareness of one's inability to deal with the prominent threat. This in turn may lead to a vicious circle characterized by an obsessive quality. According to Barlow: '[T]his shift to a self-evaluative focus of attention in which evaluation of one's (inadequate) capabilities to deal with the threat is prominent . . . this shift to a self-focused attentional state further increases [anxious] arousal and negative affect thus forming its own small positive feedback loop' (Barlow 2000: 1250). In such a state of anxiety, one is obsessively vigilant for those salient features one associates with the source of anxiety, to the extent that anxiety can become an incessant, self-feeding system that disrupts one's emotional agency. In *Pi*, Max's anxiety saturates his total existence in such a way that this state dominates in several situations. In other words, his anxiety does not merely concern his migrainous pain; he becomes overanxious about the world in general, and he attempts to cope with the resulting feelings of helplessness by attempting to gain control of the world through mathematics. However, this project is hindered in turn by his anxious anticipation of cues that evoke migraine, paranoia and social panic attacks, such as his hallucinations, amplified hearing, trembling hands and blurry vision. In addition, there is the intrusive presence of other people and their apparently random (but actually deliberate) unsolicited attention, with which Max is faced, but tries to avoid at any cost. During these scenes, the spectator too is triggered into a state of anxiously anticipating pain, not only by the sound cues of the film, such as white noise, ticking rhythms and pulsating tunes, but also by the nervous, scrutinizing movement of the camera, which mimics Max's state of mind. In the chase scene, Max's anxiety is embodied in the transformation of the urban setting into a nightmarish blur. During this scene, the image gets even darker, grainier and richer compared to the rest of the film, creating a truly claustrophobic effect. This is how anxiety structures the spectator's experience of *Pi* as an emotional event.

Barlow writes that anxiety is connected to early life experiences and the incomplete development of a sense of control over salient events. Those events that appear to be unpredictable and uncontrollable contribute to a vulnerability to anxiety (Barlow 2000: 1254). Lack of emotional control thus lies at the heart of anxiety. The origin of Max's anxiety, which results in his migraine, is the childhood event that made him temporarily blind after staring directly into the sun too long without blinking. The film's high contrast and harsh lighting visualize the way in which Max's impaired vision during his childhood accident is constantly present in his daily existence as the source of his anxiety. These filmic elements are prominent every time Max suffers a migraine attack, especially at the moment when the pain reaches its peak. It is the force of light that breaks open Max's door, filling his apartment with its blinding intensity, and it is blinding light that attacks him in the form of the headlights of an approaching train, after which the frame goes white. Before Euclid's second crash, Max stares at a glowing digit on its screen, which grows to fill his whole field of vision, as well as ours. And during his final migraine attack, a white light engulfs Max entirely; it is an image that perhaps suggests enlightenment of some kind, but is nevertheless too powerful for him to bear (figure 1.2).[7] The scene is very quiet, in contrast to the overall noisiness of the rest of the film. Thus the image could also be interpreted as a void of nothingness, an absolute and terrifying absence of the world as opposed to the multiplicity of noise. And of course Max's state of consciousness could be explained by referring to the mystical experience many migraine sufferers associate with their attacks, especially in the form of migraine auras resulting from more acute sensory awareness. Some migraine sufferers describe these epiphenomenal events as spiritual, transcendental, cosmic, psychedelic and consciousness-altering experiences.[8] In *Pi*, the blinding burst of light in which Max finds himself engulfed triggers him to change his situation – drastically.

**Figure 1.2.** White void or enlightenment? Screen capture, *Pi* (1998).

Anxiety is generally considered a psychic disturbance with a highly salient bodily component. Anxiety is a clearly embodied mental state, in which the mind and the body constantly fold over each other in negation, forming a transactional whole. In Max's case, the psychic disturbance is embedded in his migraine, his pain. The film's gestural and postural rhythm is characterized by intense throbs and pulses, created by sound, music and editing. Together with the harsh quality of the image, this rhythm attunes the spectator to the affective effects of his condition, as well as to its significance. As argued above, Max's proneness to anxiety results from his ultra-sensitivity to the world in general. Within the cinematic event, the spectator is directly induced into this state of anxiety by the anxiety-ridden aesthetics of the film. Max's anxiety seems to fall outside of what Søren Kierkegaard (1964) calls dread and Jean-Paul Sartre terms anguish, which is anxiety in the face of one's own freedom, 'the recognition of possibility as *my* possibility' (Sartre 1992: 73, italics added). Rather, it is anxiety borne out by the limitations of knowledge, which for Max is restricted to the mathematical. Serres describes this type of anxiety in relation to noise as follows: 'What terrifies is not the meaning of the noise . . . but the increasing multiplicity that says it. Fear comes from the swarming, the tide, the dread multiplies like flies, knowledge through concepts regiments this nauseous herd under the pure generality of the one. . . . Rationality was born of this terror' (Serres 1995: 66–67).

Similarly, Angela Woods argues that Max's madness originates from his knowledge crisis, and more specifically from the exclusively cerebral – anticorporeal, anti-instinctual and anti-emotional – method by which he links the subject and object of knowledge (Woods 2012: 5). She refers to psychologist Louis Sass, who argues that madness is not the result of alienation from reason, but from the body as the seat of emotions and instincts: 'What if madness, in at least some of its forms, were to derive from a heightening rather than a dimming of conscious awareness, and [were] an alienation not from reason, but from the emotions, instincts and the body?' (Sass 1992: 4).

In this light, Max's anxiety stems from his uncompromisingly cerebral approach, which disturbs his lived-bodily presence in the world. It is the intertwining of body and mind in our experience of the world that is the precondition for all knowledge; otherwise, knowledge and reason can turn into madness. In Serres's thinking, for example, knowledge cannot be found in a single organizing principle such as mathematics. Rather, knowledge is a disorderly process of interaction in a world of flow: 'Knowing this requires one first of all to place oneself between [the things of the world]. Not only in front in order to see them, but in the midst of their mixture, on the paths that unite them' (Serres 2008: 80). This is the reason why Serres prefers 'ecology of knowledge' to such concepts as epistemology or ontology. It is from this fluid 'ecological melange' of inside and outside, subject and object that hybrid forms emerge, which Serres (2007) calls quasi-objects in his book *The Parasite*. [9] The term *quasi-object* is meant to convey how manmade objects have agency of their own and act upon us. This means that things are neither absolute objects, nor 'neutral vessels through which human agency flows' (Adamson 2011: 144). Object-ness is rather a matter of resonance, of the human and non-human resounding with each other, where the object itself shows agential properties. I propose that, in general, cinema can be seen as a quasi-object, given that the spectator brings films to life by watching them, while at the same time films exercise their agency upon the spectator. Films move us – or resonate with us – with a greater or lesser degree of success within an emotional gamut that runs from horror through amusement to consolation. Films have an operational, intentional and affective structure of their own. This structure directs the spectator's attention not only towards visually salient features, but also towards those features that are not in plain sight – those that can only be detected by means of an affective sharing of experience between cinema and the spectator. Thus, understanding cinema as a quasi-object entails understanding of the participatory process between the film and the spectator in their mutual constitution. This is the reciprocal way in which the spectators are shaped by the filmic event, and simultaneously shape this event with their emotions in a process in which both are indispensable to each other.

Leaving this aside, in Serres's thinking, the haphazard flow of the world is irreducible to causal order and one can only know of the world through gestural metamorphosis and postural movements of the body mingling with the world. In this view, the senses are not merely channels of perception and sensation, but spaces of negotiation between the self and the world. This is why Serres advises us to throw ourselves 'into the ocean of the world' in order to feel its membrane, its fabric forming around ourselves, the 'invisible veil' (Serres 2008: 36). For Karen Barad, too, knowing comes 'from a direct material engagement with the world' (Barad 2007: 49). In contrast, Max aims to detach himself from the world of flow and scrutinize it from a mathematical distance. Max can therefore be seen as a modern Galileo according to Roger Poole's description:

> [He] shears away the entire world of sense-impressions, emotions and all the realities that make up our everyday world. Then, he substitutes a knowledge of the mathematical properties of the world for that complete, total human world that we knew before, and counts himself richer by the exchange. . . . In fact, he carries out a double retreat from the totality of lived experience, and then from the totality of knowledge as such. (Poole 1972: 82)

The emotional effects of Max's 'double retreat from the totality of lived experience' are vividly captured in the SnorriCam scenes. These signify the extent to which Max attempts to avoid a sensuous encounter with the disorderly flow of the world, an attempt that is the origin of his pain, his migraine. In other words, Max's migraine seems to originate from the vehemence with which he attempts to exclude everything in the world that does not fit into the rigid order of mathematics. Ultimately this vehemence turns inward, mirroring the ferocity with which Max rejects the touch of the world, just as he rejects Devi's touch, while he also clearly longs for her. He hallucinates waking up in her arms after his last horrendous headache, but he actually wakes to the reality of his cold, lonely, isolated existence.

By attempting to isolate himself from the world, Max reaches an opposition between 'interior' (knower, the subject) and 'exterior' (known, the object) knowledge, without acknowledging the relationship between the two, which plunges him into a spiritual and emotional vacuum. This is, of necessity, an ethical problem, since, as Barad points out: '[E]thics is not simply about the subsequent consequences of our ways of interacting with the world, as if effect followed cause in linear chain of events. Ethics is about mattering, about taking account of the entangled materializations of which we are a part' (Barad 2007: 384).

In *Pi*, Max declares to the Wall Street executives that he does not want to deal with petty materialists like them because he is just 'trying to understand our world'. But this understanding does not come with any responsibility for the world of which he is a part. Perhaps his enlightenment is precisely his realization of this problem. Thus, his intellectual suicide would be a mode of acceptance of an uncertain, unalterably hybrid and plural world – the world of multiplicity, as Serres calls it. There is actually a strange tranquillity in the way in which Max stares at the top of a tree that appears to have worm holes in its leaves. The hectic rhythm of the film ceases. Max does not seem to be upset at all about the loss of his ability to perform complex mathematical calculations in his head. In fact, he is seen smiling for the first time in the film. Through the act of self-trephination, Max discards his former attitude, which Sartre would have called the spirit of seriousness (Sartre 1992: 626) – an attitude that considers mathematical values as transcendent givens, independent of the mathematician's own subjectivity. However, it remains difficult to anchor any interpretative claims about whether or not Max also discovers responsibility for the world at the end of the film, beyond loose, contestable associations. Therefore the ending of *Pi* – as well as the film in its entirety – is best understood to epitomize what Janet Wolff (2008) terms the 'aesthetics

of uncertainty'. It eludes interpretation by avoiding clear coordinates of signification, and speaks directly to the spectator instead. Like Serres's chaos, the
ending of *Pi* is an open instead of a closed system of signification, epitomizing
a kind of knowledge that can never come to the point.

## Notes

Many thanks to Toni Mazel and Patricia Pisters for their helpful comments on the
earlier version of this chapter.

1. *Pi* was shot in reversal film (instead of negative film) in order to achieve a high-
   contrast look that would resemble the aesthetics of Frank Miller's neo-noir comic
   *Sin City* (1991–2000).
2. D. Harvey, 1998, 'Review: *Pi*', *Variety*, 19 January. Retrieved 3 October 2012 from
   http://www.variety.com/review/VE1117436848?refcatid=31.
3. Furthermore, Marie Thompson draws an interesting comparison between noise
   and affect insofar as affect is understood as a pre-semantic and trans-corporeal
   'swarm' of intensity in comparison to emotion that is meaningful, semantic and
   orderly: '[Affect] is unqualified, intensive, synaesthetic, insomuch that affect involves the participation of the senses in each other. Moreover, affect is synony-
   mous with noise in that it may be thought of as excess; it is that which is prior to,
   or the residue after intensity's qualification as emotion' (Thompson 2012: 208).
   Noise can also be seen in relation to nonlinear time, which Gilles Deleuze (1977)
   calls *aion*, the floating, non-pulsed time of 'pure becoming', which is the opposite
   of the linear and cumulative construction of time (*chronos*, clock time). These two
   temporalities are discussed in chapter three on *The Fountain*.
4. Laura Marks (2010) also proposes privileging noise as a creative strategy to connect with the infinite insofar as noise is understood as an index or the trace of the
   whole universe.
5. This perverted figure is a recurring character in Aronofsky's oeuvre, always played
   by actor Stanley B. Herman. He first appears as 'Pervert' in Aronofsky's short film
   *Fortune Cookie*, then as 'Moustacheless Man' in *Pi* and finally as 'Uncle Hank' in
   *Requiem for a Dream* and *Black Swan*. Originally *Black Swan*'s script ordered the
   character to do exactly the same thing as in *Pi* – to burst into show tunes suddenly
   on a subway train – but in the end the character 'merely' ends up harassing Nina
   with obscene gestures. I. Radford, 2011, 'Strange Perve on the Train – *Black Swan*'s
   Uncle Hank', *iflicks*, 24 February. Retrieved 23 July 2012 from http://www.i-flicks.
   net/blog/49-features/2295-strange-perve-on-a-train-black-swans-uncle-hank.
6. Just like Joseph Plateau, a Belgian physicist whose studies on the effect of after-
   images was crucial to research into the persistence of vision in the 19th century. A

pioneer of cinema, Plateau was the first to demonstrate the illusion of the moving image by means of phenakistoscope. Fascinated by the persistence of luminous impressions on the retina, he performed an experiment in which he gazed directly into the sun for 25 seconds. Consequently, he lost his eyesight later in life. 'Joseph Plateau', n.d., *Wikipedia*. Retrieved 26 April 2012 from http://en.wikipedia.org/wiki/ Joseph_Plateau.

7. Perhaps the scene could be interpreted as an example of what Kant calls the 'mathematical sublime', which consists of a painful experience of the 'inadequacy of the imagination' in the face of the world of multiplicity (Kant 1968: 91). In such an experience one tries but fails to explain this multiplicity fully. Instead, one discovers a transcendent event for the sensory imagination, which 'feels like an abyss in which [one] fears to lose [oneself]' (Kant 1968: 97). But as the concept of the sublime is extensively dealt with in chapter five on *Black Swan*, I will not continue to explore the implications of this interpretation here.

8. See for instance *Migraine Aura Foundation,* 2007. Retrieved 9 March 2012 from http://www.migraine-aura.org/content/index_en.html.

9. Serres's example from a soccer game illustrates the deconstruction of the subject-object dichotomy as follows: 'A ball is not an ordinary object, for it is what it is only if a subject holds it. Over there, on the ground, it is nothing; it is stupid; it has no meaning, no function and no value. . . . Let us consider the one who holds [the ball]. If he makes it move around him, he is awkward, a bad player. The ball isn't there for the body; the exact contrary is true: the body is the object of the ball; the subject moves around this sun' (Serres 2007: 225).

CHAPTER TWO

# Rhythm
## *Requiem for a Dream*

*Requiem for a Dream*, the hyperkinetic second feature film by Aronofsky, is based on Hubert Selby Jr.'s 1978 novel of the same title. It follows the spiralling plunge into desperation of its four main characters, whose lives closely inter- twine through varying phases of drug addiction. This emotionally exhaust- ing descent is presented to the spectator from within by means of the film's affective-aesthetic system, which is best characterized as overwhelming in a particularly negative way. The film begins in summer, with its hopeful protago- nists starting out chasing their dreams, a quest in which drugs – amphetamines and heroin – play a central role. The first narrative thread centres on Sara Gold- farb (Ellen Burstyn), an elderly widow living in Brooklyn, who becomes patho- logically obsessed with regaining her youthful figure after receiving a hoax invitation to participate in a television game show. In order to fit into her best bright-red dress, she starts on a regimen of amphetamine weight-loss prescrip- tion pills throughout the day, combined with a sedative at night to cancel out the effects of the amphetamines. Meanwhile her son Harry (Jared Leto) and his best friend Tyrone (Marlon Wayans) enter into illegal heroin trading in an attempt to get rich quickly. *Requiem for a Dream* expresses the protagonists' accelerated journey from bliss ('Summer') through purgatory ('Fall') to hell ('Winter') with particularly unsettling corporeal aesthetics that leave the spec- tator emotionally shattered for a long time after the film has finished. Spring is noticeably missing from the film, and thus it refuses to give any promise of the rejuvenation or rebirth associated with this season, which would provide the spectator with a sense of catharsis.[1] In fact, quite the opposite is true, since the film's ending brings about a particular affective dissonance, an assault on the spectator's senses, disturbing in a very primal way. *Requiem for a Dream* is clearly a film with 'afterlife', as Jane Stadler calls this, 'an influence that remains with us when we are affected by the sensory impact of films' (Stadler 2012: 2).

    This chapter argues that the affective dissonance in *Requiem for a Dream* is achieved by means of its rhythmic progression. This develops from a compulsive 'euphoric' to a discordant 'dysphoric' rhythm, a process that directly addresses the spectator's own corporeal rhythm. As Karen Pearlman argues, 'by creating the waves of tension and release, the spectator's body rhythm is drawn into a kind of synchronization with the film's rhythm' (Pearlman 2009: 248). Precisely in this way, *Requiem for a Dream*'s rhythm creates a contagious circuit between the aesthetic system of the film and the spectator's affective experience. In other words, the film evokes different sensuous responses from the spectator, ranging from congruent to incongruent, until, in the end, its painful, affective-aesthetic system overwhelms the spectator as part of its nightmarish crescendo.[2] *Sight & Sound* critic Xan Brooks describes *Requiem for a Dream* as follows: '[The film] runs on a flurry of split-screens, extreme close-ups and rapid edits (the average feature boasts between 600 and 700 cuts, this one has 2000). The result is highly impressive: a swooping, gut-churning assault on the senses, all underpinned by Clint Mansell's mesmerizing string score' (Brooks 2001: 49). This chapter argues that rhythm is both an intrinsic quality of film and the foundation of affective operation between the cinematic body and the lived-body of the spectator within the cinematic event. I shall employ the notion as an analytical tool for understanding the operational structure of *Requiem for a Dream* in the spirit of Henri Lefebvre's 'rhythmanalysis'. First I shall explain what the relationship is among rhythm, emotion and film aesthetics. Then I shall present a more detailed analysis of the film and its rhythmic fluctuation between natural (variable, non-metronomic) and artificial (invariable, metronomic) bodily rhythms, which incites progression from euphoria to dysphoria, as in the two phases of drug addiction. In the end I shall show how the film evokes a sense of emotional urgency by its painful affective-aesthetic system, which undermines both the affective and cognitive agency of the spectator.

## Rhythm, Emotion and Film Aesthetics

Of course, the concept of rhythm as a means of evoking emotions is not new in theories of affective elicitation in the aesthetic experience. It has fascinated filmmakers, film scholars and philosophers alike. For instance, Siegfried Kracauer wrote about the 'resonance effect' between the spectator and cinema, which in his view provokes kinaesthetic bodily responses such as 'muscular reflexes, motor impulses or the like' and causes 'a stir in deep bodily layers. It is our sense organs which are called into play' (Kracauer 1997: 158). It is this kinaesthetic resonance that brings the spectator close to 'poetic emotion' (Kracauer 1997: 175). Philosopher Susanne Langer observed similarities between music and emotion based on their rhythmic patterns of motion and rest, tension and release. Music and emotion share a dynamic structure that reveals 'the rationale of feelings, the rhythm and pattern of their rise and decline and intertwining' (Langer 1976: 222). More recently, Janet Harbord has defined cinema as a medium that is sensitive to the world's flow of energy, due to the rhythmic quality inherent in the creation of affective significance (Harbord 2007: 146). And Yvette Bíro argues that rhythm is the basic strategy of organizing all cinematic elements into an affective-aesthetic whole, and that in fact rhythm itself is the 'dramatic design' of cinema (Bíro 2008: 232). Filmmakers, such as Sergei Eisenstein, have also been intrigued by rhythmic sound-and-image experiences and their relation to emotions as based on mutual resonance (Eisenstein 1957: 71). In his metrically assembled cinematic works, Jean Epstein aims to reach the spectator's emotions by means of rhythmic velocities, movements and vibrations (Epstein 1993b: 244). Germaine Dulac writes about cinema as a visual symphony made of rhythmic images that 'feel' and 'think', and that, by doing so, move the 'soul' of the spectator (Dulac 1978: 37). For Ingmar Bergman, film is mainly rhythm, affecting the spectator's emotions directly by means of its 'inhalation and exhalation in continuous sequence' (Bergman 1960: 7). And finally, Michael Haneke too has argued that it is through rhythm that a filmmaker is able to impact the spectator more deeply, because 'basically film is about rhythm'.[3]

As argued in the introduction, Aronofsky is a filmmaker who values visual style over 'traditional' story development or character identification. Rhythm seems to be a central strategy by which he orchestrates the composition of imagery, cinematographic framing, editing, sound and music. It might even be said that Aronofsky's films function as pieces of music insofar as they move the spectator directly: physically, motorically, affectively and intellectually, since intellect is a matter of the body. The rhythm of cinema in general and of Aronofsky's films in particular resonates in the spectator's heart rhythms, felt as muscular tension and skin crawling. As we have seen in the previous chapter, in *Pi* there is an organic or dynamic tension, based on an anxious rhythm that affects the spectator at a nervous, sensorial and sensual level by means of kinetic audiovisual noise. In *Requiem for a Dream*, such 'rhythmic aesthetics' are taken to the extreme, rhythm being the most salient organizational strategy of stylistic elements in the film. Therefore, the central argument in this chapter is that the film's rhythm evokes emotion because its rhythm *carries* emotion and vice versa, and all sensuous dynamics between the film and the spectator seem to originate from rhythm. The rhythmic progression in *Requiem for a Dream* epitomizes a change in the sense of self, from intentional to non-intentional in the face of growing addiction. The resulting loss of agency makes the body no longer function as a lived-body, but as a 'thing-body', open to systematic abuse, withdrawn from the flow of the world and from authentic relations with others (Kemp 2009: 130).

But what is rhythm, and how can rhythm 'carry emotion'? One definition in Webster's dictionary identifies rhythm as 'the aspect of music comprising all the elements (as accent, meter and tempo) that relate to forward movement'. In his book *The Philosopher's Touch*, François Noudelmann discusses Roland Barthes's sensitivity to (musical) rhythm in relation to movement in the sense of bodily engagement, vibration and performance: rhythm is 'what beats in the body, what beats the body or better . . . this body that beats' (Barthes cited in Noudelmann 2012: 137). Similarly, emotions are patterned and progressive changes in the body, variations in valence, energy and tension. Rhythm and emotion are related, as they share affective variables such as regularity (regular-irregular), smoothness (smooth-rough), energy (alert-weary), complexity (simple-complex), valence (pleasant-unpleasant), tension (tense-relaxed) and so forth (Keller and Schubert 2011: 142). These affective variables also have a distinctive bodily dimension reflected by changes in the embodied appraisals of a person in a given situation (Prinz 2004: 163). Regular, smooth rhythms are associated with 'easy' emotions and irregular, rough rhythms with 'uneasy' ones. Thus emotions emerge as rhythmic changes in the individual's affective bodily valence, energy and tension as he or she engages with the environment. For instance, Jesse Prinz explains how surprise emerges as an embodied appraisal after a violation of expectation has taken place (irregularity). Some surprises involve an intrusion of harmful entities (alertness, tension, unpleasantness), while some others involve beneficial opportunities (arousal, smoothness, pleasantness) (Prinz 2004: 163–64). This is the way one affectively experiences the world in general and cinema in particular – through rhythm. In this context, the following passages from John Dewey seem worth quoting in their entirety:

> The first characteristic of the environing world that makes possible the existence of artistic form is rhythm. There is rhythm in nature before poetry, painting, architecture and music exist. Were it not so, rhythm as an essential property of form would be merely superimposed upon material, not an operation through which material effects its own culmination in experience. The larger rhythms of nature are so bound up with the conditions of even elementary human subsistence [which] induced [man] to impose rhythm on changes where they did not appear. . . . The formative arts that shaped things of use were wedded to the rhythms of voice and self-contained movements of the body, and out of the union technical arts gained the quality of fine art. . . . Underneath the rhythm of every art and of every work of art there lies . . . the basic pattern of the relations of the live creature to his environment. . . . The supposition that the interest in rhythm which dominates the fine arts can be explained simply on the basis of rhythmic processes in the living body is but another case of the separation of organism from environment. . . . [Rhythm is] the condition of form in experience and hence of expression. But an esthetic experience, the work of art in its actuality, is perception. Only as these rhythms, even if embodied in an outer object that is itself a product of art, become a rhythm in experience itself are they esthetic. And this rhythm in what is experienced is something quite different from intellectual recognition that there is rhythm in the external thing. (Dewey 1958: 147–50; 162)

Rhythm is movement, a series of developments with a particular tempo, from impetus to rest, from ascension to descension. It is a dimension of cinema that, perhaps due to the influence of Eisenstein, is often associated with editing and the way in which filmmakers manipulate the duration of shots in relation to one another. For instance, David Bordwell and Kristin Thompson distinguish between metrical and dynamic rhythmic relations between shots, based on duration. Dynamic rhythm for slowing down the film's pace is created by steadily lengthening shots. Shortening the shots will result in acceleration. Metrical rhythm is established by keeping the duration of the shots approximately the same (Bordwell and Thompson 2001: 257). A similar distinction can be made between 'upbeat' and 'downbeat' shots, which are respectively shots accented by a greater affective impact and shots that are not (Van Leeuwen 1985: 216). But as Theo Van Leeuwen points out, the shot itself is already rhythmic, both on the level of image and on that of sound ('profilmic' rhythm). There is the rhythm of dialogue and narration, the rhythm of accompanying music and sound effects. There is the rhythm of movement both within the frame and in framing mobility (the movement of camera), as well as the rhythm of image composition. According to Van Leeuwen:

> [It] is these rhythms, separately or in combination, which originate and determine the filmic rhythm. Rather than that film editors impose their rhythm on the images, the images and sounds impose their rhythms on the editors, restrict them as to where and how the film can be cut and the sound effects positioned ('layed'), furnish the potential cutting points for which the good film editor is said to have a 'feeling'. (Van Leeuwen 1985: 217)

Van Leeuwen distinguishes between rhythmic accents and rhythmic junctures, which determine the location of potential cutting points. Rhythmic accents consist of the cyclical alternation of accented and non-accented sensations – the rhythmic contrast between long and short, strong and weak, tense and lax, active and dormant, etc. Rhythmic junctures are filmic units that form rhythmic groups within the cyclical alternation. These are marked by a momentary interruption in the organization of the accented and non-accented sensation, such as a pause in speech or music, or a cessation of body movement. Furthermore, in the process of synchronizing profilmic rhythm with the editing rhythm, the editor needs to choose one of the profilmic rhythms as the initiating one to which other profilmic elements are subordinated (Van Leeuwen 1985: 217–18). The resulting cinematic rhythm can have at least two functions. The first is a cognitive function, which aligns the fluctuation of cinematic rhythm with the spectator's attentive focus. The accented moments help to keep the spectator's attention focused on the filmic event. The second one is the expressive function, which holds that rhythm articulates the film's affective mood and emotional atmosphere. Marcel Martin explains this as follows: '[A] slow rhythm may give an impression of yearning . . . of sensual immersion in nature . . . of powerlessness before a blind destiny . . . or the hopelessness and monotony of the search for simple human contact. . . . A fast, nervous, dynamic rhythm gives an effect of anger . . . of speech, of feverish activity' . . . (Martin cited in Van Leeuwen 1985: 221).

In addition, Van Leeuwen proposes two further functions for cinematic rhythm under the categories of ranking and grouping. Ranking is the process of making certain cinematic elements prominent at the expense of others by means of their rhythmically accented position. Grouping is the way in which rhythm provides 'frames' for the cinematic elements, for instance according to their dramatic ('micro' level) and thematic ('macro' level) function (Van Leeuwen 1985: 222–23). In *Requiem for a Dream*, the rhythmic dynamism is established from the very beginning of its opening scene. The film starts with television footage of a (fictitious) daytime game show. This show deals with such issues as dieting and self-improvement, and is hosted by a character called Tappy Tibbons (Christopher McDonald) in front of an overzealous live audience. The initiating rhythm of this footage is the frenzied, intense, non-natural chanting of the diegetic audience: 'Juice-by-Tappy! Juice-by-Tappy! Juice-by-Tappy! OooooOOOOH-Tappy's-got-juice! Tappy's-got-juice! Tappy's-got-juice! OooooOOOOH-Tappy!' This initiating rhythm is accompanied by another rhythmic carrier, the way in which the show's credits appear in quick succession on the diegetic television screen.

The opening has several functions. First, it establishes a rhythmic mood characterized by affective falseness as opposed to emotional sincerity in seeking human contact. For Sara is addicted to this ridiculous show, believing that it represents a utopian realm of perfect happiness where everyone has an equal opportunity to occupy the spotlight, to have dreams come true and to 'create excellence' in life.[4] Secondly, the artificial energy and forced cheerfulness of this show stands in harsh contrast to Sara's everyday dreary ('natural') life rhythm, which is mostly spent indoors in a scruffy apartment in Brighton Beach, Brooklyn. Her drug-using son Harry only comes to visit with the purpose of stealing her television set, which he takes to the pawnshop for ready cash. The first rhythmic juncture is the abrupt and unexpected cut to a close-up of the television set's electric cord being pulled out of the wall socket in the course of this theft. It epitomizes the ferocity with which Harry's unfilial act snaps Sara out of her artificial utopia and back into the dreary rhythm of her reality. Rhythmic conflicts of this kind structure *Requiem for a Dream* throughout, epitomizing a clash between the natural rhythms of everyday life's bodily motion, and drug-induced, artificial rhythms, which eventually dominate the former.

## Artificial Rhythm

In the dreary flow of her life, Sara can find consolation only by relishing high-calorie comfort food, especially chocolates, which she sensuously feels with a feathery touch of her fingertips before she slips them into her mouth. This is a guilty pleasure she has to give up if she is to fit in the elegant red dress she optimistically plans to wear on the television game show in which she believes she has been invited to participate. Like *The Tappy Tibbons Show*, the red dress symbolizes the good life that is out of reach in Sara's current reality. In that life, her son would be a successful member of society who purposefully realizes his potential through happy marriage and a decent job. The red dress also creates a contrast between Sara's past happiness and the bleakness of her present circumstances, characterized by her wardrobe of graceless, oversized cardigans and skirts in the unassuming, washed-out colours that also dominate the décor of her apartment. Thus the red dress in itself could be seen as a rhythmic accent in the colour design of the film, marking further rhythmic conflicts yet to come. There is the conflict between her mental hunger for weight loss and her physical hunger for comfort food, which is made rhythmically palpable in the scene in which she stares at half a grapefruit, a boiled egg and a cup of black coffee, the only foodstuffs allowed for breakfast on her rigorous diet. The breakfast suddenly disappears with an emphatic, gluttonous slurp.[5] These rhythmic accents stand in harsh contrast to the monotonous rhythm of the clock ticking in the background, epitomizing the way in which time always seems to drag for a person who is on a diet. Hallucinations of juicy, sizzling hamburgers, platters filled with aromatic dishes and cupcakes with decorative,

sugary icing appear out of nowhere to torment Sara, signs of her body struggling to adjust to a changed eating pattern.

Unable to stick to her diet, Sara then starts to take weight-loss amphetamine pills throughout the day. The effect of the amphetamines is overwhelming, as depicted in an accelerating montage sequence. Sara is first
shown dancing around her apartment to a silly, upbeat Latin number that
Aronofsky defines as 'cha cha played by Bugs Bunny'.[6] Next she is neuroti-
cally sipping coffee, and finally she is seen trying to watch television but unable to sit still under the influence of the drug. In another scene, the camera
pans across her apartment while she is shown cleaning up in a frenzy. This is
realized in time-lapse photography and accompanied by fast-motion television noises, highlighting her new bodily 'energy' in contrast to her previous
physical passivity. Unable to relax under the influence of the amphetamines,
she has to take a sedative before bedtime, with the effect that the rhythm of
the world seems to slow down, epitomized in Tappy Tibbons's stretched-out
speech that Sara listens to before she passes out. This is clearly a situation in
which the body is forced to adjust to an artificial rhythm, instead of following
its own biorhythmic cycle.

Similarly, the first scene in which Harry and Tyrone are shown shooting
up is done with a very quick hip-hop montage sequence that lasts no more
than five seconds, with a series of extreme close-up shots at the rate of twelve
frames per second. These include sharp images of a mouth tearing open the
plastic bag containing the drugs, heroin dissolving in liquid, a lighter heating
the drug solution, the solution boiling up, the piston of the syringe drawing up
the drug, the iris of an eye widening and the heroin circulating in the bloodstream. The sequence is accompanied by jagged sound effects that express
audibly – or rather, 'audiolize' – the extreme physical rush of getting high. This
rush gives Harry a feeling of empowerment, an illusion of being capable of doing anything. In this state, he imagines grabbing a policeman's gun and tossing
it between him and his friend. This scene, which takes place in the realm of
mental subjectivity only, is accompanied by a brisk techno track that emulates
Harry's mental state. But it does not correspond with his physical state, as his
body has grown sluggish and lethargic as the drug wears off. The juxtaposition of high and low rhythm in this scene defines the affective development of

*Requiem for a Dream* in its entirety, while creating an ever-increasing contrast between the two ends of the high/low, natural/artificial spectrum.

Despite the weary effects of the drug, the feeling of empowerment in the rush scenes plants the seed of ambition in Harry's mind. As a result, he and Tyrone enter the illegal drug trade in an attempt to realize their dreams. This is depicted in the fantasy scene in which Harry visualizes his girlfriend Marion (Jennifer Connolly) waiting for him at the end of the Coney Island pier with a wide seascape view in the background. This is a typical emotional-metaphorical image.[7] It combines the metaphor of love as a physical force, as Harry is magnetically drawn to Marion, with the metaphor of ambition or potential opportunity. The world behind Marion is thus wide open. Their ambitions seem to be realized rapidly at first, as represented in the montage sequences which cut quickly among shots of drugs exchanging hands, drugs being consumed and Marion working on her fashion designs, accompanied by the emphatic sound of a cash register or a police siren. The rhythmic thrill in these sequences is contagious, because their audiovisual cadence directly draws the spectator into their energetic staccato, evoking an emotional rush.

Getting high for the rush is the reason for Marion's drug abuse as well, at least in the beginning. In the scene in which she is introduced, Marion is first shot from a high angle, her gaze directed to the top of a many-storey building. The next, low-angle shot is from her point of view. The composition of this frame, with rows of windows ascending towards the bright blue sky in the background, clearly communicates her desire to 'shoot up' in order to escape the conventional life offered her by her financially well-to-do but emotionally detached parents. The rush and the excitement of going against the mainstream are also conveyed by the techno music that accompanies Marion and Harry's escape from the security staff of the same building, where in a previous scene they had broken a security lock in order to enter a rooftop terrace. In another scene, there is an electrifying tune on the sound track while Marion, Harry and Tyrone get high on ecstasy. This scene is filmed with an extreme wide-angle lens to create a fish-eye effect, while time-lapse photography done in waves transmits the euphoric effect of being 'on speed'.

The increased level of pleasurable psychological and physical arousal in the 'high' phase of drug abuse is considered the basis for addiction. Drugs narrow attention to the here and now, which leads to the experience of 'an increased responsivity to immediate external cues to the exclusion of other past or future events' (Wilson 1987: 346). Drugs are addictive because they transform negative emotions into positive affects by restricting perception to immediate cues, among other things. They reduce cognitive processing to the most salient aspects of experience at the expense of dispositional self-consciousness. In *Requiem for a Dream*, the linearity of time gives way to time-lessness in the euphoric drug scenes. These scenes are characterized by the compulsive rhythm of a techno beat that is seemingly devoid of any linear progression. The (extreme) wide-angle lens reduces the protagonists' world to an isolated bubble, while time-lapse photography condenses temporal du-ration to a single moment. But this kind of artificial flow is in harsh contrast to the agonizing crescendo towards the end of the film, which epitomizes the way in which their drug addiction eventually overwhelms the affective agency of the characters, leaving them thoroughly shattered. In *Requiem for a Dream*, it is precisely this conflict between artificial, drug-induced rhythm and natural rhythm that fascinates. As argued, the film is about the disruption of the lat-ter, while at the same time it creates frenzied, intense rhythmic experiences for the spectator. As Henri Lefebvre points out, non-human phenomena are also made up of rhythm – measures, beats, motifs and harmonies. In the filmic event, these may become more complicated than natural human rhythms, with powerful, unsettling consequences when the cinematic rhythm gains dominance over the spectatorial rhythm (Lefebvre 1991: 206), as I hope to be able to demonstrate in more detail later on.

The conflict between artificial, drug-induced rhythm and natural bodily rhythm in *Requiem for a Dream* has its counterpart in the way in which the af-fective development of the film progresses from a euphoric phase of drug ad-diction to dysphoric devastation. The coexistence of euphoria and dysphoria is represented, for instance, by the continuous use of split-screen in the film. Its opening scene, in which Sara hides in the closet while Harry steals her tele-vision set, concretizes Sara's desire to escape into some utopian realm, away from dreary reality. Split screen often gives the effect of two things being stuck together in eternal separation. This is also the case in *Requiem for a Dream*, such as in the scene in which Marion and Harry, after having taken ecstasy, are lying on their bed, gently caressing each other's naked bodies. As the frame is a split screen, one sees Harry's face on the left with Marion's face on the right,

Marion's face on the right with her finger caressing Harry's belly or earlobe on the left (figure 2.1) or Harry's face on the left with his hand stroking the palm of Marion's hand on the right in (extreme) close-up. The split becomes a form of touch, in which separation enables an opening up to the touch of the other, which is also felt as such by the spectator.

Furthermore, this pleasurable haptic effect is often associated with the drug ecstasy, which is known to increase physical sensitivity and feelings of intimacy (euphoria). At the same time, the split screen communicates the existential distance (dysphoria) between Harry and Marion, even in the most intimate moments. The smooth rhythm of bodily movement accompanied by the ambient score has a soothing effect, while the discontinuity between the scenes disrupts the affective flow between the two characters. In another scene, Marion is shown shooting up in front of a mirror, and she continues to watch her reflection while the scene slowly fades out into an engulfing whiteness. This epitomizes the pleasurable experience of being embraced by one's surroundings as she feels it under the influence of drugs. In this way, the film invites the spectator to participate in the euphoric rush from within, only to disrupt the experience abruptly by showing the painful effects of physical

**Figure 2.1.** Split screen as a form of touch? Screen capture, *Requiem for a Dream* (2000).

dependence on drugs in the second act of the film, entitled 'Fall'. This is how *Requiem for a Dream* as a bodily event can be understood in relation to the cognitive processes at work in addiction, as it covers an affective gamut that runs from initial rush to high phase, only to end in drug tolerance, withdrawal and the ultimate crash.

The development of *Requiem for a Dream* thus progresses from one phase of drug addiction to another, brought about by the simultaneous and analogous development of the film's idiosyncratic rhythmic pattern, as created by music, sound and editing. This rhythmic progression develops from a metrical, continuous note towards an explosive dissonance, with devastating effects. In the film's prologue, the scene in which Harry steals Sara's television set, there is high-pitched sound of orchestral string instruments tuning up on the sound track, as at the beginning of a concert. This sound has a metaphorical function, underlining the discord prominent in the scene and the dysfunctional mother-son relationship. And of course there is a reference to the title as it creates an association with *requiems*, musical compositions expressive of death and mourning in religious services and especially the Catholic Mass. Not only does the sound of the orchestral tuning enforce this religious association, it also turns into a morbid narrative expectation. The opening credits alternate with shots of Harry and Tyrone wheeling the television set along the Coney Island Boardwalk. This is accompanied by the most famous number on Clint Mansell's soundtrack, entitled 'Lux Aeterna' ('eternal light'), which is the leitmotif of the film. This number, performed by the Kronos Quartet, first creates the unsettling emotional effect of increasing rhythmic anxiety, evoking the spectator's expectation that the film's characters are inevitably heading towards an impending disaster, an expectation fulfilled in the later stages of the film.

'Lux Aeterna' combines a sparse, repetitive melody with an intense, rhythmic crescendo and a sharp pitch of string instruments with scratchy undertones. Its musical properties are best characterized as unpleasant in their valence, although enjoyable to some extent, alert in their energy, and edgy in their tension. Thus 'Lux Aeterna' complements all narrative turning points in the film, such as when Harry and Tyrone get ready for their first drug deal, when Sara posts her application for a guest appearance on the television show, and when Marion leaves her psychiatrist's apartment. At the beginning of the film, the music operates through what Jeff Smith calls polarization, 'an audiovisual interaction in which the affective meaning of the music moves the content of the image towards the specific character of the music' (Smith 1999: 160). In *Requiem for a Dream*, 'Lux Aeterna' first shifts the affective meaning of the visual event closer to the menacing emotional properties of the music. This happens when one watches the 'unruly' image of Tyrone and Harry wheeling the stolen television set past the vast hulk of an old rollercoaster and an odd red tower.[8] Later in the film, the same tune acquires the function of what Smith calls affective congruence, when 'the matching of affective meaning in both music and visuals heighten[s] the spectator's experience of the overall effect' (Smith 1999: 160). Thus, as the protagonists sink deeper into devastation, 'Lux Aeterna' intensifies the affective quality of the cinematic image, which is terror and desperation. Take, for instance, the scene in which Sara walks the streets of New York City, totally confused but determined to find her way to the television studio. She has withdrawn both from her own natural body rhythm, and from the rhythm of the world around her. As Lefebvre would have it, there is a conflict between Sara's bodily space and bodies-in-space. This state is directly experienced by the spectator due to the polyrhythmic quality of the image.

This scene is also an example of how a feeling of impending disaster streams as an emotional undercurrent through the whole film, embodied in its audiovisual flow, which oscillates between rhythmic highs and lows. Mellow, pleasant, ambient melodies and the electric energy of the techno tracks, are closely followed by more sorrowful, ominous tunes and sound effects. The rhythm of the scenes 'on drugs' is joyful at first, energetic, electrified, laid-back and fun, but this feel-good effect quickly gives way to nervousness and restlessness as the protagonists appear unable to keep their drug habits in check. This is enacted by lengthy, highly repetitive hip-hop montage sequences, in which temporal and spatial specificity is torn apart, graphic clashes are preferred to graphic matches and regular shots are combined with time-lapse and still photography. In addition, the sound in these sequences is extremely layered, combining Mansell's percussive score with diegetic and non-diegetic sound effects. The outcome is chaotic and controlled at the same time, implying a situation just about to skid out of control. Thus, the hip-hop montage in *Requiem for a Dream* interweaves many diverse narrative layers with distinct affective qualities in such a way that the film as an aesthetic whole embodies a gamut of addiction phases, from smooth rush through repetitive obsession, to loss of control and self-destruction.

Repetitive obsession is evident from the way in which the film depicts Sara's extreme pill popping, which quickly becomes a routine for her. The film repeats her daily activities in quick succession, accompanied by a sound of distant giggling that underlines her growing insecurity. For Lefebvre, rhythm is linked to needs as biological instincts. The rhythmic repetition in this scene is an intrinsic part of Sara's need for a fuller life, which she believes can be achieved through a television appearance. This need is progressively trans-formed into insatiable desire, and finally into a pathological obsession. The progression is accompanied by lack of control over her natural rhythm, which she has given up to amphetamines. Frequently she is seen unscrewing the cap of a jar, throwing a pill into her mouth, attempting to zip up her red dress, weighing herself on the scales, checking her mailbox for the game show invita-tion and repeating the cycle all over again. Loss of control of her natural bodily rhythm is palpable in the scene in which Sara is busy housecleaning. Superim-posed by a close-up of a clock ticking away frantically, the scene shows Sara making the bed, organizing the contents of her drawers, sweeping away cob-webs, vacuuming the floor, dusting the bookshelves, removing stains from her carpet and throwing away stale food from her refrigerator. This is clearly the portrayal of a phase in which the body's natural rhythm has been taken over by the artificial, chemical rhythm of the drug. In other words, the hyperactive rhythm produced by amphetamine overrules Sara's own bodily rhythms, or-chestrating her actions and redirecting her energy to the point of exhaustion. This 'rhythmic clash' – or polyrhythm – is also embodied by the sound track, which here combines the peacefully ambling 'Lux Aeterna' with rapid-tempo sounds originating from *The Tappy Tibbons Show* on television. This scene cre-ates a circuit of contagion between the aesthetic system of the film and the affective experience of the spectator, as it disturbs the rhythm by which the spectator takes in the film, literally making the spectator edgy and uneasy.

This kind of narrowing of priorities – compulsive cleaning – at the expense of responsible self-determination that Sara exhibits is valid for Harry's situation as well. His worrying about his mother's drug abuse is quickly subdued by his craving for his next heroin fix, as depicted in a mental flash-forward to the act of shooting up. Both Harry and Marion are now preoccupied with heroin, yet their shared addiction no longer brings them together, but starts tearing them apart. This change in their relationship is illustrated by an altered split screen technique: now there is no rhythmic synchronization between the two screens, which both show the same thing – heroin dissolving in a liquid, the shot being prepared, the drug entering the bloodstream and Harry and Marion's irises widening. This sequence is followed by one that is filmed from above with a slowly rotating camera, moving upwards from a medium close-up to a long shot of Harry and Marion lying with their heads together in a kind of yin-yang formation. Marion's utterance 'I love you, Harry' is rendered totally meaningless because the cinematic image contradicts it by suggesting that Marion and Harry are now 'together alone' in their drug abuse. As Peta Malins writes, 'when a body becomes a "junkie", when it becomes "dangerous", "diseased", "dirty" or "addicted", its connections with other bodies are disrupted' (Malins 2005: 493).

For Sara, the disruption of bodily intentionality increases as her tolerance for amphetamines builds. As she is unable to experience the same type of high as in the beginning, the dreariness of her life returns with a vengeance. Her brand-new, switched-off television set, which was a gift from Harry, looms like a colossal monster in a corner of her darkened apartment, while she sits in front of it apathetically despite the stimulants in her system. Richard Schusterman, among others, has pointed out that sensorial intensity caused by drug abuse can quickly become dull and meaningless, because 'intensification of pleasure cannot simply be achieved by intensity of sensation. Sensory appreciation is typically dulled when blasted with extreme sensations' (Schusterman 2008: 37). Thus Sara increases the dosage of her weight-loss pills on her own initiative and starts suffering from amphetamine psychosis, hallucinating that she is appearing as a guest on *The Tappy Tibbons Show* in her red dress as a much younger and more extroverted version of herself. The distorted image created by an extreme wide-angle lens conveys the sense of her warped, mind while her refrigerator 'comes alive', threatening to attack her. She mixes different kinds of drugs and the situation gets even worse: trapped in her own mind, she can no longer find safety either inside or outside her home. The fish-eye effect in a scene in which she is waiting for her turn at the doctor's office illustrates the way in which she experiences her being-in-the-world. Enclosed in her own drug-induced psychosis, Sara becomes increasingly isolated from her physical environment, which is also emphasized by the use of sound. The sounds of the world speed up or slow down randomly, while the sounds from her own mind are amplified, terrorizing her to the point of ultimate paranoia.

In the meanwhile, Tyrone is arrested in the middle of a drug gang shoot-out, and Harry has to use most of their money to bail him out. The ongoing war between drug gangs makes it hard to obtain drugs, and both Marion and Harry are forced to go 'cold turkey', constantly suffering from withdrawal symptoms characterized by dysphoria, as opposed to the euphoria that typifies the 'high' phase. According to Jon Elster, in this phase of addiction the individual's craving for the drug turns into an attempt simply to avoid dysphoria, instead of attempting to reach euphoria. The craving itself becomes an unpleasant experience instead of pleasant one, as it was at the beginning of the addiction (Elster 1999: 63). The change in colour design in the film runs parallel to this altered drug experience. The first part of *Requiem for a Dream* is dominated by warm, inviting colours and natural light, and the image is filled with hope for self-fulfilment. In the second part, the dominant colour theme is cold and bluish, with artificial light that instantly creates a despairing mood. The time lapse photography, which in the first part of the film created an effect of euphoric rush, now has a juddering rhythmic effect, which, combined with a dominant buzzing sound, conveys an experience of tremors and chills, thus enacting the experience of a heroin addict going through withdrawal symptoms. Harry convinces Marion to have sex with her psychiatrist in exchange for money to buy drugs, and when she is leaving the man's apartment she is filmed with a SnorriCam, the lens facing her directly. This provides a sense of her emotional numbness, which results from her awareness that she is capable of doing anything to finance her addiction. The SnorriCam conveys a sense of blocked intentionality. This is directly transmitted to the spectators as they engage with the film as a bodily event that in this scene has become frozen and arrested. Here the film embodies how heroin has dampened all other aspects of her life, including her human dignity as an emotional agent, her life now revolving around getting the next fix.

## Dysphoric Rhythm

As suggested throughout this analysis, the progressive drug addiction of the protagonists duly disturbs their 'rhythmic relationship' with the world, which results in loss of their agential control. Agency itself implies rhythm, but the more one's own natural rhythm is subdued by unnatural rhythm, the less sensitive one becomes to the flow of the world. Glen Mazis explains this as follows:

> [T]here is a pulse, a rhythm given by the background of a planet full of myriad other timings which give it a relentless beat, but we have to enter its patternings through our own timing in order to experience this. It is a two-sided game of existence and being alive: what brings pain and destruction is the same marrow of events that brings joy and building – a tide of risky potential joinings. (Mazis 2002: 36)

Sara's pain is caused by the disturbance of this rhythmic bond with the world, for instance. First her physical adjustment to amphetamines brings her life's rhythm to a standstill, as epitomized in the silent, darkly lit shots of her sitting immobilized in front of the mute television set. After she starts exceeding her prescribed dosage, her natural rhythm gets more and more out of joint, which drives her to go around in circles in her apartment compulsively and nervously to the rhythm of an irregular metronomic beat, while lights flicker around her. The rhythm of the world gets increasingly warped for her as well (figure 2.2), randomly speeding up, slowing down, threatening to overwhelm or come to a halt altogether. 'Everything is all mixed up', she complains to her unconcerned physician.

For Harry and Marion, the thrill of taking heroin, followed by a restful feeling, is abbreviated as the periods of craving grow longer. Their cold turkey does not simply result in a painful, nauseating feeling, but it also has the frenetic rhythm of an (impossible) attempt to escape one's own body, an experience that Jamie Skye Bianco describes as 'the body's forcible attempt to re-member a prior sensate balance' (Bianco 2004: 388). So the deeper the protagonists move towards drug-induced oblivion, the farther they jerk away from 'devoting' themselves to the world as 'eurhythmic' bodily subjects – to use Henri Lefebvre's term – to the point of no return. According to Lefebvre:

> The body consists of a bundle of rhythms, different but in tune. . . . The body produces a garland of rhythms, one could say a bouquet, though

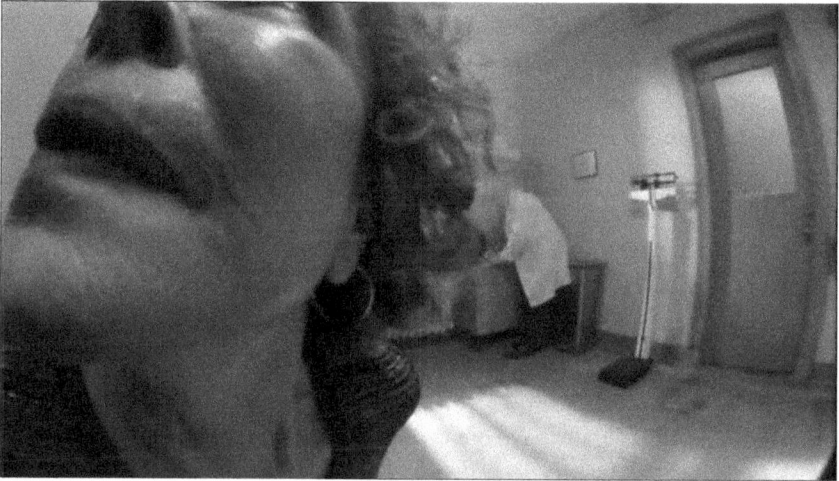

**Figure 2.2.** Sara's warped world. Screen capture, *Requiem for a Dream* (2000).

these words suggest an aesthetic arrangement . . . the harmony of the body. . . . What is certain is that harmony sometimes (often) exists: eurhythmia. The eu-rhythmic body, composed of diverse rhythms . . . keeps them in metastable equilibrium, which is always understood and often recovered with the exception of disturbances (arrhythmia) that sooner or later become illness. (Lefebvre 1991: 20)

In *Requiem for a Dream*, the descent of the protagonists can be understood as a progression from a eurhythmic to an arrhythmic bodily state, which is re-lentlessly embodied in the film's own rhythm. This rhythm starts off as a met-ronomic flow, but as the film progresses, it transforms into a cacophonic and disturbing beat that has a particularly unsettling effect. The film forces upon the spectator the effects of arrhythmia, the physical condition experienced as an irregular heartbeat. The cacophonic effect is especially efficacious for the climactic last part of the film, in which all the different arrhythmic patterns that epitomize the protagonists' pain come together in a discordant whole. The effect is built up gradually. There is a dissonant musical melody that consists of a quick succession of percussive string strikes in different force-ful sonorities, bathing the scenes in a catastrophic mood. The cutting rhythm progressively increases in tempo, synchronizing with the accelerating pace at which the characters' destinies approach each other and eventually collide violently. Since we have a natural tendency to entrain our bodies, our senses, feelings and movements to the rhythms of the world, we cannot help but tune in to the cacophonic rhythm of the film's climax as well. Similarly, John Dewey writes that an aesthetic experience is only possible in a world patterned by the punctuation of pain and pleasure, which we experience rhythmically. In pleasure there is harmonic adjustment to the conditions of existence, while pain has to do with perturbation and conflict (Dewey 1958: 17). Similarly, experiencing art 'is a rhythm of intakings and outgivings. [Its] succession is punctuated and made a rhythm by the existence of intervals, periods in which one phase is ceasing, and the other is inchoate and preparing' (Dewey 1958: 56). If the world of *Requiem for a Dream* is punctuated by conflict and harmony in Dewey's sense, this has to do with the alternation of natural and unnatural rhythms. And unnatural rhythms become more and more dominant as the film gets increasingly addiction-infused. As Bianco puts it, 'we *sense* and *feel drugged* in this explosion of intensive powers [of the film and its] relentless organization of non-organic rhythms, temporalities, diffractions and affects decentring the capacities of the [spectator]' (Bianco 2004: 388).

The descent of the protagonists to rock-bottom culminates in the third part of the film, entitled 'Winter'. Here, Sara's hallucinations become more severe, her whole apartment buzzing with electricity to illustrate the extent to which drugs have poisoned her whole being. This disturbing effect reaches the spectators from within through a combination of the SnorriCam technique and point-of-view shots, so that it feels as if they were affectively positioned inside Sara's embodied mind. This is not a question of emotional identification, but affective mimicry, in which the spectator responds to the film's 'muscular gesture', as Jennifer Barker calls this (Barker 2009: 78). The participants on *The Tappy Tibbons Show*, including Sara's own alter ego, wearing an over-the-top red glitter dress with a Bride-of-Frankenstein hairdo, enter her living room, definitively disturbing the inside/outside distinction in her personal experience, a situation that can only be explained by psychosis. These creatures of her own imagination mock her modest belongings and then ridicule her to her face, giving flesh to her insecurities, while the walls of her apartment break down and the whole place is transformed into a television studio. A bizarre and chaotic fantasy sequence then follows in which Sara is surrounded by dancing game-show guests who demand to be fed by her until her suddenly anthropomorphized refrigerator threatens to swallow her and she escapes the apartment, screaming in terror.

By far the most disturbing part of *Requiem for a Dream* is the infamously painful montage sequence towards the end of the film. It cuts among Sara in a psychiatric hospital undergoing electroconvulsive treatment, unanesthetized; Marion performing an 'ass-to-ass' sexual act in a private sex show for a cheering group of investment bankers; Tyrone in jail somewhere in the American South, mashing boiled potatoes in a huge pan with a hand beater while a prison guard (a cameo appearance by Hubert Selby Jr.) laughs at his predicament; and Harry getting his gangrenous arm amputated. In this sequence, the sound resists being magnetized diegetically by the visual, but it transgresses the different spatial and temporal planes.[9] As a result, the spectators get entrapped between different narrative trajectories, which causes confusion about their own position in a troubling network of connecting scenes. Perhaps it could be said that the spatial and temporal dynamics in this sequence are based on a polyrhythmic relation between sound and image, which severely disturbs the rhythm of spectatorial engagement. Thus, for instance, we hear the bankers cheering while we see Sara suffering from convulsions after an electric shock. Consequently, the fates of the characters overlap in time, and we too get caught up in the intersection at which the different spatial and temporal planes meet. The emotional effect is still intensified by the sharp, disjointed and brutal string score, which has a harsh and thwarting effect, and which carries all the misery that has been accumulated in the course of events. The cutting frequency accelerates rapidly as the various situations come to a climax, so that it becomes almost impossible to distinguish among any of the spatial planes, until the image mercifully fades to white. In *Pi,* the engulfing white light can be considered to convey some kind of transcendental experience – albeit not unambiguously. In *Requiem for a Dream,* any such transcendence is falsified, which is in agreement with the anti-cathartic function of the film, insofar as its ending results in loss of agency – or insofar as the lived-body gives way to thing-body and to pain that swells to contaminate the protagonists' consciousness, as Scarry would have it. The only possible future for the protagonists is a further decline, either into self-deception or into insanity, which has led some critics to label the film one of the most despairing in history.[10]

Much attention has been paid to film openings as 'watching instructions' that give the spectator a sense of what the inner dynamics of the film will be (Kuntzel 1980; Elsaesser 2012). But as Yvette Bíro reminds us, the ending is just as important in the internal assemblage of each and every cinematic element of the film. As she puts it, '[T]he ending has the charge to sum up the whole' (Bíro 2008: 204). The ending of *Requiem for a Dream* is best characterized as what she calls turbulent, a moment when the film's internal affective tension reaches a 'boiling point' (Bíro 2008: 232). This boiling point is the reason why *Requiem for a Dream* becomes an overwhelmingly painful experience that paralyses our emotional agency in a fashion analogous to the incapacity of the characters to experience themselves as intentional agents. Thus, as they end up in humiliation and pain, stripped of any agential integrity, it is this same effect, if not the very experience, that the film forces the spectator to feel as well. This is caused by the film's affective parameters – especially its rhythm – which are organized in such a way that they first generate a sense of flow, but at some point disrupt this flow abruptly as the protagonists slide deeper into addiction.

Danielja Kulezic-Wilson writes that the musical flow of hip-hop, on which the audiovisual style of *Requiem for a Dream* is based, simultaneously creates and disrupts continuity. The repetitive 'breaks' and 'scratches' in this musical style rupture the melodic flow in such a way that the ruptures themselves become a systematic rhythmic pattern (Kulezic-Wilson 2008a: 27). Nevertheless, this 'rhythmic flow of ruptures' is regularly cut abruptly towards the end of the film, which epitomizes the lack of synchronicity not only in the bodies of the protagonists, but in the cinematic body as well. Lara Thompson makes a similar claim when she writes that the experimentation with rhythm in *Requiem for a Dream* draws the spectators into the drug-induced psychic disruption of the protagonists, but I feel that she wrongly concludes that consequently the spectators become empathetically bonded to them (Thompson 2011: 8–11). Empathy is considered a sharing response to the suffering of a cinematic character. This stands in contrast to sympathy, in which narrative alignment and moral allegiance (Smith 1995) – liking the character and what he stands for – are the most important parameters. With empathy, an 'imaginative reconstruction of another person's experience' (Nussbaum 2001: 302) appears to be the main variable. But empathy can actually be an impertinent reaction to somebody's suffering, especially if it lacks respect for the *otherness* of that person's experience. As Nussbaum puts it, with empathy, 'one must be aware both of the bad lot of the sufferer and of the fact that it is, right now, not one's own', for otherwise 'one would precisely have failed to comprehend the pain of another as *other*. One must also be aware of one's *qualitative difference* from the sufferer' (Nussbaum 2001: 327–28). Without such awareness, or even the effort to gain this awareness, empathy is merely a 'self-involved feeling' (Solomon 2007: 67) resulting from 'emotional contagion', which affects the other on a pre-reflective level. This kind of empathy is an appropriation of the other's experience by the self, a feeling that Bertolt Brecht termed 'crude empathy' (Brecht 1976: 518).

In *Requiem for a Dream*, the spectator's emotions are founded neither on such emotional contagion nor on the imaginative reconstruction of the other's experience. In fact, the quality of the film's unbearable ending causes the spectators to feel concern about their *own* peace of mind, rather than the suffering of the characters. This self-directed concern results from the direct, sensuous and rhythmic properties of the film, as registered in their affective intentionality, which induces pain in the spectator. This complicates, rather than enables, empathy. It is pain that is experienced as something that must be disposed of, not embraced.

Thus, the horror of the film's ending is not a matter of (true) empathy, because empathy necessarily requires distance, one's awareness of oneself as another person, different from the person for whom one feels empathy. In contrast, the emotional effect of the film's ending consists of direct engagement with pain. This is registered in the affective intentionality of the film's aesthetic system, which itself 'suffers' from drug-induced bodily asynchronicity.[11] Bianco calls this type of film 'techno-cinematic'; she also emphasizes the centrality of rhythm in her Deleuze-inspired analysis of *Requiem for a Dream* as a 'bombardment of affect' that is felt in the flesh. She writes that the film ends 'with a relentless 'hip-hop montage' of bodies-come-undone to an erratic and crashing techno-aural rhythm. . . . The rhythmic and resonant centrifugal attraction that keeps bodies whole is put out of sync and loosened from the organic threshold. They and we are caught up in an unbalancing sensation of forces, in the deterritorialization of the human body' (Bianco 2004: 391–92).

In *Requiem for a Dream*, there is a clear difference in rhythm among the three acts – Summer, Fall and Winter. The Summer segment is dominated by smooth rhythms characterized by mellow energy and hardly any tension, which promptly give way to irregularity and nervousness in the Fall segment, only to skid into rough, alarming, psychotic asynchronicity in Winter. This development does not merely function as a metaphor for the downfall of the protagonists, but it also embodies the affective intentionality of the film itself towards the spectator. As Teresa Brennan notes, rhythm plays a significant role in intersubjective affective exchanges, because various rhythms are tools for expressing *agency* (Brennan 2004: 70). *Requiem for a Dream* as an 'emotive agent' guides the spectator through all stages of addiction, from enticement and pleasure, through craving and withdrawal, to full despair and humiliation, felt directly in the flesh as it responds to the film's rhythm. The rhythmic asynchronicity at the end of the film is thus felt as painful humiliation, not only because humiliation is what the protagonists feel, but also, and more importantly, because the film itself 'humiliates' by outweighing the spectator's own emotional agency. Evelin Lindner defines this experience as follows:

> To be humiliated is to be placed, against your will and often in a very hurtful way, in a situation that is greatly inferior to what you feel you should expect. . . . It often involves force, including violent force . . . the idea of pinning down, putting down, or holding to the ground. Indeed, one of the defining characteristics of humiliation as a process is that the victim is forced into passivity, acted upon, made helpless. (Lindner 2002: 126)

The ending of *Requiem for a Dream* clearly imprisons its protagonists in pain and humiliation, while they suffer loss of agency, the feeling of the body being acted upon beyond control. First Sara is attacked with ridicule, scorn and disdain, both by Tappy Tibbons and by her own 'ego ideal' – her personal image of a perfect self appearing as a guest on the game show. Then her humiliation is mercilessly exposed as her personal space dissolves into the televised reality, leaving her totally open to invasion from the outside world, even though this takes place only in her imagination. The registration of Sara's humiliation – imaginary or not – functions as a multiplier of her loss of agency, resulting in a painful, even obscene conflation of her social isolation and public exposure. Isolation and exposure are humiliating sanctions, because they convey a painful message of subordination as well as social rejection, injuring the individual's self-respect. The fantasy scene in the television studio both isolates and exposes Sara in two ways: it subjects her to the intrusive presence of a television crew, chorus girls and the audience on the one hand, and it shows how her humiliation is filmed under bright studio lights on the other. Furthermore, the scene alternates between point-of-view shots and reaction shots in such a way that it makes the spectator, too, vulnerable to the ridiculing invasion of the outside world.

The scene in which Sara confusedly walks the streets of wintry New York City, dressed only in her (now dirty and shabby) red dress, can be seen as another emotional-metaphorical image that embodies humiliation both as downward orientation and exclusion. The downward orientation is concretized in the high camera angle that convincingly suggests looking down on Sara contemptuously. The exclusion is expressed in the way in which Sara stands out from the image as an abject stain that does not belong in the picture. The image is predominantly grey, and the passers-by speed past Sara as shadows in fast motion, while her own movement is slowed down. In the metro scene, this idea of exclusion is even more evident, with the passengers turning away in disgust from Sara's pleading.

The downward orientation of the camera becomes increasingly prominent towards the climax of the film. We are looking down from directly above at Sara being taken to hospital, and at Marion in her bathtub keeping her face under the water; this is a response typical of humiliation avoidance – a desire to hide one's face or sink out of sight. The same camera angle is used when Sara is being force-fed with a tube down her throat, and when she receives electroconvulsive shocks. In jail, Harry and Tyrone are literally excluded from the societal world. In addition to the constant pain caused by withdrawal symptoms, they endure intentional humiliation as well as violence from the prison guards, which is once more emphasized by the vibrating camera that epitomizes their out-of-joint situation. Here, rhythm is an agential force that not only expresses the humiliation of the protagonists, but also induces a state of humiliation in the spectators by overpowering their affective agency. Humiliation, rhythm and (loss of) agency are linked, because humiliation is always a painful reminder of one's lived-body as surrounded by the rhythm of others. In the words of Raoul Vaneigem: 'The endless minuet of humiliation and its response gives human relationships an obscene hobbling rhythm. In the ebb and flow of the crowds sucked in and crushed together by the coming and going of suburban trains, and coughed out into streets, offices, factories, there is nothing but timid retreats, brutal attacks, smirking faces and scratches delivered for no apparent reason' (Vaneigem 1967).

From a dynamic point of view, Lefebvre defines agency in terms of a living organism that captures positive energies and defends itself against negative energies that are active in its vicinity. For him, the lived-body is a recipient and reservoir of massive, rhythmic energies and through this rhythmic energy, all lived-bodies are internally and externally present for each other by means of a positive energetic flow (love, respect) or a negative one (hatred, humiliation). In this vein, Lefebvre continues:

> [S]urplus energy ... relates on the one hand ... to the body which stores it, and on the other hand to its 'milieu'. . . . In the life of every 'being' ... there are moments when the energy available is so abundant that it tends to be explosively discharged. It may be turned back against itself, it may spread outwards, in gratuitousness or grace. . . . Excesses of all kinds are the result of excess energy. (Lefebvre 1991: 180)

Perhaps it could be said that the 'explosive discharge' at the end of *Requiem for a Dream* is the result of negative, destructive surplus energy. This explodes inside the physical and psychological turmoil of the protagonists, and it also spreads outwards towards the spectator through the film as a bodily event or milieu.

But perhaps even more importantly, in *Requiem for a Dream* it is the protagonists' very bodies themselves that are rendered agents of self-destruction and self-humiliation, as their bodies indeed turn against them. As a result, they surrender both their agential dignity and their ability to overcome their addiction, as well as their capacity to stand up in their own physical and psychological defence. Scarry writes that in pain, individuals may be overwhelmed by a sense of 'internal agency', experiencing their own body hurting them. As a result, the individual feels acted upon, simultaneously tormented from the inside (the body) and from the outside (an external cause, such as electrical shocks). According to Scarry: 'This dissolution of the boundary between inside and outside gives rise to . . . an almost obscene conflation of private and public, . . . isolation and exposure . . . physical pain [and] intense moments of humiliation (Scarry 1985: 53). The obscene exposure of pain felt by the protagonists in *Requiem for a Dream* turns their bodies inside out as it were, revealing the most inward part of them. Therefore, the logic of humiliation is a scene of exposure, and the spectator's discomfort with the film's corporeal aesthetics during the climax of *Requiem for a Dream* is the consequence of negative emotion at being unable to stop watching what one no longer want to see. This means that we, too, feel acted upon by the film in ways that paralyze our sense of agency. Philip Fisher writes that in such moments of 'vehement passions' as captured in the ending of *Requiem for a Dream*, we feel 'overwhelmed by something outside ourselves or by something else we believe may damage or destroy us . . . we are the victim or the potential victim of something coming towards us in the world, something that undermines, for at least the moment, our capacity to think ourselves as agents' (Fisher 2002: 15).

The ending of *Requiem for a Dream* brings an overwhelmingly negative, painful, humiliating bodily sensation, which undermines both the affective and cognitive agency of the spectator. This sensation is embodied in the affective-aesthetic system of the film itself, which efficiently inhibits conversion of the negative into anything positive, such as a feeling of cathartic pleasure as soon as the scene of suffering has come to an end. Indeed, in *Requiem for a Dream*, the reciprocal, affective attunement is organized in such a way that the film's agency outweighs the spectator's agency, and there is an agential (power) asymmetry between the film and the spectator. However, in my interpretation of the overpowering effect of the film, I do not mean to suggest that the spectator of *Requiem for a Dream* is a passive victim of the film's intentional attitude. The overwhelming experience of watching *Requiem for a Dream* does not equate to passivity, since the spectator's affect remains continually directed towards the film, or rather, it is bound up or formed in tandem with the film. A truly passive response would be a lethargic, apathetic one, insofar as lethargy and apathy are the opposites of activity and motion as well as emotion. Even being humiliated does not equal being passively at the mercy of this negative experience; rather, it is to be situated inside the film's 'force-field' as a weakened, overwhelmed emotional agent, in which context 'weakened' and 'passive' are not the same. This negative emotion is not a consequence of passivity, since it is a form of reception that arouses vivid consciousness, even if it is painful. Instead, it is the result of the film's rhythmic, affective power that draws the spectator into its life-space in a process that involves active surrender, as Dewey argues. According to him, an aesthetic experience 'is an act of the going-out of energy in order to receive, not a withholding of energy' (Dewey 1958: 53). And of course we always remain free to refuse to yield to the film's overwhelming intrusion by deliberately directing our attention to something else, however infrequently we may choose to do so.

As argued above, humiliation seems to be part of the film's affective intentionality, turning the film, and especially its ending, into a particularly overwhelming experience that works to entrap the spectator within this strong sensation. In other words, the affective intentionality in *Requiem for a Dream* is premised on the notion of inducing pain in spectators, so that the film tangibly overpowers their sense of agency, compromising their ability to respond. This is analogous to the way in which the protagonists of the film are kept captive by their own pain and humiliation, as the film refuses the spectator any gratifying release. Instead, it emphasizes a progressive, rhythmic descent into the sensorial and affective situation of pain and humiliation without reprieve. This is why the spectators' negative emotions endure, prompting them to feel the painful effects of disturbance in their sensuous relationship with the world, even after the film has finished. This pain circulates in *Requiem for a Dream* as a discerned loss of agency, which is felt by the spectators in the flesh, and leads to acknowledgement that they too are vulnerable to humiliation and exposure, which they experience as a tangible inability to regain agency themselves. As an agential counterpart to the bodily event, the film's discordant, dysphoric rhythm wins out over the spectator's rhythm aiming at harmony, which results in powerful, unsettling effects. In this way, the film virtually functions as an 'electroconvulsive shock' in itself, provoking us to reflect on what the film makes us feel: a profound loss of agency and painful bodily disconnection.

## Notes

Many thanks to Tina Kendall for her helpful comments on the earlier version of this chapter.

1.  Some critics have claimed that spring is there for the viewers to create for themselves. Thus, the final shot of the film, taken vertically from directly above Sara,

Harry, Marion and Tyrone, all four in foetal position, could be seen as a possibility for rebirth after a requiem for the dead. See for instance Moreno (2009: 226).

2.  In a similar fashion, Jean Jackson speaks of chronic pain sufferers who experience their selves as overwhelmed, possessed even, saying that their bodies are taking over and driving them crazy. Yet she emphasizes that this is not a question of mind-body dualism, since such pain is 'by definition simultaneously bodily experience and mental-emotional experience' (Jackson 1994: 209).

3.  Haneke in a DVD interview with Serge Toubiana on his film *The Seventh Continent* (1989).

4.  The show is called 'Juice' after the acronym for the slogan 'join us in creating excellence'.

5.  The scene is an homage to Czech surrealist filmmaker Jan Svankmajer. Stop-motion and exaggerated sounds are trademarks of this filmmaker, especially in eating scenes, which create strange effects imitated by Aronofsky in the breakfast scene.

6.  The song is called 'Bialy & Lox Conga' by The Moonrats, with Darren Aronofsky in vocals.

7.  On emotional-metaphorical images in cinema, see Bartsch (2010: 240–60).

8.  This red tower, which is seen in the background of many scenes in the film, is an old amusement park ride called the Parachute Jump. It is a landmark of Coney Island, where the film was shot almost entirely, as an homage to Aronofsky's geographical background. *Requiem for a Dream,* 2012, The Worldwide Guide to Movie Locations. Retrieved 13 June 2012 from http://www.movie-locations.com/movies/r/requiem.html.

9.  Michel Chion speaks of spatial magnetization in the film theatre. Normally the image of the sound source will be associated with the sound, as though magnetically, so that the spectators mentally situate the sound where they see its source on the cinema screen (Chion 2009: 491–492). I adopt this term to describe the sound that disrupts the diegetic continuum by moving from one spatial and temporal plane to another in ways that are too complex to be described by the term non-simultaneous sound.

10.  For instance, *Empire* film magazine ranks the film the number one most depressing film in the history of movies. S. Braund, 2009, 'Top Ten Depressing Movies', *Empire*. Retrieved 25 June 2012 from http://www.empireonline.com/features/top10/depressing-movies/.

11.  In discussing the score of Stanley Kubrick's *The Shining* (1980), Kevin Donnelly makes a similar claim about film music: 'Music is related to bodily and life rhythms, through the essence of volume, beat and pulse perhaps more that timbre, pitch and harmony. . . . Music in horror films often attempts a direct engagement with the physical, [being] tied to the intrinsic sounds of the human body: the high buzz of the nervous system and the deep throb of the bloodstream and heart' (Donnelly 2005: 95, 105).

CHAPTER THREE

# Grief

## *The Fountain*

The visually and symbolically rich third feature-length film by Aronofsky, *The Fountain*, contains three intertwined storylines with different sets of characters all played by the same two actors, Hugh Jackman and Rachel Weisz. The characters are Tommy, a modern-day neuroscientist, and his wife Izzi, who is fighting brain cancer; Tomás, a Spanish conquistador, and his queen, Isabel; and Tom, a space traveller who has hallucinations of his lost love Izzi/Isabel. The narrative tension both within and among these storylines is based on thematic juxtapositions, such as mind and body, science and spirituality, and finitude and infinitude. In addition, just like in *Pi*, there is a conflict between the search for an ultimate scientific solution to the mysteries of the world and the chaos of pure multiplicity. In this film, the conflict between the persistent human desire to know everything and the world of accident and chance that refuses to be reduced to human order is epitomized in the mystical Tree of Life. The Tree of Life is a common mystical motif in various world religions and philosophies, as well as in science, where it describes the interconnectedness of all life on Earth.

The first shot of the film is a handwritten quotation from Genesis, inscribed in ink on a piece of parchment: 'Therefore the Lord God banished Adam and Eve from the Garden of Eden and placed a flaming sword to protect the Tree of Life' (Genesis 3:24). This quotation is a reference to man's first act of disobedience to God, known as the Fall, when Adam and Eve ate from the forbidden Tree of Knowledge. It undermined the relationship that should have existed between Adam and Eve and God. By disregarding His command, Adam and Eve (creation) appropriated God's authority as Creator, asserted their independence from God, and grasped at an imagined equality with Him (being 'like God' in knowledge). This was punished by both physical and spiritual death. Adam and Eve lost their innocence, and were reduced to mere suffering earthly mortals by God. In *The Fountain*, Tommy can clearly be seen as a modern-day Adam who suffers but refuses to accept this human condition, and feels compelled to find the Tree of Life – that is, to 'play God' in order to return to the Garden of Eden. His surname, 'Creo', which means 'I believe' in Spanish, may be seen as a direct reference to the duality of Creator/creation. This duality acknowledges that there is a likeness between the Creator and the created, but that they are not identical. Man is fundamentally the useless passion (to be God), as Jean-Paul Sartre has famously argued.[1] On the narrative level, this duality is embedded in a juxtaposition between desire for immortality and acceptance of mortality, which is dealt with in the contrasting narratives of Tomás's mission as a conquistador and Tom's search for inner peace. This same opposition is emblematic of Tommy's inner struggle, caused by his inability either to find a cure for Izzi's illness or to accept or acknowledge his loss, until he finally reconciles himself to his fate.

This chapter, however, approaches *The Fountain* from a different perspective, because the film is not at all about dualism. On the contrary, it is about all things being interconnected, and it actually resists any dualistic 'either/or' readings. The film does, however, remain open to multiple interpretations, which to some extent might explain its divided critical reception. I shall attempt to define the film's impact from its metaphysical vision, which is immersed in sensory details of lived experience, as expressed in its visual style. I shall focus on the juxtapositions of mind-body, science-spirituality and finitude-infinitude, as well as on the emotional effects caused by these juxtapositions. I hope to show that instead of denoting coeternal binary oppositions, these juxtapositions represent a multifaceted structure that can best be understood as the emotional core of pathological grief. It is this emotional core that is felt by the spectators, not so much as a result of narrative processing, but by means of 'kinetic' cinematic aesthetics that directly transmit to them the painful emotional logic of the film. Furthermore, the juxtapositions that are apparent in *The Fountain* are comparable to the inherent dichotomy embodied in the emotion of grief. This dichotomy consists of simultaneous awareness and denial of loss, and urgent experience of pain and the corresponding act of dissociating from pain. It is encountering a world one cannot fully inhabit after the loss of a loved one – or even the loss of self in the face of approaching death (Tanner 2007). This chapter describes such dichotomy as it presents itself through visual symbolism in *The Fountain*. It shows how grief shapes the sensory and affective dynamics of human experience, but also what is required to process and work through grief, so that something new might emerge, a 'fresh kind of *carrying forward*' as Denise Riley describes this (Riley 2012: 73). Thus, for me, the impact of *The Fountain* stems from its poignant visual imagery, symbolizing the struggle of its protagonists to come to terms with the stubbornness of grief borne out by denial. In the end, the film's philosophical standpoint, as revealed in its visual style, embraces rather than disavows the juxtaposition between finite human embodiment and infinite spiritual transcendence.

For the sake of clarity, a preliminary summary of the film's complex narrative structure seems in order. *The Fountain* unfolds in a non-linear fashion through three temporal layers, each separated by five centuries. These cyclically interwoven layers are: the past, with Tomás the conquistador searching for a Maya pyramid; the present, with Tommy the neuroscientist diligently searching for a cure for his wife's brain cancer; and the future, with Tom the space traveller floating in lotus position in outer space with the dying Tree of Life. This structure could signify that past, present and future are parts of the same continuum, rather than separate entities. However, one must take into consideration that the segment of the film set in the past is based on a fairy tale Izzi writes down in her notebook. In addition, Tom, the space traveller, is constantly haunted by earthbound Tommy's memories instead of his own. This is why it might also be appropriate to claim that Tomás only exists in the realm of imagination, and that Tom is merely an external projection of Tommy's internal emotional state. It may even be claimed that the layer featuring Tom is the final chapter of Izzi's (fairy tale) book, which she constantly urges Tommy to finish for her. Although the film does not directly imply this, I shall return to this proposition at the end of the chapter, because it is key to understanding the emotional effect of grief in *The Fountain*.

This interpretation would suggest that all events in the film take place in the present. In that case, the events in the 'past' and the 'future' could best be understood as occurring in 'no-time', instead of as part of continuous, linear time.[2] Laura Tanner calls this kind of temporal structure the 'expansiveness of the present' in the phenomenological experience of grief (Tanner 2007: 234). It anticipates future absence by preserving the past in (mental) representation. Thus the threat of Izzi's death in the present serves as a channel through which Tommy's imagination converts his memory of her into the essence of an image in the future – represented by the haunting vision of Izzi in her winter coat urging Tommy to 'finish it'. In other words, Tommy's grief puts him in an out-of-joint temporal and spatial reality. However, the intertwined narrative strands in *The Fountain* can also be seen as cellular layers, functioning as membranous interfaces, through which pain and emotion can be transmitted from one layer to another. In this chapter, I approach the film from all these possible perspectives, respectively identifying the three narrative strands as three mental dimensions (imaginary, actual and mnemonic), membranous interfaces (epidermal, dermal and hypodermal) and temporalities (past, present and future) in relation to the juxtapositions of mind/body, science/spirituality and finitude/infinitude. Not only are these juxtapositions deeply embedded in the narrative of this film, they are also prominent in its visual style. In the end, I conclude that the aesthetic complexity of the film is structured around the dissociative logic of grief, an emotion for which classical Greek had no other word than for pain (Gustafson 1989: 457). In *The Fountain,* pain signifies the affective progress of working through grief felt in and through the body. For the spectator immersed in the spatio-temporal layers of the film, the experience of bodily dissociating and re-connecting may lead to a heightened appreciation of the ability to re-attune with one's temporal and spatial environment after the loss of a loved one.

There seems to be an inherent paradox in the experience of grief that manifests itself in dichotomies. Donald Gustafson (1989) argues that grief is conditioned by a 'counter-belief desire', which involves belief that a loved one is dead, and an (irrational) desire that this may not be the case. Tanner speaks of grief as entrapment in the urgent bodily experience of pain on the one hand, and a sense of bodily separation from the world in which one is located on the other. As one simultaneously lacks the agency to participate in this same world, she calls this experience 'intimate detachment' (Tanner 2007: 243). And Denise Riley describes grief as an altered condition of life that is experienced as arrested, frozen time. To her, grief is a feeling of being cut off from the flow of time, resulting from an act of dissociation that shields one from the reality of the death of a loved one. Writing about the death of her own child, Riley recalls how she experienced this painful event so intensely that she sensed that a part of her had died instantly: 'So you are both partly dead, and yet more alive. You are cut down, and yet you burn in life' (Riley 2012: 14).

Grief involves knowing and not knowing that the loved one is dead, a sense of identification with and separation from him or her. Furthermore, in grief one finds oneself on a threshold between inside and outside: 'The light contact of your senses with the outer world, and your interior only thinly separated from it, like a membrane resonating on the verge between silence and noise. . . . Far from taking refuge deeply inside yourself, there is no longer any inside, and you have become only outwardness. . . . I work to earth my heart' (Riley 2012: 19).

In *The Fountain*, the inability to process grief, the feeling of being torn or frozen between life and death, acknowledging and denying bereavement, becomes a question of enforcing dichotomies of mind and body, science and spirituality, finitude and infinitude. These are related to the incompatibility of desire and belief in Gustafson's model of grief, in which desire can never be satisfied, as belief dictates desire will never be true. In *The Fountain*, such desire takes the form of denial of pain. What *The Fountain* depicts is the dissolution of the conflict between denial and the reality of emotional pain, and as such it becomes a grief-stricken event that directly and palpably engages the spectator affectively. In *The Fountain* there is an inevitable movement towards loss, and the collection of images and memories that would resist such loss, resulting in an altered temporal experience. Not only does this strategy serve to hold grief at bay, but it also preserves it, yielding torment as well as consolation, until one finally allows the dead to be dead. This is why the final scene of the film shows Tommy at Izzi's grave uttering a goodbye, after having 'finished it'.

## Mind and Body

To argue that Tomás and Tom are solely products of the brain suggests a strict separation of body and mind. Tomás exists in the realm of imagination, while Tom comes into being as a result of Tommy's denial of his physical and emotional pain. Tommy denies that his lived-body is in pain, and isolates his grief so that its core is embodied elsewhere, namely in a memory dissociated from awareness, which is Tom. In other words, Tom is the product of Tommy's psychic negation of Izzi's anticipated death, designed to counter his lived experience of embodied pain. In fact, the idea of mind/body dualism is clearly present in the film, and its fundamental Christian meaning is articulated in the inquisitor's speech during the execution of the heretics: 'Our bodies are prisons for our souls. Our skin and blood, the iron bars of confinement. But fear not. All flesh decays. Death turns all to ash, and, thus, death frees every soul.'

At the same time, both the 'past' and the 'future' layers of the film are borne out by the body in pain, which eventually dissolves such mind/body dualism. Izzi is dying of brain cancer, and her handwritten fairy tale is thoroughly structured by her pain, which not only explains the Maya creation myth, but also anticipates her own death. The film opens with this narrative strand, and the sense of lurking death is immediately present. In the first scene of the film, Tomás and his two companions attempt to enter a Maya pyramid deeply hidden in the dark jungle, while a sense of threat surrounds them. In an ensuing attack, Tomás's companions are speared by sharp lances while climbing a wooden fence. Tomás himself meets a violent death at the hands of a Maya priest, who is armed with a flaming sword. In another painful scene that is part of this narrative strand, tortured heretics are lifted to the ceiling of the Inquisition courtroom by their feet and then dropped to their deaths. They are shown groaning in agony, with heavy spasms running through their bodies. These extreme pain sensations, which Izzi describes in her book, are sharply contrasted with the fact that she has lost her sense of touch for hot and cold. The pain that she describes may thus not only signify her own physical pain, but also her longing to be in the world as a whole, sensing bodily subject. Through her fairy tale, she lends intense sensory materiality to her weakened experience of the present and her anticipation of a future without pain.

While Izzi's fairy tale accentuates her sensory experience of pain, shaped by her somatosensory present, Tommy denies his. Refusing to accept the imminence of his wife's death, Tommy is obsessed with finding a cure for her illness. Yet the harder he fights against death, the more fundamentally death becomes part of his innermost self. In other words, Tommy's effort in the fight against death attaches him to death in such a way that the attachment itself becomes his reason for being. This is a form of entrapment, epitomized in the scene in which Tommy leaves the hospital where Izzi is recovering from a seizure. The camera follows Tommy in one long take as he crosses the road, passes a construction site and almost gets hit by a car. The scene is completely silent until the abrupt sound of the skidding car and its blaring horn.

The silence represents Tommy's engulfment in emotional pain, as he is expelled from the sensory realm of time, unable to recover his corporeal agency. Riley defines this experience as time that is not 'fully lived' (Riley 2012: 14). Tommy can only overcome this by accepting his helplessness in the face of Izzi's illness, and by acknowledging that the body is not mere matter, subject to scientific intervention and human choice. Similar to the character of Max in *Pi*, Tommy's scientific pursuit seems to alienate him from his emotions, his instincts and the body, thus preventing him from processing his grief.

In *The Fountain*, tattooing is emblematic of Tommy's resistance to his emotional and bodily reality. This takes the form of adorning the body with tattoos, which Tom executes with a dip pen. Tommy is also shown tattooing his ring finger to replace his lost wedding ring after Izzi's death (figure 3.1). This tattoo obviously reflects the eternity of its subject – Tommy's love for Izzi. But it especially symbolizes his enduring grief, which results from refusing to process his pain emotionally. This is why Tom is doomed to repeat the original tattooing act endlessly, inhabiting a prolonged, unlived time overshadowed by the consciousness of his loss. In such emotional pain time becomes a 'plateau', as Riley describes it (Riley 2012: 20), with no sense of duration or future, epitomized in the 'timelessness' of a tattoo. In tattooing, the ink must penetrate the top layers of skin and enter the dermis. Obviously this process is not painless, but pain is necessary for the formation and preservation of the tattoo. In *The Fountain*, Tommy is under the illusion that he needs physical pain to preserve his love for Izzi, since pain is an experience in which bodily and mental 'components' are inextricably intertwined. At the same time, this reasoning prevents him from working through his grief. This keeps him entrapped in disembodied, atemporal pain, which disrupts the intentionality of the body. In other words, Tommy is unable to work through his grief, because he externalizes his emotions through his scientific project and through self-induced physical pain. It is only when he allows his pain to emerge on the inside that the emotional healing can begin.

As mentioned above, the narrative structure of *The Fountain* can be conceived as a configuration in which past, present and future coexist. Considering the centrality of tattooing to the film, I propose that its narrative structure could also be considered as a set of membranous interfaces analogous to the three layers of human skin. These three layers consist of interconnected

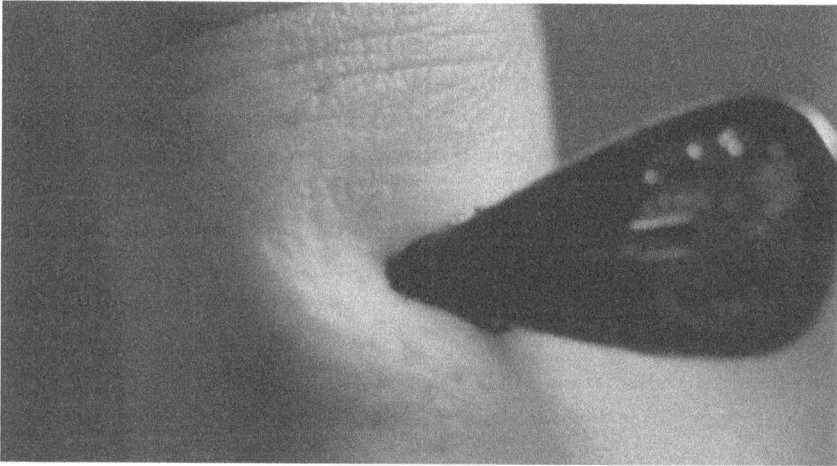

**Figure 3.1.** Pain preserved in ink. Screen capture, *The Fountain* (2006).

membranous tissue, permeated by pain receptors, and always in the process of renewal. Thus, Tom's journey through a nebula, a huge cloud of stellar plasma that the dying star Xibalba emits into space, might be compared to the migration of dead skin cells through the epidermis towards the skin's surface. The form of the nebula is duplicated in the image in which light filters through snowflakes covering the skylight in Tommy's lab. This visual effect even resembles membranous tissue composed of cellular layers that fold into one another in a kaleidoscopic fashion. Tommy's emotional turmoil, which keeps him imprisoned in his pain, imprints the layer of skin that preserves painful memories and emotions, just like the subject of a tattoo is preserved in skin by ink. There is a connection between skin and emotion. Claudia Benthien speaks of the correspondence between semantic and somatic emotion, inner feeling and external touching, and of the reciprocal relationship between affect and touch. According to her, the emotional and the psychic dimensions, such as memory, 'quite simply cannot do without recourse to the tactile dimension' (Benthien 2002: 187).

If the future narrative strand stands for the outermost layer of skin (epidermis), and the present strand for the second layer (dermis), then the past strand stands for the 'core' of the skin (hypodermis), the 'raw' tissue that lies below modern Western culture. In this layer, the story of the Spanish inquisition and the search for the Tree of Life are connected as paths to sanctity and eternal life. The practice of mortification of the flesh as a path to sanctity is painfully depicted in the scene in which the inquisitor is shown whipping himself in a long shot, while the camera rapidly moves into a close-up of his open, bleeding wounds. In Christianity, pain has been seen not only as the compulsory condition of humanity after the Fall as a result of the Original Sin of Adam and Eve, but also as the 'primary medium for divine-human communication' and 'integral to salvation' (Schoenfeldt 2009: 20).[3] Pain has also been considered a source of spiritual enlightenment within the Christian framework, as it is a way of imitating the suffering of Christ, and so it offers an avenue to a mystical union with him (van Dijkhuizen 2009: 208). Scarry remarks about self-flagellation as a religious practice:

> The self-flagellation of the religious ascetic, for example, is not (as is often asserted) an act of denying the body, eliminating its claims from attention, but a way of so emphasizing the body that the contents of the world are cancelled and the path is clear for the entry of an unworldly, contentless force. It is in part this world-ridding, path-clearing logic that explains the obsessive presence of pain in the rituals of large, widely shared religions. (Scarry 1985: 34)

The very idea that skin is an organ that preserves emotional memories on the one hand and disperses them on the other demonstrates the extent to which mind and body are inextricably entangled. Tommy/Tom's act of tattooing is comparable to religious self-flagellation, insofar as both are means to cancel out the 'contents of the world' – in Tommy's case, his emotional pain. But in the end, *The Fountain* rejects such mind/body dualism. On the contrary, the film presents the spectator with a view of corporeal subjectivity in which mind and body are so intimately intertwined that they cannot effectively be separated. This is how the film shows that (emotional) pain can point the way to redemption, since pain can have another function apart from Scarry's 'cancelling out the contents of the world'. Pain can also be an avenue for radical self-transformation ('rebirth'), since it can redirect one's way of life, if only one chooses to surrender to it instead of resisting its transformative power. This idea of pain as transformative power is especially present in mystical discourse, in which pain can become 'an alchemical force, like the forger's fire, which magically transforms its victim from one state of existence to a higher, purer state' (Glucklich 2001: 25).[4] Pain as an 'alchemical force' is epitomized in the climax of *The Fountain*, in which Tom floats into the gravitational field of Xibalba. In this scene, his body is stretching indefinitely, like matter swirling into the event horizon of a black hole, while at the same time the Tree of Life bursts into new life. This dissolves the mind/body juxtaposition insofar as it presents the body as an attribute of spiritual substance from which new life flows.

## Science and Spirituality

The second juxtaposition in *The Fountain* is science versus spirituality. This is already established in the opening shot of the film, when the handwritten Genesis quotation promptly dissolves into a close-up of an elaborately decorated sun cross, or rayed cross. The centre part of such a cross resembles the sun, and the glass ball in the middle of this specimen contains a lock of hair belonging to Tomás's liege, Queen Isabel. Kinich Ahau is the sixteenth-century Yucatec name of the Maya sun god, and it is in these parts of the world where Tomás, who is seen kneeling in front of the cross, is in search of the Tree of Life. As it predates Christianity by thousands of years, the use of a sun cross here may suggest that the Maya and Christian religions have common roots from long before the Spanish conquest of Maya society. This in turn would signify that the origin of faith is not the sole province of any one established religion, as beyond religious myths there is a primordial fundamental quest from which all religions spring. Religion shares this common ground with the sciences, to the extent that both address the question of the origin of the universe.

In its turn, the image of the rayed altar cross dissolves into a close-up of Queen Isabel of Spain – actually Tomás's memory of the queen handing him her ring, which he now holds. Rings are another recurring mise-en-scène element in the film, along with other circular motifs. These include Tom's bubble floating in outer space towards the dying star Xibalba, which, in the film, shares the name of the underworld to which, in the Maya religion, dead souls go to be reborn. There are also the armband tattoos that circle Tom's arms like growth rings of a tree, as well as recurring visual effects that designate 'wormholes', cinematically created by means of macro photography of fluids. In quantum mechanics, wormholes function as hypothetical 'shortcuts' through the space-time continuum that potentially enable time travel – at least in science fiction.

There is thus the possibility of interpreting the film's structure as a wholeness of three intertwining yet separate temporal layers: past, present and future. Viewed from this perspective, one could conclude that the function of wormholes in *The Fountain* is indeed to connect these different time layers. This enables organic entanglement of the time layers in a fashion similar to the ways in which the strands of a triple helix intermingle. This would result in the eternal intertwinement of spatial and temporal specificity, after which the narrative unfolds from any temporal point, while the coexisting past, present and future are in constant redevelopment. Thus emerges a narrative strand in an alternative universe, where Tommy leaves his lab and does take a last walk with Izzi in the snow. In this same universe Tommy also receives a tree seedpod from Izzi, which he plants on her grave in the 'real' universe. Tommy's change of mind-set from one universe to another invites one to think about the choices that can be made in matters of both spirituality and of science. It may also suggest, however, that past, present and future can only reconnect after time has resumed its flow, which allows the dead to be committed to memory, instead of to a prolonged presence, as Riley proposes (Riley 2012: 46).

The film's different time layers are not united merely on the narrative level; they are also connected visually, by the image of the wormhole for instance, or by the use of graphic matches between shots. There is a scene in which the camera following Tom's hand gliding over a tree trunk continues in the next shot, showing Tommy soaping Izzi's arm in a bath. The rotating space bubble dissolves into a shot in which Tommy circles along a round floor pattern, filmed from above. The movement of Tommy's hand filmed in close-up, lingering on the new tattoo on his finger, is continued as Tom probes his own, similar tattoo. A stylistic trick, in which the camera rights itself from an upside-down position while shooting Tommy rushing to his lab, is repeated in the scene in which we see Tomás galloping towards the inquisitor's castle. This trick suggests that their missions are interconnected, as they are both in search of scientific knowledge about the natural world. However, in both cases this pursuit is converted into a spiritual quest, which ends differently for each of them. Tomás drinks the sap from the Tree of Life and turns into vegetation, literally 'pushing daisies', while Tommy comes to terms with the finitude of life and overcomes the pain caused by losing Izzi. This coming to terms is brought across to the spectator by a visual metaphor in which a shot of a ceiling lamp in Tommy's lab first brightens and then fades out to white, only to fade into the following shot of Tom's space bubble leaving the nebula and entering into the bright photosphere of Xibalba. In this way, an epiphanic scientific or spiritual experience is emulated by means of the same visualized metaphor – namely 'seeing the light' – that also occurs in *Pi* and *Requiem for a Dream*. But in contrast to the two earlier films, the white light in *The Fountain* seems to suggest a transformative enlightenment, instead of some falsified transcendental experience.

As the film progresses towards the completion of Tommy's mourning process, the circularity in the film's mise-en-scène becomes striking, perhaps symbolizing Tommy's grief coming full circle perhaps. The circularity is continually emphasized by means of the framing of the image, either straight from above or straight from below the objects that are filmed. This angle often emphasizes the round shape of objects, such as the circular floor patterns, the hem of Queen Isabel's gown on the floor, the gate to the hidden Maya pyramid, the shape of a seedpod in the palm of Izzi's hand, and the pattern of glowing light filtering through snowflakes on top of a skylight, an image representing a dying star surrounded by a nebula. In the beginning, the film is rather darkly lit, but lighting gradually brightens as the main characters come closer to their scientific and/or spiritual goals. The climax of the film shows an extremely luminous stellar explosion that radiates gold across the different narrative layers. Throughout the film, images are often bathed in a golden glow, the most salient illumination technique in *The Fountain*. The colour gold is an important aesthetic element in Buddhist mysticism, and indeed there is a sprinkling of Buddhist symbols throughout the film's visual design. Gold also symbolizes the sun, and thus Buddhist elements in the film are connected to the Maya sun cult, offering the spectator a holistic spiritual experience. Both in Buddhism and the Maya religion, death is not considered the end of life, but the beginning of a journey that includes the possibility of reincarnation, which is also the conclusive insight offered to the spectator by *The Fountain*. In this way, the colour gold resonates with the spectator's 'colour consciousness', as Joshua Yumibe puts it, referring to the work of Technicolor supervisor Natalie Kalmus. According to Yumibe, this resonance of colour addresses the spectators' senses directly and thus enhances their experience of cinema cognitively, physiologically and emotionally (Yumibe 2012: 8–9). In *The Fountain*, the sensuous nature of gold clearly corresponds with the mystical and emotional significance that the film conveys, soliciting the spectator directly into a spiritual experience. Furthermore, the stellar explosion scene functions in a way similar to that of the aesthetics of the cinema of attractions, astonishing the spectator with an intensively colourful, unworldly view.

In her analysis of the film, Patricia Pisters (2010) has paid attention to its 'neuroaesthetical' elements, but perhaps *The Fountain* could more rewardingly be understood in terms of neurotheology, as the film finally offers a spiritual experience, directly relayed to the spectator by its aesthetic system.[5] This system reveals spiritual awe or oneness with the universe, for instance by the use of 'divine light', a salient aesthetic element in the film that emerges at the moment of approaching death. Thus, the juxtaposition of science and spirituality in *The Fountain* may prompt one to ask whether mystical experiences are 'genuine', or merely neural phenomena that correspond with subjective spiritual events. This is also the central question in William James's (1997) psychological study into the variety of religious experience, first published in 1902. James makes a remarkable distinction between a possible scientific explanation for the origin of spirituality and the spiritual value of religious experience itself. In fact, he comes to the conclusion that, in the end, it is not the origin of religion that is most relevant, but rather the extent to which a spiritual experience can change people's moral behaviour or their concept of reality. Such experiences do not necessarily arise from practising religious acts, but they often evolve from the psychological state of a believing person who may be in deep emotional pain – after losing a loved one, for instance.

James's insight that there is a relationship between a spiritual experience and the emotional inner self of the believer becomes particularly relevant when one interprets Tom in *The Fountain* as an embodiment of Tommy's emotional state. Tom is Tommy's attempt to externalize his pain, a distanced representation in the future that reflects his agential inability to work through his pain as a lived-body in the present. Tom experiences hallucinations that he himself creates, the intensity of which yields torment as well as consolation, like a spiritual experience. The hallucinations are a strategy to preserve presence against the flow of time, with Izzi eternally alive in her winter coat, in her hospital bed. But this also imprisons Tom in the timelessness of the present, leaving him unable to sense any progress into emotional healing, until he finally submits to Izzi's insistence to 'finish it'. Thus in Tom's experience, at first time is arrested as an incorporate atemporality, but this actually leads to a new kind of opening that enables him to carry on and also leads to post-traumatic growth. As Lynn Bridgers points out, there is a correlation between (post-) trauma and James's description of religious experience, insofar as trauma and faith can both be transformative events: '[T]raumatic experience may create the possibility of simultaneous maximal discharge [of affect] and may give way to a kind of spillover effect, or sudden affective change. Subjectively, such an experience would be described in terms of a sudden transformative experience, including the kind of [spiritual] conversion James addresses' (Bridgers 2005: 170).

From this angle, *The Fountain* elicits a (quasi-)spiritual sense of transformation in response to a traumatic event. Thus, towards the end of the film, Tom enters a smaller vessel to separate himself from the arrested time of the space bubble – his trauma – and heads towards the divine light emitted by Xibalba. Tom is filmed in a silhouette shot, sitting in lotus position, an image which makes an association with Buddhism especially hard to avoid (figure 3.2.). This association is further confirmed in the next shot, which shows Tom bathing in strong frontal key light, while the space bubble that contains the Tree of Life rotates in the background. This Mandala-like image is centrally composed, with tree branches right behind Tom, and the whole frame is saturated with golden light, while a rim light effect illuminates the edges of both bubbles. The excessively decorative style of this image is clearly reminiscent of Buddhist art, and the obvious question that arises is one regarding the extent to which the use of Buddhist aesthetics in *The Fountain* is an example of cultural appropriation. Indeed, the film could be criticized for superficially requisitioning the visual style of a particular culture, as if this style were merely a commodity. Leaving this question aside, however, my main point about this scene is that it aims to inspire spiritual awe, which in Ed Tan and Nico Frijda's definition is something that emerges in a larger-than-life situation. Confronted

**Figure 3.2.** Buddhist symbolism in *The Fountain*. Screen capture, *The Fountain* (2006).

by awe-inspiring scenes like these, one feels a desire to lose oneself in a sensation of 'eternity' – a sensation that Sigmund Freud defined as an oceanic feeling (Tan and Frijda 1999: 62–63). Michel Serres interprets these sensations as being like swimming in an 'indeterminate place' that 'takes us back to a time before we were born', freed from gravity (Serres 2008: 321). In that analogy, the decrease in gravity in the scene originates from Tommy's body in pain and leads to his body leaving the body in order to return to the body through (spiritual) rebirth. Thus the affective quality of the scene is more in line with a spiritual experience in William James's sense than founded on claims about the truth of religion. The ending of *The Fountain* dissolves the science/spirituality dichotomy, because it directs the spectator's attention to the lived-body as a fundamental reality, in which the two paradigms are not mutually exclusive.

## Finitude and Infinitude

The third juxtaposition that can be discerned in *The Fountain* is finitude/ infinitude. This overlaps to some extent with the juxtaposition of science/ spirituality, as it deals with questions concerning the mythical dimension of time, circular repetition and the endless return of the same, a finite figure of the infinite and the search for eternal life. As mentioned, the unfolding of *The Fountain*'s narrative is best characterized as a nonlinear repetition of story elements across co-existing temporal, mental, or membranous planes. As a result of this intertwined narrative layering, Tom can feel Tomás's pain, for instance, when a Maya priest attacks him with a flaming sword. The scene with the priest cuts abruptly to an extreme close-up of Tom's wide-open eyes, while he screams in terror and agony as if he himself were on the receiving end of the attack. Events and situations that are part of one time layer are frequently echoed in another. The warning sign on Izzi's electrocardiac equipment is first heard by Tomás in the past and then by Tom in the future, before it finally wakes up Tommy inside her hospital room in the present. Snowflakes from the present fall onto the rootstalk of the dying Tree of Life in the future. Tommy's memories from the present become Tom's hallucinations in the future. Tom picks up the ring in the future that Tomás dropped in the past. And finally, Tom travels to the past and appears in front of the Maya priest as the mythical 'First Father'. This vision prevents the Maya priest from killing Tomás, who then finds the Tree of Life. He drinks the sap of the Tree of Life, and his body yields growth to countless flowering shrubs, converting his finitude into infinitude.

At the level of image, we are also presented with similar intertwining planes. There is, for instance, the frequent use of deep space in which the shot contains a large numbers of layers in sharp focus, such as in the scene in which Tomás visits the queen in her castle. The scene is shot in a decorative, church-like hall with enormous pillars, walls embellished with rich ornaments and hundreds of lanterns suspended from the ceiling. The scene creates the effect of Tomás walking through stars, drawing a visual comparison with Tom floating in outer space. During most of the scene, Queen Isabel, who wears a dark-brown gown with a golden tree branch pattern, remains veiled behind a wrought-iron screen. The scene in which Queen Isabel is shot in focus and the screen out of focus, in particular, draws the spectator's attention to the layering itself. The scene has extraordinary beauty, but the layers also lend the images a tactile quality that moves the spectator directly. As a result, the scene not only emanates visual pleasure, but it also evokes haptic, sensual sensations. This idea of haptic pleasure or haptic aesthetics is prominent in Laura Marks's (1999, 2002) research on 'the skin of the film' and touch as a mode of spectatorship. In contrast to optical visuality, a mode of seeing that masters and represents, haptic visuality is tactile, kinaesthetic and functions like the somatic senses, including touch and proprioception. In *The Fountain*, the haptic layering of the image is even extended across the past, present and future strands, and thus connects one temporal dimension with another. In one tricky scene, we are first shown a very lifelike drawn image of a medieval castle in close-up (the past), after which the camera tracks backwards through a long hall in Tommy and Izzi's apartment (the present). This trick clearly brings across the temporal entanglement of past and present, 'condensed' in a single image.

A similar kind of intertwining is created by means of visual motifs that are prominent in one temporal dimension and repeated in another. These include the golden embers slowly drifting away from the dying star Xibalba as it extends its outer photosphere into the surroundings. This 'sparkle effect' is replicated in the silent scene in which Tommy passes a construction site from which welding sparks fly into the night. The same gestures, utterances and objects appear interchangeably and with the same significance in the different temporal layers. For instance, the act of touching has the same affective significance regardless of whether it is Tommy touching Izzi's neck, or Tom touching the dying Tree of Life, its bark grey and brittle. It signifies the way in which Tommy's recollection of Izzi is immersed in the sense of touch. In the same vein, the film regularly uses dissolves, in which the first shot 'blends' with the second shot by means of a graphic match. In scenes like these, the circularity in the first shot, such as the shape of the rayed cross, is superimposed with a similar shape in the second shot, such as floor tiles arranged in a circular pattern. All of this creates the effect of the cyclical interconnectedness of the three time layers, and of a cyclical vision of life itself.

The cycle is completed in the film's climax, in which the past and the future merge to become the present. In this sequence, Tom is approaching Xibalba in lotus position while the camera zooms in on his forehead – his third eye, perhaps. By means of the wormhole effect, the scene makes a transition from the future to the past, where Tomás is invading the Maya pyramid. He approaches the Tree of Life, which is surrounded by stunning scenery – the symbolic (?) return to the Garden of Eden – and then proceeds to pierce the bark of the tree, after which he gluttonously drinks its thick, milky sap. Right before he collapses and is buried under flowers at the foot of the tree, Tomás gets a vision of Xibalba. The narration then promptly shifts to the future, transitioning with the ring, which Tomás drops and Tom picks up. Finally, the scene culminates with a stellar explosion. This is how, through its entanglement of narrative strains and visual elements, *The Fountain* communicates to the spectator the (popular) scientific notion that the model of the universe is cyclic. In this theory, the universe is considered to consist of an infinite sequence of cycles. It repeatedly collapses on itself, comparable to a massive star turning into a supernova, and then re-emerges in a new, expanding Big Bang. This claim is supported by the end of the film, a fade-out in white that could represent the event at the 'beginning' of the universe. After the fade-out, the white areas in the image start to condense, a reference to the formation of stars, until the credits end with an image of the universe full of galaxies.

In *The Fountain*, this cyclic model is contrasted with another concept of existence that is passing from the finitude of death to the infinitude of life. I argue that *The Fountain* proposes that finitude and infinitude are inseparable. The ring as a salient motif in the film is emblematic of this vision. A ring symbolizes infinitude, because it has neither a beginning nor an end, but its rim constitutes a finite border. The lifetime of a star is finite, but the remnants of the star, such as carbon, oxygen and iron, are the building blocks for new celestial bodies such as Earth – our planet is made of recycled stardust. Yet the film does not actually presume to resolve the enigmas upon which it touches, such as what the origin and purpose of life are. Instead, *The Fountain* raises questions that seem of greater weight than any film could seriously propose to answer.

Nevertheless, the juxtaposition of finitude and infinitude in *The Fountain* also pertains to something profoundly different, namely the eternal return of emotional pain in the experience of traumatic grief. Referring to Pierre Janet, Jill Bennett writes that extreme affective experience, such as grief, resists cognitive processing in a way that subjects it to uncontrolled repetition (Bennett 2005: 23). Such uncontrolled repetition and the constant return of pain are embodied in *The Fountain*, until the cycle is broken and Tommy finds a way to get over his pathological grief. The spectator too feels the effect of this cyclical repetition and can 'tune in' to what is the emotional core of the film as it unfolds as an affective-aesthetic event. This is why in the remainder of this chapter the focus will be on the process of working through grief, and the way in which this process is embodied in the aesthetic style of the film.

## Working Through Grief

In his *Rhetoric*, Aristotle writes that grief over a deceased person is often mingled with pleasant memories of what he or she was like when alive: '[T]here is an element of pleasure even in mourning and lamentation. There is grief, indeed, at his loss, but pleasure in remembering him' (Aristotle 2010: 29). By contrast, in *The Fountain*, Tommy's grief takes a pathological form that admits no pleasure, and that is enhanced by feelings of guilt and frustration, as he has been unable to find a cure for Izzi's condition in time to save her. Tommy is entrapped in guilt, which manifests itself as a painful, recurring memory that resists narrative processing, which could help him to overcome his grief. Tommy's emotion does not fit Aristotle's description, but it is rather closer to the definition offered by Martha Nussbaum, a philosopher with a particular interest in Aristotle's philosophy. In her *Upheavals of Thought* Nussbaum describes grief as a repeatedly encountered affective frustration entwined in the grieving person's cognitive fabric (Nussbaum 2001: 80). This concept of affective frustration was already part of Freud's famous distinction between mourning and melancholia. He defines mourning as a psychic response to loss that does reach a definite end (working through grief), while melancholia is a crippled emotion that is comparable to long-term depression, and that is characterized by inability to establish a sense of separateness to the lost person. As a result the loss becomes constitutive of the mourner's self, as the mourner seeks to regain the lost person through emotion (Freud 1957: 237–58). Similarly, Riley describes her grief about the loss of her son as sharing his death, as a form of not abandoning him, '"just because he is dead". [ ... ] I tried always to be there for him, solidly. And I shall continue to be. (The logic of this conviction: in order to be there, I too have died)' (Riley 2012: 21).

In *The Fountain* the process of melancholia is embedded in time and memory, and represented by the interweaving of actual and imaginary, mnemonic narrative elements. Here the virtual and the actual correspond to Gilles Deleuze's distinction between nonlinear (*aion*) and linear (*chronos*) time. This notion helps one to understand how Tommy's self is saturated by his memory of Izzi. On the level of *aion*, Izzi is constantly present, which makes it impossible for Tommy's consciousness to process her as an object of memory in his consciousness on the level of *chronos* (the past). Thus Izzi has turned into a 'melancholic fetish', essentially there to preserve Tommy's memory of her by means of obsessive disavowal or counter-belief desire: 'I know my wife is deceased (belief), but by "reproducing" her as a mnemonic fetish I can deny this fact' (desire).

Therefore Tommy is at once restless and strangely frozen, arrested in his grief, pathologically fixated by his memory of Izzi, which he can neither relinquish nor work through. Janet writes that this kind of affective failure occurs when the effects of overwhelming emotional experience are stored in somatic memory instead of semantic memory. Semantic memory is a dimension of memory that processes an emotional event by means of distortion. This locates the event chronologically and positionally (*chronos*), and ensures that it is differentiated from current reality (*aion*). Somatic memory resides in the sensorimotor, bodily sensations that are related to the experienced emotional event. According to Janet, extremely painful emotional events resist processing by semantic memory. As a result, they are persistently stored as visceral sensations and visual images, such as nightmares and flashbacks, in the somatic memory: '[C]ertain happenings . . . have indelible and distressing memories – memories to which the sufferer continually returns, and by which he is tormented by day and by night' (Janet cited in Van der Kolk 1994: 258). In *The Fountain*, it is the future strand in particular that is full of haunting visual flashbacks of Izzi. These include her standing in the doorway to Tommy's office or sleeping in a hospital bed. In addition to these visual hallucinations, there are also sensations conveyed through the sense of touch and manifested in numerous bodily gestures.

In this thematic approach to working through grief, there is yet another claim that can be made about the complex structure of *The Fountain* – namely, that the future layer embodies Tommy's somatic memory, the present his current reality and the past his semantic memory. It is in the future layer (somatic memory) that Tommy would try to narrativize and work through his grief, constantly urged on by his hallucination of Izzi urging him to 'finish it'. But in order to 'finish it', Tommy has to acknowledge and feel his emotional pain, which instead he denies. This denial leads to his failure to integrate Izzi's death with semantic memory. According to Janet, such failure is based on dissociation. This occurs when affect is pathologically separated from consciousness, leading to hypermnesia, an abnormally vivid recurrent memory of the past.

In such cases, emotion emancipates itself, becomes independent and develops on its own account: 'The result is, on the one hand, that it develops far too much, and, on the other hand, that consciousness appears no longer to control it' (Janet cited in Putnam 1989: 415). Izzi's death is such a moment of dissociation, a scene in which the efficacious use of sound is revealing. The alarm sound of her electrocardiac equipment is heard simultaneously in all temporal layers, at first suggesting the full integration of Tommy's somatic and semantic memory, as well as his reconciliation with present reality. But this is promptly followed by their strict separation, as triggered by Tommy's uncontrollable emotional distress. This next stage is visually presented to the spectator in a scene in which Tommy desperately – and to no avail – attempts to reanimate Izzi. It is as if the room temperature suddenly drops below freezing point, causing the condensation of Tommy's exhaled breath, another visual metaphor for his emotional frozenness. Through a graphic match, the scene cuts to the future layer, which suggests that Tommy's grief is also channelled and preserved (frozen) there. This idea of emotional frozenness is equally captured in the imagery of the ensuing wintry funeral scene, which likewise spreads out from the present into the future layer.

Nussbaum speaks of grief's disorderly motions and kinetic properties, which our rational faculty is unable to house, because such internal properties of grief seem to lack intentionality (the 'aboutness' of emotion) and evaluative judgment (Nussbaum 2001: 44–45). In addition, there is the cessation of time's flow and the emergence of immobile non-time that further isolates the person dwelling in grief (Riley 2012: 24). In accordance with these properties, the much commented-on disorderly spatial and temporal movement in *The Fountain* seems to escape the organizational control of the narrative. This reflects Tommy's struggle to get control over, or work through, his grief. The spectator is invited to feel the emotional effects of this struggle through participation in the affective system of the film, in which the narrative layers get randomly entangled, as an attempted endeavour at processing grief. In other words, as Tommy attempts to work through his grief, the spectator is invited to experience the film by letting go of narrative control as the strategy to 'semantically process' a painful emotional event. Therefore, the intentionality of *The Fountain* is not about generating narrative meaning, but about experiencing the film directly in order to allow for its affective propensities. The 'disorderliness' in the entanglement of the narrative strands in *The Fountain* emulates how painful emotions can sometimes result in a disorderly relation- ship with the world. This is because painful emotions make us feel vulner- able and powerless, incapable of regaining a sense of agency in a difficult life event despite our best attempts. Thus the narrative tension in *The Fountain* is analogous to Tommy's inner struggle, which alternates between losing and regaining control, but ultimately keeps him persistently captive (frozen) in the eternal return of grief. However, it is this very idea of letting go of control that the film offers as a plausible strategy for re-channelling pain in productive, transformative ways.

Nussbaum writes that emotions often link us to the objects and persons in the world 'that we regard as important for our well-being, but do not fully control' (Nussbaum 2001: 43). Of all emotional experiences, it is perhaps in that of grief that this conflict between vulnerability and control is clearest, and it is this notion that structures *The Fountain* as an emotional event through- out. The conflict is epitomized in Tomás's quest as a conquistador, which can only be successful if he chooses to expose himself to unknown hazards such as those posed by the dangerous jungle and the hostile Maya.[6] Thus Tomás is surrounded by a threatening soundscape that seems to arise from the im- mersive environment of the jungle, and that includes animal vocalizations and other natural elements (vulnerability). This is accompanied by forceful move- ments of the camera, affectively emulating Tomás's determination (control). In contrast, the frenetic dynamism of the scene in which he single-handedly fights the Maya epitomizes his lack of control over the situation. Then, shortly afterwards, it is as if the camera itself urges him to regain his lost control, to restore his composure, and to climb the steps of the Maya pyramid. On top of the pyramid he is confronted by a Maya priest armed with a flaming sword – again a direct reference to Genesis and the Biblical cherub that guards the en- trance to the Garden of Eden. Not only does this priest put an end to Tomás's life, but his violent act also ends the entire (future) narrative thread. It is only Tom's acceptance of his past vulnerability and lack of control that will reverse this 'ending' at a later point in the film.

Similarly, the future layer contrasts imagery of yoga poses and ascetic prac- tices, showing control of mind over body, with images of vulnerability. These are Tom's hallucinations issuing from his somatic memory, thus representing control of body over mind. As suggested before, Tommy's self-induced pain in the tattooing scene could be seen as a 'world-ridding' act of control aimed at cancelling out his emotional pain, which equates to his vulnerability. The entire emotional trajectory of the film seems to revolve around control and vulnerability as affective qualities at the core of (unresolved) grief. This is corroborated by the desperate but futile attempt of the three narrative layers to catch up with one another just before the terrible event of Izzi's death.

In purely visual terms, control and vulnerability are especially prominent in the future layer. It contains an important juxtaposition between grief and consolation, embodied in dark (grief) and luminous (consolation) visual elements. In the future layer, the darkness of the image reflects only grief at first, as do the depicted ascetic practices that are designed to keep affect at bay. But a promise of hope gradually enters the scene with references to Xibalba and its golden embers that disperse the dark clouds of the nebula, which in turn gradually enables movement out of the dark into more benign lighting. But then death occurs before the space bubble has penetrated the last dark cloud. Through this event, Tom is enclosed in an irreparable finality of loss at first. This is why the golden embers do not actually enter his bubble to illuminate it with hope. This scene is analogous to the one that shows Tommy grieving in his and Izzi's bedroom, isolated in his emotion, while glowing snowflakes fall outside the window. It is only when the nebula around the bubble 'collapses' that it is fully illuminated and melancholia gives way to mourning. This change entails acceptance of one's helplessness before the all-powerful natural world. The insight that seems to be conveyed by the visual symbolism of *The Fountain* is that in order to work through grief, one has to learn to depend on forces beyond one's control for well-being, and to acknowledge a certain vulnerability in front of the world, as Nussbaum would have it (Nussbaum 2001: 43). Tomás, who refuses to acknowledge this, nevertheless loses his self in the eternal flow of nature's force. Catherine Lord argues that in this scene, Tomás is 'rebooted into a type of Deleuzian "becoming tree", his organic humanity absorbed' (Lord 2009: 167). But he does not consciously *seek* this experience of 'natural connection', in contrast to Tom, who voluntarily allows himself to be disintegrated by the gravitational force of Xibalba. As suggested in the beginning of this chapter, it might be agreed, at least for the sake of argument, that the narrative strand in which Tom figures is actually the last chapter of Izzi's book as written by Tommy. Within this interpretation, I propose that by integrating Tom into the storyline with Tomás, Tommy finally succeeds in integrating his somatic memory with his semantic memory, and participating in the flow of time again. As a result, Tommy writes off his obsessive need for scientific control by allowing Tomás to 'become nature' and by accepting his own fundamental vulnerability, which is necessary to distance himself from his pain, his grief.

If the spectators are successfully invited by the visual symbolism of *The Fountain* to assume the affective postures of a grieving person, their mediating emotions may well show them their own possibilities in the face of a great loss. However, judging from the ambiguous critical reviews and audience comments on the film, the inherent symbolism and affective quality of the film's visual style are not readily accepted by every spectator. Despite acknowledging the film's visual and stylistic merits, many critics describe *The Fountain*'s operative agency as 'metaphysical muddle', 'blatant airheadedness', or 'navel-gazing' and 'mind-numbing blur'. Other critics admire the film for its 'textural richness' and 'sensual potential' as well as its 'Zen directedness', and consider the tale to be told in an 'awe-inspiring', 'profoundly moving' way.[7] A lively discussion on the Internet Movie Database shows a similar division of audience comments into two camps. There are reactions that emphasize the film's poetic, metaphysical, transcendental and mythical qualities, but there are also reactions that reject the film as stylistically overdone, kitschy, overtly sentimental, quasi-spiritual and faux-philosophical.[8] Such reactions raise interesting questions about aesthetic appreciation in relation to visual style, spirituality and metaphysics. In her book *Pretty*, Rosalind Galt describes precisely this 'quality of discomfort with a style of heightened aesthetics that is too decorative, too sensorially pleasurable to be high art, and yet too composed and "arty" to be efficient entertainment' (Galt 2011: 12). In the same vein, one could argue that *The Fountain*'s controversial reception means that it is considered too stylistic for its own good, or stylistic in the wrong way, not truly philosophical but pseudo-metaphysical, and too 'flirty' instead of serious in its dialogue with science and spirituality.

Leaving this aside, I propose that the aesthetic merit of *The Fountain* is there when the film directly and palpably engages the spectator with its affective quality. This results in a direct experience of the reverberating repetitive logic of grief beyond the diegetically coherent flow of narrative information. Despite its alleged artistic flaws, the film shows an important insight into the operative logic of pathological grief, as well as into what is necessary to overcome the accompanying painful emotions. But these insights may only be available to those who willingly open themselves up to a somatic experience of the film's emotional core. Again, the film's merit lies in its affective insight into such notions as somatic and semantic memory, an insight that is embodied in the way the film presents itself to spectators as lived-bodies. This in turn renders the film anything but pseudo-philosophical, since it invites them to participate in an emotional discourse on the effects of grief. Due to the spectators' engagement with the film's aesthetic system, this takes place at the level of the sensuous, the true seat of affective cinematic experience.

## Notes

Many thanks to Laura Copier for her helpful comments on the earlier version of this chapter.

1.  '[The] fundamental project of human reality is to say that man is the being whose project is to be God' (Sartre 1992: 724).

2.  Patricia Pisters argues that the temporal layers of *The Fountain* exemplify Deleuze's theory of time. In her Deleuzian reading of the film, the 'future' is understood as what Deleuze terms the 'third time'. This is a form of temporality in which 'all times' – historical Isabel from the past and Izzi from the present – come together (Pisters 2010: 246).

3.  According to Michael Schoenfeldt, for this reason it is not a coincidence that in Christianity an instrument of 'torture and death' – a crucifix – serves as a central symbol (Schoenfeldt 2009: 20).

4.  Yet as Jan Frans van Dijkhuizen points out, it takes a deliberate effort to remain aware of the transformative power of pain, for otherwise pain can easily lead to enduring despair (Van Dijkhuizen 2009: 200).

5.  Neurotheology is a neuroscientific study of religious experiences and the extent to which they correspond with neural phenomena, such as in the work of Eugene d'Aquili and Andrew Newberg. In their book *The Mystical Mind* (1999), they describe how emotive and cognitive parts of the brain allow people to have spiritual experiences.

6.  Of course this is in stark contrast to historical conquistadors, who used their Western war tactics and weaponry against indigenous peoples of Central America who were mostly unprepared.

7.  See, for instance, *Rotten Tomatoes,* 2010, *The Fountain.* Retrieved 6 May 2012 from http://www.rottentomatoes.com/m/the_fountain/reviews/.
8.  *Internet Movie Database,* 2012, *The Fountain.* Retrieved 9 May 2012 from http://www.imdb.com/title/tt0414993/reviews.

# CHAPTER FOUR

# Masochism
*The Wrestler*

In *The Wrestler*, Mickey Rourke plays Randy 'Ram' Robinson, a wrecked star of the eighties' professional wrestling scene, who, twenty years later, is still performing for a handful of nerdy wrestling fans in high school gyms and community centres around the state of New Jersey. After a horrendous wrestling match that involves staple guns, barbed wire and broken glass, Randy suffers a severe heart attack and is ordered to quit wrestling by his doctor. Outside the wrestling world, Randy's only 'real' human relationship is with the aging stripper Cassidy (Marisa Tomei). She advises Randy to re-establish contact with his estranged daughter Stephanie (Evan Rachel Wood), but this turns out to be a painful, impossible undertaking, which ends with Randy losing both his daughter and (apparently) Cassidy too. Meanwhile, Randy is forced to take a 'normal' job at the deli counter of a supermarket, where he has to deal with fussy customers and wear an awkward hygiene cap. After having been recognized by one of the customers as Randy the Ram, he deliberately cuts his hand and quits his job in a rage. Unable to deal with life outside the wrestling world, Randy agrees to fight a big rematch with his glory-days enemy, The Ayatollah, despite his heart condition, and even without payment. The fight ends, as his fights always do, with a 'Ram Jam' manoeuvre in which he leaps off the top rope of the ring onto his opponent – this time, presumably to his death.

The last 'Ram Jam' manoeuvre is done in a Christ-like pose, and biblical associations are hard to avoid with *The Wrestler*. The film even contains a direct reference to Mel Gibson's *The Passion of the Christ* (2004).[1] But this chapter discusses Randy's suffering, his *passion* in the original Latin meaning of the word, from a different point of view. I refer to the way in which *The Wrestler*'s corporeal aesthetics directly induce pain in the spectator. This pain functions to draw the spectator's attention to the difference between the non-diegetic and the diegetic audience. The diegetic audience, the audience in the film's story world, is the audience demanding pain. It is this audience Randy addresses, and for which he performs. By contrast, the non-diegetic audience, the spectators of the film, are invited to observe Randy's pain very closely, but without ever getting really close to the character. It is the contradictory dynamics between diegetic and non-diegetic audiences that draws one's attention to the discrepancy between spectatorial and performative pain, with important ethical consequences. As such, the film functions as a violent thought provocation, pushing the limits of our viewing position, so that we become positionally conscious of our own responsibility as spectators of pain.

The film achieves this by staging a drama of the flesh, borne out by a conflict between a vulnerable lived-body and a 'tough' body-as-an-object – a conflict that is closely linked to masochism in a Sartrean sense. Further-more, it is linked to Sartre's notion of bad faith, because Randy's masochism serves to distance him from responsible self-determination, and offers the means for self-deception and self-objectification instead. In this course of action, the spectator is treated as an accomplice, instead of a mere witness, and the ethical challenge offered by *The Wrestler* seems to acknowledge this. In other words, the spectators are not allowed to forget the conditions under which the objectification of another person takes place, including their own role as witnesses in the process. This chapter explores how the film confronts spectators with painful imagery, forcing them to acknowl-edge the pain of another, while simultaneously exposing them to the im-possibility of such acknowledgement. *The Wrestler* demands spectatorial engagement, while simultaneously complicating it. By doing so, it provokes the spectators into an interpretation aimed at self-reflection, which does not, however, lead to purging of the negative affect. This spectatorial en-gagement has to do with the juxtaposition of distance and proximity. In *The Wrestler*, flesh opens and bleeds (proximity), while the victim is objectified (distance). In this way, the film forces its spectators to look in a mirror, thus presenting them with an image of a crowd cheering at the sight of pain and objectification in the name of entertainment, while compelling them to acknowledge the correspondence between the diegetic and non-diegetic audience.

## Nostalgia in Denial

The film opens with a black screen. On top of this, the comic strip-like opening credits unfold over the noise of a cheering audience and Quiet Riot, an eighties heavy metal band, revving up. The camera glides over numerous professional wrestling posters and tabloid clippings, all about Randy the Ram's fights, showing sensational slogans and photos depicting oiled, naked torsos and faces grimacing with triumph and pain. The aesthetics of this opening sequence are heavily saturated with testosterone-laden masculinity, referring to a world in which values related to emotional toughness, endurance of pain, brazenness, casual sex and pumped-up muscles rule over interpersonal relationships and familial responsibilities. The image fades into black, and on the audio track a sound of someone coughing can be heard before the next shot appears, a contrasting scene twenty years after Randy the Ram's days of glory. He is shown sitting in a space that appears to be an elementary school classroom in some suburb, waiting for his fight to begin. The setting of this fight is both geographically and symbolically far removed from Madison Square Garden in New York City, where Randy's famous victory over The Ayatollah took place. In this alien setting, Randy is shot from a low angle, with his back to the camera and his head buried in his arms, while we hear him sigh deeply. As he heads home later on, there is only a heavy metal song on his car radio to remind him of his past fame.

Heavy metal rock from the eighties, diegetic and non-diegetic, is an important auditory motif throughout the film.[2] Often referred to as glam metal, this music genre is characterized by a tough, thick, loud, massive sound and extended guitar solos, and is generally associated with aggression and virile masculinity. The music is combined with a theatrical style of performance, long hair and heavy make-up, as well as gaudy accessories and flamboyant clothing made of materials like tight, colourful spandex. These 'softer' features, whether intentional or not, are often associated with a camp attitude, and here they are associated with the world of professional wrestling, too. In the film The Wrestler, this juxtaposition of toughness and softness becomes a constant struggle, in which the one always cancels out the other. It could be said that Randy lives in two separate worlds that can never meet. In the world of wrestling, Randy still enjoys the admiration of his peers, his loyal middle-aged fans and young boys, while in the world outside the wrestling ring he is financially broke and forced to tolerate constant humiliation from his boss at his low-paid job. In front of the audience, his muscular body can still take every blow, but offstage he has to submit to its vulnerability, as is evident in the backstage scenes in which medics stitch him up. Outside the wrestling scene he is very lonely, and can only encounter his love interest Cassidy at a strip club, where female desire is typically measured against male sexual pleasure instead of by its own standards. This becomes clear in the scene in which young club patrons ridicule the aging stripper, declaring Cassidy too old and sexually unappealing to perform a lap dance. At first Randy displays to Cassidy his old wrestling scars as badges of honour, but later in the film the scar resulting from his heart surgery testifies to his mortality. His body can no longer manage the demands of professional wrestling, and requires maintenance by means of a substantial amount of drugs, including painkillers and steroids. The heart surgery scar is not one of which Randy is proud; it is, rather, a source of shame that Randy can only overcome by means of self-delusion and bad faith.

This juxtaposition of pride and shame, toughness and softness, evokes negative emotion by means of painfully direct cinematic features. The most painful sequence, by any standard, in *The Wrestler* is the agonizingly long fight scene with Necro Butcher. This sequence is approximately seven minutes long, but it feels endless, as it is saturated with relentless negative emotion throughout. As with the ending of *Requiem for a Dream*, the Necro Butcher scene in *The Wrestler* evokes discomfort, which is a consequence of the spectator's inability to stop watching an unpleasant, painful scene. The narrative structure of the sequence is rather complex, consisting of three temporal layers before, during and after the fight. It starts with a flashback of Randy and Butcher discussing the most efficient and spectacular ways of inflicting pain. After this, the narration leaps to the end of the fight, showing Butcher lying on the floor with bloody incisions all over his body caused by broken glass and barbed wire. His toothless mouth is twisted in a hideous scowl, while the crowd is chanting 'you're so dead'. He gets up with much difficulty, only to get a windowpane smashed on his head, after which Randy floors him violently with his knee. Then we follow the exhausted Randy backstage, and we notice that his body too is covered with wounds, staples and broken glass, as the camera lingers over the bloody mess. A flashback brings us back to the beginning of the fight, which had started out with Randy and Butcher slapping each other's faces. The shot reverse shot of this scene sees to it that we feel as if we were on the receiving end of the blows, until Butcher ends the slapping by spraying insecticide on both Randy's and on his own face. The sequence then continues with Butcher using a staple gun on Randy as well as on himself, fastening a dollar bill to his brow and digging a deep wound in Randy's forehead with a fork. These shots alternate with shots from after the match, in which the medics are removing the staples and trying to patch up the contestants. All this is filmed with agonizing proximity in close-ups that 'bring the eye where it would not normally look . . . the close-up thus creates uncanny intimacies and shows us the body as we rarely dare look at it – as an organic mass bearing the marks of decomposition that is barely visible to the naked eye' (Beugnet 2007: 91). Jean Epstein also associates close-up with pain: 'The close-up is an intensifying agent because of its size alone . . . this magnification acts on one's feelings more to transform than to confirm them. . . . The close-up modifies the drama by the impact of proximity. Pain is within reach. . . . As an emotional indicator, [the close-up] overwhelms me' (Epstein 1993a: 239).

The close-ups in *The Wrestler* induce pain directly by lingering over sharp items that are shown first as they penetrate the skin and afterwards as they are being removed (figure 4.1). The close-ups magnify the bruises, thus drawing the non-diegetic audience's attention to the vulnerability of the body, which is not witnessed by the diegetic audience. In addition, we can hear the pained moans, groans, grunts, gurgles and whinges in aural close-ups that bespeak bodily vulnerability, while these sounds are apparently inaudible to the crowd cheering and booing in the background. Finally, the Necro Butcher sequence denies the spectator any sense of catharsis or relief, as it ends with Randy throwing up in a corner backstage and then collapsing on the floor, while a sharp chirping sound indicates his heart failure. Often catharsis works by configuring violence and pain in the service of enjoyment, as Brian Price points out (Price 2010: 42). Like *Requiem for a Dream*, *The Wrestler* is explicitly anti-cathartic, offering no narrative satisfaction or purifying release of tension for the spectator. One reason for this is that *The Wrestler* does not function affectively through empathy, which is an essential element of catharsis. In the experience of catharsis, the spectators are invited to empathize with the suffering of a tragic hero(ine), while identifying with the 'metaphysical truth' of the drama (Nietzsche 1999: 31). In contrast, *The Wrestler* regularly evokes pity for its main character, but since pity is associated with superiority, it is, by definition, not an empathetic reaction. Pity always involves looking down upon the pitied, even when one is feeling genuinely sad about the other's misfortune (Solomon 2007: 66). This anti-cathartic operative logic in *The Wrestler* potentially invites the spectator to reflect on the very conditions of viewing the film, as will be argued in the final part of this chapter.

After Randy has a heart bypass, there is an immense contrast between his (past) athletic image as a professional wrestler leaping off the top rope, and his current reality as a wrecked, aging, frail man wearing a hospital gown, which embarrassingly reveals his buttocks as he is struggling to get out of bed. At first, Randy seemingly tries to come to terms with the certainty of his bodily deterioration: he gives up wrestling and accepts a daily job at the deli counter of a local discount supermarket. He performs his duties with apparent satisfaction until one day a customer recognizes him, after which he deliberately thrusts his hand into a cold cuts machine, bleeding all over the place. Again, the violence of the moment is emphasized by a close up of the wound, by the suddenness of Randy's gesture, and by the shaky, handheld camera that follows Randy as he rages his way out of the store, while the framing fiercely alternates between frontal and rear angle. This too is a painful scene, not only because it renders Randy's pain tangible for the spectator. The scene also marks a defining moment of bad faith that will lead to Randy's definitive self-destruction, instead of to any kind of responsible self-determination. He

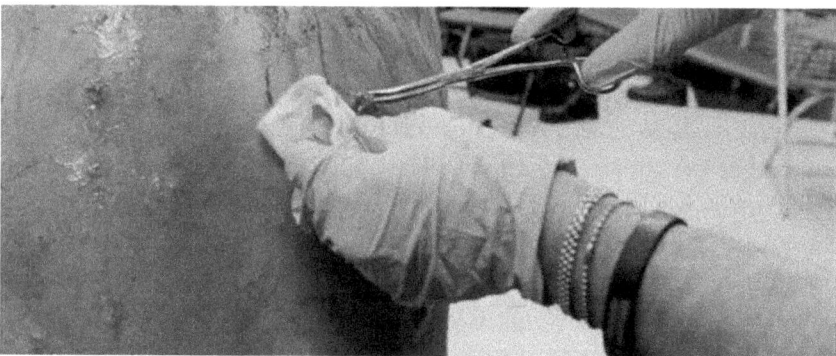

**Figure 4.1.** Close-up as an instigator of pain. Screen capture, *The Wrestler* (2008).

returns to negotiating about the wrestling match with The Ayatollah, and is shown preparing for the match in a montage sequence accompanied by loud heavy metal music. This is a scene that does not inspire admiration, as might be said of similarly structured scenes depicting (anti-)heroes preparing to face inescapable dangers, such as the ending of *The Wild Bunch* (Sam Peckinpah, 1969). Instead, it evokes pain due to the inevitability inherent in the scene, which is saturated by lack of hope that a 'happy end' might still be possible.

In contrast to earlier wrestling scenes in the film, during the last fight pain is not clearly visible on the bodies. There is no show of blood, for instance. Even though one occasionally recognizes pain in Randy's facial expressions, one is invited to imagine pain from the inside, as evoked by the sounds that accompany this scene. There is the sound of Randy's heavy breathing, but it is the piercing electric sound that comes and goes that particularly embodies Randy's painful sensation that his heart's electrical circuitry is about to fail. The film ends with Randy leaping off the ring's top rope for the last time, accompanied by an accelerating, ethereal score that is in delicate contrast to the harshness of the setting. The music stops abruptly and the final shot is cut to black, denoting the lethal stroke for Randy's heart. In his recent book, Sam Girgus writes about 'cinema of redemption' in which a hero goes through an ethical struggle but ultimately accepts 'a total commitment to an ethical order of belief and action, one that makes ethical relations with others more important than personal demands, success and wealth' (Girgus 2010: 25). In contrast, *The Wrestler* can be seen as an example of cinema of relapse, and its avoidance of catharsis changes the spectator's relationship with the film. The lack of ethical struggle in *The Wrestler* does not mean that the film itself is not ethical, however. Its ethical dimension is found in the way in which the film positions the spectator as an accomplice in Randy's objectification, as will be demonstrated later.

Perhaps *The Wrestler*'s lack of catharsis is partly explained by the observation that it is not an aesthetically pleasing film, as are Aronofsky's preceding film, *The Fountain*, and his next one, *Black Swan*. In fact, *The Wrestler* is downright ugly in a way that does not pretend to aim at 'true' beauty with transformative value. In this, the film resembles social realist ('kitchen sink') filmmaking on location in drab (post-)industrial landscapes, which can become true spectacles of enigmatic squalor for those who do not have to inhabit them (Hill 1986: 136). As Julia Hallam and Margaret Marshment point out, this approach may well result in what John Urry terms a 'tourist gaze' – not unrelated to the voyeuristic gaze discussed later on in this chapter – which involves 'a fascination with difference that enables the lives of unknown people and the places they inhabit to be represented as a commodity, a spectacle for consumption' (Hallam and Marshment 2000: 195). This results from the strong emphasis in social realist filmmaking on the link between deprived, ugly environmental conditions and the psychological makeup of the characters, combined with observational camerawork. Social realist filmmaking features landscapes of the marginalized underclass, spaces that 'international capitalism can no longer find a use for . . . abandoned inner city areas, satellite housing areas built to rehouse those displaced by earlier urban regeneration schemes . . . industrial towns where the industries that once provided jobs and relative affluence have moved to new locations' (Hallam and Marshment 2000: 193).

As a marginalized, socially isolated figure, Randy spends most of his time indoors, in spaces that have little or no natural light – community centres, discount stores, gyms, strip clubs and sleazy bars – and often he finds himself in the backrooms of these unappealing locations. These are settings that altogether lack beauty or charm, exuding instead either a cold, industrial feeling, or shabbiness and gaudiness that are hardly masked. The backstage rooms of such venues where Randy is still invited to perform are untidy, messy, cramped spaces with cheap, clunky furniture and tasteless décor made from laminated plywood and plastic in earthy, muddy colours. The wrestling ring itself is a stiff construction that tends to look out of place in its environment, its floor covered with loud sponsor logos. The discount store where Randy works has not invested in interior decoration: it is a plain, grey, dreary, factory-like hall, the complete opposite of fashionable delis or elegant food halls that one may come across in luxurious department stores. Randy's abode in a trailer park close to an abandoned railway line is a closed, desolate, depressing space that does not radiate joy or cosiness, and the strip club he frequents is a stuffy, dark establishment with garish neon lights. All the film's settings are hopelessly enclosed, alienated environments, and even the outdoor shots have a dispiriting affective quality due to the choice of locations, such as drab parking lots, dying city centres and dull suburbs. This effect is enhanced by the fact that the film was shot in early spring, with mostly grey skies and almost all the snow melted away, but no blossoming trees yet in view.

Costume adds to the overall aesthetic unpleasantness of the film: most characters wear cheap-looking, badly fitting practical clothing with no sense of style: quilted jackets, lumberjack shirts, loose-fitting jeans, large college shirts, hooded sweatshirts and track pants, in unassuming colours such as dark grey, navy blue and army green. Cassidy's scanty strip-club outfits have little elegance or allure, and Randy's professional wrestling gear consists of brightly coloured tights made of glossy spandex. The wrestlers' bodies are brawny but not particularly lean, showing muscles that would be hard to build without steroids, and sporting poor-quality tattoos. Randy has an artificial tan resulting from frequent visits to tanning parlours and the use of self-tanning lotions. His badly bleached, flat, volumeless hair hangs limply around his face when not pulled up in a slapdash bun.

The wrestling itself, although it requires athleticism and skill, is not an elegant sport compared to, say, gymnastics. The manoeuvres, although discussed in advance by the wrestlers, still look improvised and never show poise or elegance. Rather, they lack control and co-ordination in order to provide the sport with an unpretentious, raw quality. Similarly, Cassidy's 'erotic' high-heeled tottering to music in the strip club is hardly graceful, especially as she looks rather bored most of the time. All in all, the deliberately unappealing mise-en-scène elements in *The Wrestler* create aesthetics that are as awkward and outdated as the clumsy 'pixel' design of Randy's Nintendo game, which is based on his famous first match with The Ayatollah. These images create aesthetic displeasure rather than contentment, resulting in feelings of discomfort, embarrassment and negative astonishment.[3]

In this context it is interesting to notice how the film introduces its main character, played by Mickey Rourke. Randy is first shown in a static long shot filmed at a low angle and in a 3/4 rear view, sitting as far as possible from the camera. In the following shots, a handheld camera follows him closely either from a full rear or 3/4 rear angle, then stops and lets him move out of sight. This recurring technique has a symbolic function: it operates by inviting the spectators to put themselves in the character's place on the one hand, and blocking access to the character on the other. This strategy epitomizes Randy's isolation from any social contact, including the spectator. But it has another, more tactical function as well, which is to avoid showing the character's face at first. The film refuses to show us Randy's face either through a 'badly' chosen camera angle, or through lack of light in the image. It is only at the seven-minute mark of the film that we get a full, clear view of Randy's face, as he rushes out of the back of his van, where he was forced to sleep after having been locked out of his trailer by his landlord. He then pretends to attack a group of noisy trailer park kids outside his van, as if he were some kind of monster.

In her discussion of Mickey Rourke's performance in the film, Keri Walsh (2010) states that the strategy of withholding the view of his face from the spectator creates a combination of desire for the gorgeous young Rourke of the 1980s and dread for the monstrous Rourke of the 2000s.[4] Watching Rourke's disfigured face in this film, it is indeed hard to avoid the association of beauty turned into beast. In the 1980s, Rourke enjoyed the status of sex symbol, especially after his leading role in Adrian Lyne's erotic drama 9 1/2 *Weeks* (1986), and he was considered one of the best-looking actors in Hollywood. A trained boxer, Rourke returned to the boxing ring in the 1990s, but suffered a number of severe facial injuries. He allegedly had to undergo reconstructive surgery more than once, which left his face hideously disfigured. A lively Internet discussion on the subject describes Rourke's new face as 'horrifying', 'strange', 'scary', 'awful' and 'gruesome'. *The Wrestler* seems to exploit fully Rourke's present appearance, with its noticeable cheek, chin and lip implants, as well as the unnatural shape of his eyes. This ugliness is mirrored on the level of human feelings. It is disturbing to watch Randy's deliberate self-destruction, how he persistently endures humiliation by his employer and resentment by his daughter. The same holds for the scene in which Randy is crassly seduced by a woman in a bar, with whom he ends up having sex in the restroom. And there is the bloodthirsty audience in attendance to see pain, not a solid performance by a wrestler. This renders the wrestling scenes painfully self-reflective, compelling the spectators to scrutinize their own viewing position from the inside. This scrutiny is borne out by direct bodily engagement with the film, which proposes contemplating the spectators' accountability for the violence, prompting them to ethical judgment.

These situations are so profoundly ugly in themselves that it becomes nearly impossible to distance oneself emotionally. The only moment of beauty and serenity in the film is the scene in which Randy visits the deserted New Jersey shore with his daughter. Now there is spaciousness in the frame, and the boarded walkway forms harmonic lines, while the image bathes in natural, soft lighting. They visit a derelict but picturesque old casino, exuding old-fashioned charm with its wooden construction, which stands in stark contrast to the rest of the film's scenery. The beauty of this scene suggests a moment of potentiality in Deleuze's sense, a defining moment when life opens itself to multiple possibilities. In Randy's case, these possibilities include acknowledging that he is needed, and that he is in need of others too, beyond his emotionally superficial wrestling acquaintances. However, in *The Wrestler,* such potentiality is converted into a possibility lost forever and sensed as emotional pain. The spectator feels this pain precisely because Randy denies his. Philip Fisher defines aesthetic moments like this as follows:

> What happens in these cases is a blank spot where the reader or spectator volunteers passion, stepping in to supply the missing fear, grief, shame, or anger. Volunteered passion is a stronger demand on the spectator and a more perfect aesthetic strategy for the eliciting of passion than sympathy, understood in the narrow sense of feeling alongside another's explicit emotional state, can ever be. (Fisher 2002: 144)

By means of its aesthetic specificity, *The Wrestler* produces such an affective 'blank spot', which the spectators fill with their own 'passion', because the protagonist of the film is disavowing his emotions. With its effect on the spectator based on ugliness, *The Wrestler* may not be the most beautiful film in the world, but neither is the work aesthetically experimental or surprising. Nevertheless, its affective quality is extraordinarily strong, wretched and vibrant. It confronts one with a lifestyle with which one does not necessarily want to be confronted, while evoking fascination and a feeling of authenticity without making any 'truth claims'.

The opening scene of *The Wrestler* establishes a utopian, illusory space of nostalgia, fame, and belonging, echoed by the cheering crowds and the overzealous announcers from the past. It is the space to which Randy longs to return, but to no avail. The gap between Randy's utopian past and his dystopian present is already obvious from the very next shot: Randy sitting in an elementary school classroom full of scattered colourful toys and decorated with childish paintings. 'Journeyman' Randy seems rather out of place in this picture, with its references to the beginnings of life, with every possibility still open. It soon becomes clear that his own possibilities are rather limited. He

lives in a trailer park, and is unable to fulfil even the marginal social require-
ments that apply to this situation. He is repeatedly behind on his rent pay-
ments, as he has few job possibilities. A nightly scene in the back of his van
is filled with loneliness and nostalgia, as Randy studies his 'wall of fame', assembled from tabloid clippings in the scarce light provided by a torch. A mel-
ancholy electric guitar, played by Slash from Guns N' Roses, accompanies this
scene. It functions as the affective glue that binds the spectator to the scene,
resonating loneliness by means of 'affective congruence' (Smith 1999), an
aesthetic strategy discussed in chapter two on *Requiem for a Dream*.

Randy appears to be a marginal figure in a context that is marginal in itself.
Professional wrestling, even though it is popular entertainment, at least in the
US, is often seen as a suspect type of sport and a marginal form of popular culture (Mazer 1998: 5). It has its own jargon, its own logic, and bizarre dramatic
conventions that are not necessarily comprehensible to a mainstream viewer.
Randy is also isolated in his daily job as a hauler at the discount store, where he
deliberately stays in the staff-only area, out of sight of the costumers. Before
his fights, he is often given a private dressing room, perhaps out of respect for
his past fame, but this only enhances his isolation, even in the social setting in
which he belongs. Furthermore, Randy now seems to be too 'old school' in the
wrestling ring, which has become extremely hard-core in his absence. In this
hard-core world, plain wrestling is no longer enough. Audiences are now used
to seeing blood, and so Randy has to cut himself with razor blades and suffer
even more painful inflictions, until his heart finally gives up. This is also epitomized in the scene in which he plays an old computer game called 'Wrestle
Jam' with a neighbourhood boy, which, after his bypass, is all the wrestling he
is up to. The game, in which Randy himself features as one of the characters,
fills the entire frame. Then, off-screen, the boy dismisses the game as outdated and shows himself to be not really interested in winning. When the virtual Randy figure finishes the game, real Randy cheers in victory, not realizing
or admitting to himself how he has become out of touch with the real world.
This kind of 'nostalgia in denial' is in fact best characterized as a psychopatho-
logical condition that may result from painful feelings of uprootedness, social
fragmentation, isolation and alienation (Rosen 1975: 350).

These are emotions that structure *The Wrestler* throughout. As Welsh puts
it, Randy is a cliché, not realizing himself that he is one, but suffering precisely

for this reason (Welsh 2010: 132). Randy's loneliness is tangible in several other scenes that follow the bypass operation. After he has been released from hospital, there is a long shot of Randy sitting in his camper, positioned at the far end of the camera's view. Depth of field, frame composition and lack of light in the image all emphasize the oppressive feeling of loneliness, which is accompanied by the already familiar guitar tune on the sound track. Then the camera gets very close to Randy, further emphasizing feelings of being cramped in the already confined living space. This image suggests Randy's entrapment in a cocoon of loneliness, built by his own mind-set. In another scene, filmed in an extreme long shot, Randy collapses among some trees during his first jogging session after the bypass. Here it is the camera's distance, instead of its proximity, that signifies his loneliness, his fragility. It calls attention to how small this physically large man must feel at that moment, enclosed within the branches of the thicket.

Randy's moment of epiphany takes place during a poorly attended fan meeting at a community centre, where old-time wrestlers earn cash selling Polaroid pictures of themselves at eight dollars apiece. In this humiliating situation, the camera imitates Randy's wandering gaze without adopting his point of view. First there is a zoom into a close-up of a wrestler to Randy's right, dozing off at his table. The camera zooms out, passing in front of Randy, only to zoom in diagonally and focus on a forearm crutch leaning against a table, before panning to the left to catch another old wrestler yawning. Then the camera circles behind Randy to his right, zooming into a close-up of the footrest of a wheelchair, and finally settles into a close-up of Randy's joyless face. The circularity of camera movement in this scene communicates the deadened circle in which Randy now finds himself. He attempts to break free from this by accepting a steady job at the deli counter. On his first day, he is shot in medium close-up in the mirror of an unkempt toilet, trying on a hygiene cap over his bleached curls. As he walks through the service corridors, the camera follows him closely in one long take, a generic technique unmistakably associated with fighting films. Perhaps the most famous scene of this kind can be found in Martin Scorsese's *Raging Bull* (1980), in which the camera follows Jake LaMotta (Robert de Niro) through the bowels of a sports arena up into the glaring spotlights of the boxing ring. This association is emphasized by the non-diegetic cheering of an imaginary audience that gradually becomes more audible, only to stop abruptly with a hollow pitch when Randy enters the new 'stage'. An elliptical sequence follows, showing Randy wrapping up cold cuts, dealing with customers, oiling the grill, and learning to use the pressure cooker. Then, suddenly, he acquires a taste for customer service: his body language loosens up, he starts flirting with his female customers and bonding with the male ones; in other words, he performs. For a moment, Randy belongs to the world, only to be rejected again shortly afterwards.

A recurrent aesthetic element in *The Wrestler* is a shot in which the camera trails or follows Randy from behind. It is a technique that is often associated with character identification, because of its intimate quality. A following shot makes the spectator aware of the character's presence in the physical world of the film. This enables spectators to feel as if they are physically attached to the character by means of affective mimicry. In this mode of engagement, the camera models itself on human movement, which provokes a mimetic bodily reaction in the spectator. But this trailing technique can also be defined as a pure point of view, which has the effect of marking the camera movement solely as a presence, not as a person. Otherwise the camera assumes a subjective presence and acquires an internal vision, in Deleuze's definition of free indirect discourse in Pier Paolo Pasolini's 'cinema of poetry' (Deleuze 1989: 148). In *The Wrestler*, the pure point of view attaches the spectators to Randy, but at the same time it draws their attention to the space that *separates* them from him. This in-between space cancels out the initial attachment, compelling the spectators to feel the emotional effect of loneliness without necessarily requiring them to identify with Randy's state of mind. This juxtaposition of proximity and detachment is the operative aesthetic logic throughout *The Wrestler*. It compels the spectators to recognize Randy's torment, and it confronts them with their ultimate failure to do so, which leads to ethical questions about pain and spectatorship. This invites a reciprocal exchange between cinema and spectator. The conditions of this viewing enable spectators to reflect on the affective quality embodied in the film.

## Masochism and Spectatorship

Randy's loneliness seems to be associated with masochism, which for many theorists also draws a distance between the self and the world. Of course many practitioners of masochism seek to (re)unite with the world through (sado)masochistic acts. In this vein, Lynda Hart describes masochism as a performative, reconnective and redemptive process that enables the practitioner to access his or her 'whole' self through the senses (Hart 1998: 81). Roy Baumeister (1998) compares masochism to meditation, but also to alcohol and drug abuse, as well as to recreational activities such as watching movies. To him, it is a means of escaping from the 'burdensome' higher level of self-awareness to a 'lower' level of physical body as locus of immediate sensation.[5] And of course there is Michel Foucault, who considers sadomasochism a 'creative enterprise' used to break free from the traditional, heteronormative sexual grid (Foucault 1996: 384). In contrast, Randy's pain is neither cathartic nor transformative. It is a dissociative process that serves to distance his self both from the vulnerability of his body and his true feelings. Linda Holler describes this type of 'palliative' masochism as a means of escaping the self-world through acts that render one's embodied and intersubjective connections unavailable, and that 'deaden the flesh and remove the self from moral choice' (Holler 2002: 152–53).

Randy's masochism 'deadens the flesh' because it prevents him from seizing opportunities in the present and imprisons him in the lost glory of the past instead. His body is not a positive, enabling, instrumental subject, grasping and containing the world, but – despite its athleticism – a negative, inert, contingent object that is defined by its quickly eroding ability to entertain. This is why, before a match, he hides a piece of a razor blade in his protective gear to cut his forehead with as a form of compensation when he is floored by his much younger opponent.[6] Both for him and the audience, bleeding functions as proof that he is still tough, that he can still absorb pain and exceed his physical limits. Randy has trouble accepting his aging body and therefore takes steroids, puts himself through brutal physical workouts, bleaches his hair with strong chemicals and spends hours lying on a tanning bed. When his body ultimately fails him, he no longer knows who he is. This leads to further emotional confusion and humiliating alienation. Randy's bodily objectivity – or should one say abjectivity? – is epitomized in the contiguous following camera sequences, which regularly isolate him from the flow of the world while bringing the spectator closer to the character. The cramped settings, emphasizing his sensory immunity, also serve to divide him from the world. The only spacious

imagery in the film is found in the seashore scene, suggesting Randy's potential to open up to the world, a possibility that is eventually lost forever.

This is the reason why Randy's masochism is best characterized as a form
of bad faith in Sartre's sense, an attempt to achieve subjectivity by looking at
oneself simply as an object for the other. Sartre links bad faith to the concept
of 'facticity' – or rather to one's failure to accept one's facticity in all its potentially humiliating limitedness. Randy enters into bad faith, for instance, when
he falls victim to the temptation to identify himself entirely with his facticity
– his physical body, his past. Thus he denies himself any possibility for responsible self-determination in the present. Furthermore, for Sartre, masochism
is an exercise in bad faith 'by which the Other would found me in my being'
(Sartre 1992: 491). As a basis for subjectivity, however, masochism is ultimately
a failure, an act that causes a person to be fascinated by his own objectivity.
This is because masochists are always complicit with their own objectification.
They knowingly insist on being defined as objects, and therefore by necessity
cannot be mere objects. There are many instances of bad faith in *The Wrestler*
through which Randy attempts to hide his failure of self by becoming a pure
object for the other, a mere 'instrument of wrestling' for the audience. Right
before the rematch with The Ayatollah, Randy projects in a broken voice all
responsibility for his actions onto the audience in what is to be his last speech:

> A lot of people told me that I'd never wrestle again. . . . But, goddamn it,
> I'm still standing here, and I am the Ram. As time goes by, they say, he's
> washed up. He's finished. He's a loser. He's all through. But, you know
> what? The only ones who are gonna tell me when I'm through doing my
> thing is you people here. You people here are the ones who are worth
> bringing it for, because you're my family.

His casual sexual encounter in a bar with a woman whose brother used to have
Randy's poster on his door is not much more than masochistic self-deception.
Her sexual desire is directed at a poster from the past instead of the actual,
'original' Randy in the present. He purposely injures his hand in the cold cuts
machine, because being recognized in the 'wrong role' confronts Randy with
his self-deception, while the physical pain confirms his bad faith regarding his
'true' vocation as a wrestler. Walsh writes about the scene as follows:

> The gesture's meaning goes in two directions: symbolically, we see the destruction of the phallus, the ego, the flesh as signed by the thumb, but narratively we see the return of the phallus because this is . . . the moment when Randy has had it with his emasculating job and decides that he would rather die on his feet in the ring than live on his knees in the supermarket. (Walsh 2010: 157)

Yet she concludes that the gesture evidently enables Randy to live out the 'phallic lie' anyway. In the same vein, it could be argued that the gesture and the pain that ensue are there to give him an excuse to fall back on the original state of self in denial, after the customer's remark has forced him to take an unfavourable third-person stance towards himself. This triad structure is also present in the emotion of shame, which for Sartre is closely connected to masochism, and which will be discussed later. Randy's decision to return to the wrestling ring after the self-injury scene is thus a suicidal, passive strategy, meant to avoid a life of creative self-determination, parading as defiance.[7] Watching the development of the film as it moves towards Randy's final match is like witnessing a prolonged suicide. The montage sequence in which Randy prepares for the match conveys a sense of determination that harshly belies the weakness of his heart, as visualized in the fresh surgery scar on his chest.

This type of self-deceptive masochism is closely linked to shame. A masochist's insistence on being defined by the other as an object leads to shame, which the masochist learns to love as a profound sign of his objectivity in turn (Sartre 1992: 492). Thus *The Wrestler* emphasizes Randy's bodily vulnerability and emotional isolation, so deeply-rooted in his lived-body that he himself does not notice it any longer. The scene with the customer is exceptional, because in this scene Randy's shame becomes self-reflective, and he becomes positionally conscious of his shame, as Sartre would have it. For Randy to be recognized by this customer is a revelation of the existence of his body as an object for the other – aging, weakened and humiliated. But shame is imposed on the spectators as well. They are treated as 'involuntary voyeurs' wanting to look away, but feeling compelled to watch anyway. This produces an affective-aesthetic experience from a self-reflective viewing position, potentially with ethical dimensions.

As clichéd a concept as it is in cinema studies, voyeurism played a central role in psychoanalytic film theory during the seventies, most notably in the work of Christian Metz (1982) and Laura Mulvey (1975). Both argue that cinema is inherently voyeuristic. Darkness in the film theatre, the apparent privacy of the spectator's situation, and even the shape of the cinema screen – these taken together create a 'keyhole effect'. This is complemented by the film characters acting as if they were unaware of any spectators, while allowing themselves to be watched. Voyeurism is one of the means by which the (classical) cinema disguises its discursive nature. The basic condition for voyeuristic looking is a *distance* between the spectator and the object. According to Metz, 'the perceiving drive concretely *represents the absence of its object* in the distance at which it maintains it and which is part of its very definition: distance of the look, distance of listening' (Metz 1982: 46, my italics). From a cognitive perspective, Richard Allen argues that cinema that privileges a distanced, disembodied and acentral (as opposed to central) point of view of filmic events often gives rise to voyeurism (Allen 1995: 130–31). In contrast, for Sartre, a voyeuristic look creates intimacy between the seer and the seen: the voyeur forgets himself and 'fuses' with the object of his look:

> No transcending view comes to confer upon my acts the character of a given on which a judgment can be brought to bear. My consciousness sticks to my acts, it is my acts; and my acts are commanded only by the ends to be attained and by the instruments to be employed. My attitude, for example, has no 'outside'; it is a pure process of relating the instrument (the keyhole) to the end to be attained (the spectacle to be seen), a pure mode of losing myself in the world. (Sartre 1992: 348)

For Sartre, voyeurism is to look with fascination, a mode of losing oneself to the world in the act of looking. The object of the look exists as a spectacle for the voyeur's 'pre-reflective consciousness', or his consciousness *is* the spectacle. Thus, for Sartre, proximity is essential to voyeurism, in contrast to Metz and Allen, for whom distance is key.

Heterosexual pornography is frequently considered the voyeuristic genre par excellence, defined by 'maximum visibility', as Linda Williams puts it. Porn aesthetics aim at realizing a top spectacle for the keen voyeur, preferably using cinematic techniques that provide the most favourable view of the performers' bodies. These also include clear and close shots of genital action and actual penetration, culminating in a 'cum shot', a close-up of male ejaculation on, for instance, the woman's face, breasts, or belly.[8] Porn prefers 'close-ups of body parts over other shots, to overlight easily obscured genitals, to select sexual positions that show the most of bodies and organs . . . such as the variety of sexual 'numbers' or the externally ejaculating penis' (Williams 1989: 49). For this reason, Williams (1991) proposes the category of 'body genre' to refer to pornography, but also to horror films and melodrama, the aesthetics of which focus around images of bodily proximity and excess. However, such images may also lead to feelings of discomfort and shame, followed by rejection, a desire to turn one's gaze from the spectacle. Many pornographic conventions can be experienced as disgusting rather than sexually exhilarating. There are certain mental aspects, such as our desire to watch, that 'we just don't want to know about ourselves, and about our formations as selves', writes Laura Kipnis. 'These seem to be precisely what pornography keeps shoving right back at us' (Kipnis 1999: 171).

It is this pornographic proximity that to some extent characterizes *The Wrestler*. In this context, Walsh describes the setting of *The Wrestler* as three 'meat markets' meaning the wrestling ring, the strip club and the deli counter (Walsh 2010: 156). She associates Rourke's appearance with that of 'a pornographic, existential boxer' (131), and defines his performance as based on pleasurable submission, the intention of giving oneself up totally. Also, from the perspective of film aesthetics, *The Wrestler* shows similarities to the pornographic genre, especially in the wrestling scenes. The camera stays close to the action, much closer than the diegetic audience normally gets (figure 4.2). In this regard, Lucy Nevitt distinguishes between diegetic pain and actual pain in professional wrestling. To her, the paradox in wrestling seems to be that pain is the authentic core of the sport, but the actual bodily stress involved in the manoeuvres must be dissembled for the sake of illusion. As will be shown in the next chapter, on *Black Swan*, there is a similar contrast in ballet. Referring to Scarry, Nevitt explains that 'diegetic pain must be performed outwards [while] actual pain is an experience that tends to draw the sufferer inwards . . . and so it cannot be read clearly by a large live audience' (Nevitt 2010: 84).

**Figure 4.2.** Painful proximity. Screen capture, *The Wrestler* (2008).

This inability to read pain accurately is undoubtedly valid for the diegetic audience in *The Wrestler*, but quite the opposite is true for the non-diegetic audience. It is the film itself that visibly 'performs' Randy's inner pain and renders his diegetic pain an inward experience. The fight scenes consist of several extreme long shots showing manoeuvres in their entirety, especially the aerial techniques and throws. But they also draw the spectator's attention to the difference between a diegetic and a non-diegetic viewing position. Regularly the camera moves to a close-up of Randy's face twisted in pain, perhaps a painful equivalent of an orgasmic grimace. And there is the counterpart of a cum shot with blood as proof of authenticity that exceeds the fictive framework by its affective quality – hence my porn analogy. Even if hard-core porn can be considered a spectacle that is less 'staged' than a feature film,[9] the close-ups of pain in *The Wrestler* create a pornographic sense of 'fleshy intimacy' with unpleasant consequences. The wrestling scenes in the film are painful and discomfiting to watch, especially Randy's fight with Necro Butcher, which is mercilessly graphic in its rawness. All wounds and injuries are filmed up close and personal. Every act of violence, such as Randy's rubbing pieces of broken glass deeper into his opponent's skin, is experienced by the spectators as a physical sensation on their own skins. The close-ups of medical instruments removing staples and pieces of glass from the wrestlers' bodies and of the stitching up of their open wounds after the fight are possibly even more painful to watch than the previous shots of these injurious items penetrating their skin. But the spectator's attention is also drawn to signs of weakness by means of such things as auditory close-ups of agonizing groans, gasps and heavy breathing, inaudible to the diegetic audience.

The question that arises from this affective experience is why one keeps watching these scenes even though they are thoroughly disagreeable. The answer is not that watching equals a form of masochistic spectatorship, which Michelle Aaron defines as the 'perverse' pleasure of indulging in pain and discomfort (Aaron 2007: 51–86). In this context, Steven Shaviro has argued that cinema is a masochistic technology *par excellence*, alluring its spectators to lose control through, 'abjection, fragmentation and subversion of self-identity' that evokes visceral excitation and intensifies experiences of passivity (Shaviro 1993: 56; 64). But the displeasure experienced when watching *The Wrestler* is not about seeking passive submission; rather, it is about the way in which the film makes demands on our spectatorial responsibility, overriding our own demands for cinematic pleasure, whether masochistic or not. As a result, one feels compelled to watch even when one would rather turn away from the affectively negative fight scenes, just like the character Cassidy does.

One possible answer as to why do we keep watching could be that the spectator stays with the film in anticipation of a 'reward', such as appreciation of the film's virtuosity, or esteem for its deeply moving aesthetic force. A similar argument has already been formulated by David Hume, who stated that negative emotions from an aesthetic experience could be overcome, when pleasure and delight in its artistic expression overwhelm and absorb them, rather than simply cancel them out (Hume 2007: 237–47). Yet another explanation for the spectators opting to stay with the film is that they hope that things will eventually turn out well for the tormented protagonist; *The Wrestler*, however, never gives the spectator any (false) promise of a happy ending. Finally, one might argue that one keeps watching because the film will eventually offer one a 'purifying' release of emotional tension in the form of catharsis. In that case, when a scene of suffering comes to an end, relief from pain could discharge the discomfort that the film imposes upon us. Yet, as argued above, *The Wrestler* seems deliberately anti-cathartic, essentially lacking any transformative power that would cancel out the spectator's negative emotions. Instead, these emotions endure, prompting the spectator to feel the effects of masochistic bad faith even after the film has finished. Thus, Randy's masochism is present in *The Wrestler* as a deliberate inability to change his situation, which is felt by the spectator in the flesh, as caused by the affective exchange between the film's corporeal aesthetics and the lived-body of the spectator. This invites the spectators to adopt a (self-)reflective attitude, through which they can contemplate the conditions that are operative in this particular viewing experience.

Therefore I do not think that *The Wrestler* illuminates what Arthur Danto calls 'an uncomfortable truth in the psychology of moral perception', which is that people derive pleasure from, for instance, watching 'pornography of torn and bloodied bodies' (Danto 2005: 258). Danto seems to argue that pleasure is something inherent in the act of watching, even if the object disgusts or disturbs the spectator. In contrast, in my assessment of the film *The Wrestler*, masochism is not readily convertible into pleasurable aesthetic satisfaction. This in turn compels us to re-think the whole pleasure-displeasure binary in the context of cinematic experience. For instance, in pornography sexual excitement, disgust and shame are often inextricably intertwined, underlined and made into theme and spectacle (Kipnis 1992; Williams 2001; Kalha 2005; Paasonen 2011). With certain differences, the same could be claimed about the experience of horror. Therefore it seems that affective intensity as such is a central issue in extreme cinematic events, beyond any distinction between pleasure and displeasure, delight and disgust. It is the affective intensity of parts of *The Wrestler* as 'extreme cinema' that draws the spectators closer to the screen and simultaneously repels them.[10]

Thus the fighting scenes in *The Wrestler* can be considered events of 'pornography of pain' without gratification, which one nevertheless may value as vivid and immediate affective experiences, regardless of their non-pleasurable, non-rewarding qualities. However, this porn analogy that I am using could be considered problematic from the perspective of porn studies insofar as it may weaken the conceptual definition of pornography itself. Similarly, Rosalind Coward (1984) writes of spectacular visual presentations of cooking as 'food porn'. Furthermore, meaty and visceral close-ups are typical of horror and martial arts films, as well as sports events and reality television shows, without necessarily being 'pornographic'. Nevertheless, I consider *The Wrestler* 'pornographic', insofar as its filmic affect works simultaneously through proximity and distance. There is the proximity of the body/act in the image and sound, and the potential distance in the power of the spectator to turn away from the spectacle. *The Wrestler* also possesses the affective quality of porn, which is the combination of attraction to 'bodies in action' and revulsion at the possibility of getting too close.

Furthermore, the film's masochism also addresses our responsibility as spectators, making an ethical demand that forces us to recognize that the lived-body is more than disposable, commodified flesh.[11] It directs our attention to the fact that Randy's pain is 'constructed' for the audience, regardless of their inability to acknowledge this, because Randy does not communicate his pain. His pain is not a posture towards the world, but an inward gesture, transcending its affective expression. In other words, Randy's pain exceeds in meaning any conventional representation of pain. It becomes an 'excess' in the film's affective operation that one cannot know, but only feel. Sharon Sliwinski writes that, confronted by such painful images, we are required to recognize both the suffering of another person and the impossibility of that recognition. This in turn poses the question of how and why one is engaged in the visual spectacle as a spectator in the first place (Sliwinski 2004: 155–58).

The uncomfortable, voyeuristic proximity to Randy's mental and physical pain confronts the spectators with their own spectatorial desires in a self-reflective manner. For cinematic displeasure calls attention to itself, prompting spectators to shift their attention to their own state of emotion so that they become positionally conscious of their displeasure. This is a crucially different state from the genuine experience of pain that, according to Scarry, 'has no referential content. It is not *of* or *for* anything' (Scarry 1985: 5). Pain takes over so completely that one's consciousness is thoroughly 'contaminated' by it, with no room for (self-)reflection. In *The Wrestler* there is proximity, felt as 'pre-reflective' displeasure by the spectator and brought about by the aesthetic system of the film itself. There are scenes in *The Wrestler* during which the spectator's consciousness *is* (the spectacle of) pain. But there is also a clear affective and experiential discrepancy between Randy and the spectator. It may be a fallacy to argue that the spectator's experience is simultaneously pre-reflective ('my pain') and reflective ('not my pain'), but not if this state involves a constant shift of focus or a dual perspective.

Both our pre-reflective and reflective responses to the film are necessary to acknowledge the discrepancy between our pain and Randy's. This acknowledgement involves awareness of our own spectatorial responsibility for his pain, but also denies empathetic identification with Randy and his pain. Similarly, Nevitt writes that wrestlers complicate empathy, because they feel pain and respond to their pain according to a strange set of conventions. Wrestlers embody corporeal vulnerability shared by the audience, but this also emphasizes the way in which they simultaneously transcend their state of being in the world as lived-bodies (Nevitt 2010: 86). In *The Wrestler*, such juxtapositions between vulnerability and toughness, proximity and distance, lived-body and thing-body, agential corporeality and objectified flesh, internal gesture and external posture, do not take place on the pre-reflective level only, but they also function at the level of self-reflection. This creates an ethical space that forces the spectators to acknowledge their own role, not only as witnesses, but also as accomplices in Randy's (self-)objectification, or 'instrumentalizing self-interpretation' as Peter Lucas calls this phenomenon. It is a process that encourages individuals to interpret themselves as objects of use (Lucas 2011: 2–5). As Lucas points out, the process of objectification does not refer merely to how one treats or represents others – as objects-to-be-looked-at, for instance – but also to one's positive or negative perception of them. I propose that *The Wrestler* invites the spectator to perceive Randy both as a nonagential object and as an agential subject, because his agency is restricted to acts of instrumentalizing self-interpretation solely in the eyes of the wrestling audience, and both Randy and the non-diegetic spectator know this to be so. Michelle Aaron argues that ethical cinema always raises questions about 'looking on', and thus must be understood in terms of consent and participation (Aaron 2007: 89). I consider *The Wrestler* ethical, insofar as it pushes the limits of visual pleasure and spectatorial responsibility, asking questions about acceptable ways of looking and responding, which always lie at the core of (reenacted) scenes of suffering, as Libby Saxton (2010) points out.

According to Lorraine Code, to display an ethical attitude towards others is to acknowledge their actions as manifestations of their choices as 'active, sentient, thinking beings' (Code 1995: 84). But it is difficult to acknowledge Randy's actions as such, since they are based on 'choiceless choices'. Randy's actions are choiceless choices insofar as they express desire to be reduced to the status of an object, while he still possesses sufficient capacity for responsible self-determination. Lucas distinguishes different stages of objectification. First there is instrumentalization, a stage at which a person is reduced to being a utensil, followed by acceptation, when the person identifies with the negative and/or stereotypical image that is made available to him or her (Lucas 2011: 62–82). As already shown, the images that are available for Randy to identify with are highly limited. This restricts his capacity for undistorted self-interpretation to stereotypes of virile, testosterone-laden masculinity in the world of professional wrestling. This leads to the conclusion that objectification may involve a person's instrumentalization of himself, which carries important consequences for this person's sense of identity. In *The Wrestler*, objectification functions by means of a triangular structure in which Randy, the film itself (through its pornographic proximity, for instance) and the spectator all participate as accomplices. We are encouraged to perceive Randy as an instrumentalized object, however much we may wish not to, because as spectators, we are on the wrong side of the wrestling ring.[12] Although there is a clear difference between the diegetic and the non-diegetic audience, *The Wrestler* does not allow the latter to forget that they are the spectators and thus, by definition the instrumentalizers, whose desire to watch Randy finally contributes to his own masochistic demise. This is an insight that *The Wrestler's* cinematic masochism expresses affectively and viscerally. It is an embodied experience of 'thinking-feelingly' of the film that evokes the possibility of ethical scrutiny, however unpleasant its conclusions might be.

## Notes

Many thanks to Susanna Paasonen for her helpful comments on the earlier version of this chapter.

1. The reference occurs early in the film, during Randy's first visit to a strip club where Cassidy cites the film to him: "'He was pierced for our transgressions, He was crushed for our iniquities. The punishment that brought us peace was upon Him, and by His wounds we were healed.' . . . It's from *Passion of the Christ*. You never seen it? Dude, you gotta. It's amazing. It's, like, so inspiring. They throw everything at him. Whips, arrows, rocks . . . just beat the living fuck out of him for the whole two hours. And he just takes it – the sacrificial Ram'.

2. The soundtrack includes numbers from bands such as Cinderella, Ratt, Accept, Scorpions, Guns 'N' Roses, and Quiet Riot, whose '(Bang Your Head) Metal Health' (1983) is Randy's theme song, which accompanies him every time he enters or leaves the wrestling ring. However, for his last fight with The Ayatollah, the

introductory song is 'Sweet Child of Mine' (1987) by Guns 'N' Roses, which was Mickey Rourke's own entrance song when he was a professional boxer.

3.    In the context of kitsch, the resulting feelings can be completely opposite, of course. For instance, Charles Baudelaire wrote about the aristocratic pleasure of being displeased by objects of bad taste: 'Ce qu'il y a d'enivrant dans le mauvais goût, c'est le plaisir aristocratique de déplaire' (Baudelaire 2004: 396).

4.    In addition, Rourke's presence functions as a distancing element, as in 'Oh my God, it's Mickey Rourke'. This complicates character engagement and reflexively poses questions about desire associated with stardom and spectatorship.

5.    Even if this classification of the physical body as the seat of a 'lower' level of sensation emphasizes a hierarchy between body and mind, which does not exist in the phenomenological understanding of lived body as an intentional and transactional whole of body-mind.

6.    This is actually a common strategy in professional wrestling called 'blading': 'Blading means using a piece of a razor to open a cut and get the blood flowing. The usual place to cut [is] the forehead because the blood flows freely over the face, creating the "crimson mask" effect' (Albano and Sugar with Benson 2000: 44).

7.    Although Sartre (2012) also noticed individuals like Jean Genet, who embraced masochism and became social rebels by turning themselves into objects for society to 'spit on'. Furthermore, from an Artaudian point of view, Randy's suicide might be seen not as an act of self-destruction, but a violent re-conquest of the self, a way to give circumstances the shape of one's own free will (Artaud 2001: 56–58).

8.    According to Williams, this is the generic problem-solving function of heterosexual pornography: to disentangle the enigma of sexual difference by means of rendering the female orgasm 'visible' through this fetishizing convention (Williams 1989: 95).

9.    The reason for this is that hard-core porn promises the spectator access to a 'real' event (sex act) and its documentation/performance, while a feature film offers access to a fictive narrative and its representation. On the other hand, one might argue that all porn is staged too, because the sex can be seen as an act in the theatrical sense performed for the camera/spectator. Or, as Linda Williams puts it, 'sex . . . is the supreme fiction of hard-core pornography' (Williams 1989: 267).

10.   Extreme cinema is a category that is usually associated with Asian filmmakers such as Shinya Tsukamoto (*Tetsuo: The Iron Man*, 1989), Takashi Miike (*Audition*, 1999), Kim Ki-duk (*The Isle*, 2000) and Park Chan-wook (*Oldboy*, 2003). But I think that the fight scenes in *The Wrestler* in particular also bear similarities to this genre.

11.   Roger Poole even establishes the body as the locus of all ethical experience: 'Nothing happens to me which does not happen to my body. Insult the body and you insult the freedom within in. Attack the body, you attack the person. Torture the body, you mutilate the individual. Kill the body and you kill the spirit which

inhabits it. . . . The body is the locus of all ethical experience, and all experience is, because spatial, ethical. There can be no act which does not take place in ethical space. There can be no 'flaccid' act, no act devoid of significance, no unconditioned act' (Poole 1972: 27).

12.   This is possibly corroborated by our knowledge of the relationship between Aronofsky and Rourke. In an interview, Rourke reminisces with certain submissive pleasure: 'Darren is in your face. . . . He is the captain. He sat there the first day we met, and he pointed his little pink finger at me and he said, "You're going to do everything I say, you're going to do everything I tell you, and you're never going to disrespect me in front of the crew . . . and I can't pay you."' M. Dance, 2009, 'Mickey Rourke', *The Cinema Source*, 20 January. Retrieved 28 May 2012 from http://www.thecinemasource.com/blog/interviews/mickey-rourke-interview-for-the-wrestler/.

# CHAPTER FIVE

# The Uncanny Sublime
## Black Swan

*It is in the spirit of the theatre to express horror by the wild gestures of the body. It would be in the spirit of the photoplay to make the world around the terrified person change in a horrifying, ghastly way. The camera can do that, and the spectator would come deeply under the spell of the emotion to be expressed. It becomes his emotion, just as in the close-up it is his attention which is forced on the single detail.*

*–Hugo Münsterberg*[1]

The above quotation from Hugo Münsterberg accurately describes the emotional impact of Aronofsky's fifth feature-length film, *Black Swan*. Its story revolves around a young ballerina, Nina Sayers, who dances as a soloist in a prestigious New York City ballet company. Nina is simultaneously portrayed as innocent and devoted, vulnerable and controlled. This ambiguity in her personality is reflected by the challenge she is faced with, namely to perform the emotionally and physically demanding double role of Odette and Odile in the legendary Tchaikovsky ballet *Swan Lake*. In order to rise to the occasion, Nina must plunge deep into her uncontrolled dark side. But she is prone to mental illness, and her artistic progress is increasingly hampered by violent hallucinations and severe panic attacks.[2] It does not help that Nina still lives with an overprotective mother (Barbara Hershey) who gave up her own ballet career of some sorts for motherhood. The mother now projects all her frustrated ambition, jealousy and disappointment onto Nina. The story starts in medias res, with Thomas (Vincent Cassel),[3] the ballet company's artistic director, looking for a 'fresh face' to play Odette the White Swan and her evil twin Odile the Black Swan. Against all odds, Nina gets the role. Lily (Mila Kunis), a free-spirited dancer and new addition to the company, helps Nina to lose a measure of self-control in order to find her darker, more sensual self, as is necessary to dance the Odile part successfully. At the same time, it is obvious that Lily, as Nina's 'evil twin' in real life, wants to steal Nina's role. In a scene that takes place during the premiere, Nina finds Lily in her dressing room, all dressed up in the Black Swan costume, ready to take over her part in the next act. During the struggle that ensues, Nina stabs Lily to death with a shard of a broken mirror, and dances the Black Swan act with great triumph. Afterwards, Nina realizes that this fight was a complete figment of her own twisted imagination – but the shard of mirror is deeply lodged in her own abdomen. Ignoring her fatal injury, she nevertheless takes the stage in the last act as the White Swan, her life gradually fading away.

Both *The Wrestler* and *Black Swan* end with the protagonist presumably jumping to his/her death, and this lends the ending of both films a typical anti-cathartic quality. Like in *The Wrestler*, in *Black Swan* this anti-cathartic effect engages the spectator in affective reflection on the conflict between the vulnerability of the lived-body and the instrumentalized body-as-an-object. *Black Swan* can be interpreted as a study of female breakdown. More generally, it is a study of psychic disintegration, steadily elevated towards the sublime. This is experienced as co-existing pain and pleasure, as simultaneously awesome and awful. In her discussion of the 'disdained' concept of the sublime, Cynthia Freeland shows its relevance for the appreciation of film as a work of art, as well as for awareness of a film's aesthetic qualities, which include its moral vision. According to Freeland, with the cinematic sublime, 'we shift from the perspective *within* the film to a perspective *about* the film. This shift accompanies the shift from a predominantly emotional or imaginative experience on the sensory level to a more intellectual . . . experience including pleasurable reflection on the film's moral point of view' (Freeland 1999: 73). For Freeland, the sublime is a mediating term that connects the affective-aesthetic to the ethical-philosophical within the cinematic event. She argues that the sublime may play a vital role in accounting for certain crucial aspects of cinematic experience. On the one hand, the sublime may facilitate a more profound understanding of the appreciation of films as works of art, as well as of the role of emotions in this process. On the other hand, the sublime may help to understand how cinema provides opportunities for ethical enquiry and energizes philosophical thinking. For Kant, the sublime not only prompts Burkean 'rapturous terror' but also 'sublime reflection' as a means to make sense of one's (moral) pursuits, and to give meaning to experience beyond a 'common ground' (Pillow 2000). This chapter explores the affective-aesthetic system of *Black Swan* and how the film connects to the sublime, prompting philosophical reflection outside our 'regular' conceptual and experiential grasp, as it reaches inside the realm of animality, inside the realm of the uncanny.

As Scott Bukatman argues, the sublime and the uncanny are closely related: 'both stage a confrontation with the limits of human power and agency, and both are heavily freighted with the weight of the unknown. The sublime figures the unknown as excess; the uncanny re-presents the familiar in terms of estrangement' (Bukatman 2011: 129). In Julian Young's argument, experience of the sublime requires one's personality to be divided into an embodied self, threatened by the possibility of death (pain), and a disembodied, 'eternal' self, free from any such threat and therefore capable of feeling pleasure. Referring to Schopenhauer, Young argues that transcendence of embodied individuality lies at the core of experience of the sublime. In this experience, one is faced with one's inevitable advance into 'nothingness', while one imagines oneself to be above the body as an 'eternal subject', with nothingness merely a 'representation' (Young 2006: 137). In *Black Swan*, this eternal, disembodied subject appears literally as an uncanny other, which becomes a threat to the embodied self. Nina's personality is divided into an embodied self (White Swan) that gets swallowed by a disembodied, eternal self (Black Swan). The film is both an exploration of the sublime, and a sublime experience in itself, as the spectators also 'divide' themselves as they watch the film. It invites the spectators to think-feelingly about the conflict between the body as an instrumental vehicle for artistic expression, and artistic expression as a lived, embodied practice.

Furthermore, *Black Swan* combines excessive, sublime elements with alienating, uncanny ones, in confronting the spectator with bestial forces from beyond human reality. This is why the sublime and the uncanny are inseparable in the film. At the same time, these forces of the uncanny emerge from within the self, comparable to Freud's Doppelgänger. Significantly, in an interview, Aronofsky mentioned Fyodor Dostoevsky's short story 'The Double' as a source of inspiration for the film.[4] For Freud, the Doppelgänger is the archetypal figure of the uncanny, embodying the return of the repressed matter of the self; this thus seems another obvious approach to analysing the film. Yet as Freeland points out, both sublime and uncanny elements in cinema are often better explained by examining how the film's 'aesthetic surface' prompts corresponding experiences in the spectator. This is a method she prefers to searching for psychoanalytical themes, for instance (Freeland 2001: 34).

In this chapter, I attempt to move from a precise interpretation of the aesthetic organization of a film to larger thematic issues that deal with the uncanny and the sublime. I shall argue that these issues open up important avenues for a corporeal way of thinking about the film. From this one might gain insight into important notions, such as the interconnectedness of bodily transformation and the dissolution of self in a state of insanity. Such interconnectedness consists of a conflict between the materiality of the body and the immateriality of the soul. And it is such a conflict that is expressed in the dancer's bodily performance, independent of his or her psyche and emotions. It would be easy, banal even, to interpret the peculiarities of Nina's psychic pathology in terms of repressed sexuality in relationship with artistic performance. I approach *Black Swan* from a different perspective. I suggest that what is expressed in the film's cinematic aesthetics is a psychic-corporeal experience of self-destructive psychosis. The spectator is directly induced into this aesthetic reality, which is experienced as the uncanny sublime. This experience is clearly different from the classical Kantian account. There, the sublime pushes the limits of imagination, while at the same time it enables one to 'think' what one fails to imagine as an Idea of Reason, such as the overwhelming power of nature, or the infinity of the cosmos. In Kantian thinking, the sublime is defined as 'an object . . . the representation of which determines the mind to regard the elevation of nature beyond our reach as equivalent to a presentation of ideas' (Kant 1968: 119). The experience that I explore in this chapter is best described as that of the 'carnal sublime'. This provokes 'embodied reflection' of one's own materiality, directing one's sensual awareness to 'both the richness and fragility of material existence' (Sobchack 2011: 204). In *Black Swan* there is a blatant conflict between the richness and the fragility of material existence, which manifests itself in various ways. There is the tension between aestheticized and embodied pain, between the self and its uncanny double, as well as between pain and pleasure, all embodied in the film's audiovisual style. By virtue of its affective-aesthetic specificity, *Black Swan* communicates important insights about the relationship between body and soul. In doing so, it enables the experience of an uncannily sublime form

of filmmaking, and thus it anticipates the possibility of reflection on the distinction between 'having a body' and 'being a body'.

## Aestheticized/Embodied Pain

With music by Clint Mansell on the sound track, which re-imagines Tchaikovsky's original score,[5] *Black Swan* starts with opening credits rolling across a
black screen. As soon as the title of the film appears, we briefly hear an echoed
mechanical rattle mixed with distorted laughter. This is the first uncanny moment in the film, as a voice from outside the frame always has an inherently
uncanny effect, as Mary Ann Doane has argued (Doane 1980: 40–41). Then
the black screen gradually brightens through a fade-in into the opening scene,
which is the prologue of the Bolshoi version of *Swan Lake*. Or at least this is
what the spectator may initially understand, until other uncanny effects, such
as Rothbart's becoming an animal, destabilize this assumption and introduce
the inseparability of virtual and actual as a central topic of the film. In this
prologue, we notice Nina in the spotlight, dancing the role of Princess Odette,
while the rest of the image remains dark. There is an ethereal quality to this
scene, mostly due to its cold blue lighting, which emphasizes the weightless,
flowing movements of the dancer, who is wearing a full, multi-layered romantic tutu. But there is also a sense of eeriness, a lurking dread seeping into the
image from the dark edges of the frame. And from there, Rothbart materi-
alizes, giving flesh to this darkness surrounding Odette. He transforms into
a monstrous bird, while the scene turns into a frenzied whirlwind, until the
enchanted Odette falters and the scene fades out.

   This same sense of lurking dread noticeable in the opening scene remains
present throughout the film as a negative, sensuous undercurrent below the
surface of events. Opposite beauty is the beast. In the film, the 'beast' first
manifests itself in negative emotions such as obsession, jealousy, blind ambition, insecurity and repressed sexuality. But later, these emotions are lodged
in the physical shape of Nina's uncanny double, who at first only exists as a
reflection in the mirror, then as a hallucination outside the mirror, until finally
she literally bursts through Nina's skin. In addition, the lurking presence of the
evil double is often suggested by direct cinematic elements, such as by the

haunting, paranoid presence of the tightly framed camera, which regularly follows Nina from touching distance, in a similar manner as in *The Wrestler*, and the acousmetric bursts of laughter that emerge out of nowhere. These negative, sensuous qualities of the film directly titillate the spectator's skin, since *Black Swan* is a film that can make your hair stand on end. It is a well-known physiological fact that intense emotions, such as fear or awe, can give us goose bumps. *Black Swan* can actually evoke this so-called piloerective reaction because the film is both frightening and awe-inspiring. It imposes upon the spectator a horrendous delight of the sublime, combined with an uncanny tension between outwards appearance and inner reality.

In my carnal understanding of the sublime as an aesthetic experience, it is a bodily event that provokes overwhelming emotional reactions, combining awe and horror, beauty and pain. The combination of beauty and pain is particularly strong, as beauty will be characterized by 'profound inexhaustibility', while pain is defined by its 'excruciating particularity', as Valentine Daniel puts it. He explains that beauty extends itself and opens out to the world, inviting others to partake of its essence, while pain closes in on itself, finding affirmation in its unsharability (Daniel 1994: 233). Pain is an essential element in the aesthetic experience of the sublime, but in *Black Swan* it also functions in other ways. The sensation appears as aestheticized pain in the film, but also as embodied pain that reminds the spectator of the materiality of the body. Pain prompts one to consider one's body not merely as an object one possesses, but essentially as a 'subject that feels its own objectivity' as Vivian Sobchack argues (Sobchack 2004: 178). Tension between aestheticized pain and embodied pain is present throughout *Black Swan*, and it is the same tension that assumingly lies at the core of ballet's aesthetic ideal in general. This aesthetic ideal would be to deny the 'fragility' of the flesh. This is why many (classical) ballet techniques seemingly ignore the principles of human design, dictating the use of pointe shoes and enforcing the unnatural, nearly 180-degree straight alignment of legs and feet from the hips in the basic positions.[6] Whereas a regular ballet audience only witnesses the perfection of the final product on stage, Aronofsky's film depicts the dancers' pain from the coulisses and backstage, in such a way that it is viscerally felt by the spectator.

When Nina wakes up at the beginning of the film, we see a close-up of her feet loosening up with emphatic cracks on the sound track. Then we witness her at breakfast, which consists of half a pink grapefruit with a poached egg and nothing more.[7] It is a fragile balancing act for a ballet dancer to restrict the intake of calories and still stay sufficiently energetic during physically demanding dance training and performance. Eating disorders are a well-known risk in the world of professional ballet; Nina is also regularly shown throwing up in reaction to stressful situations. Nina's bulimia can be seen as part of the greater harm that she inflicts on herself. Self-inflicted harm is also reflected in the montage sequence that precedes the first ballet-training scene. The sequence consists of a series of (extreme) close-ups showing Nina breaking in her new pointe shoes by smashing them, bending their soles and striking them with scissors as dancers are wont to do, hoping to lessen the ensuing pain by forcing the shoes to conform to the shape of their feet. Next, Nina sews on ribbons and elastics, before taping her toes and putting on the shoes. But the sequence also has symbolic significance, with the shoes standing for the beauty and the basic physical nature of this particular art form. Significantly, these beautiful objects have to be smashed in order to achieve the aesthetic ideal of ballet. Pointe shoes as a double metaphor actually embody the paradox of ballet, in which the 'raw material' of the dancer's tangible body has to be denied for the sake of lightness, ethereality and disembodiment. In the words of Jean Epstein (2012), the pointe shoes in *Black Swan* function as objects of 'obscene sensuality', heavily invested with ambiguous emotional vigour.

In addition, the violent breaking in of the shoes is emblematic of the ruthless way in which Nina treats her own body. One instance of this occurs after Thomas has questioned whether Nina will dance well enough to convey the predatory duplicity of Odile the Black Swan. Next Nina is shown perfecting her fouetté turns in front of the mirror until she injures herself. The scene is filmed in slow motion to emphasize Nina's mental determination and concentration, which go beyond the physical limitations of her body. The framing of the image alternates between a medium close-up of Nina's resolute face and a close-up of her piroutting foot, accompanied by the amplified sound of pointe shoes clicking on a wooden floor. But Nina fails to finish the fouetté series, and she falls to the floor groaning with pain, which is followed by a close-up of her bleeding toes. This close-up is a painful reminder of the limitations of the flesh-and-blood body faced with ballet's disembodied demands. As Merleau-Ponty (1968) reminds us, the 'weakness' of the body (which he calls the 'flesh') is a necessary element in the bodily subject's ability to have an embodied, sensible as well as sensing perspective on the world. By denying the fragility of the flesh, Nina loses this ability.[8] As a result, she loses her embodied connection with the world, which ultimately causes her insanity.

At some point, Nina develops a mysterious rash on her shoulder blade as a result of self-mutilating scratching. In psychiatry, self-mutilation is considered a coping mechanism for overwhelmingly negative and intolerable affects that lead to feelings of depersonalization (Himber 1994). Thus negatively overwhelmed by her pent-up emotions, Nina scratches herself to maintain a sense of identity. According to Karen Suyemoto and Marian Macdonald, self-mutilation reaffirms the sense of identity, because skin is the most fundamental boundary of self (Suyemoto and Macdonald 1995). Reaffirmation of self is indeed the reason why Nina regularly studies her reflection in the mirror. It is as if here she attempts to find the ideal self that she has fashioned, but that keeps disappearing. Perhaps it could even be said that Nina's ultimate 'dissolution' results from her attempts to deny the flesh. The harder she tries to achieve this disembodied ideal, the more she feels the need to reaffirm the body as a true source of her self through self-mutilation.[9] But this strategy skids out of control and her body takes over, starting to injure itself beyond Nina's conscious control. She starts to experience importunate hallucinations that feel uncannily real – in which her skin is torn off for instance. These scenes are often framed in close-up, and for the spectator it is as if the film itself has become an open wound. Such scenes coarsen our aesthetic experience of the film, while deepening our understanding of its affective significance, which is rooted in the vulnerability of the lived-body.

A particularly mortifying example of this idea of film as an open wound occurs in the scene in which Nina visits the company's former principal dancer, Beth (Winona Ryder), in hospital after her horrendous car accident, which may well have been a botched suicide attempt. On the one hand, Nina is terrified by Beth's physical damage, but on the other she seems inexplicably fascinated by it. As a result, she cannot help but lift the hospital duvet to expose Beth's grotesquely mutilated leg (figure 5.1). In this scene, Nina's combined terror and fascination reflect her own physical and emotional pain. Furthermore, like Lily, Beth is another Doppelgänger for Nina, the perfect ideal for which she strives and from whom she steals. Eventually Nina replaces Beth and becomes the ballet company's face on posters where Beth's picture used to be. Beth also represents the grim reality of perfection and what has to be sacrificed in order to achieve it. This culminates in another deeply disturbing scene towards the end of the film, in which Nina visits Beth in the hospital for the second time in order to return things she has previously stolen from her. In this scene, Beth repeatedly stabs herself in the face with a nail file, morphing into Nina as she does so. Not only does this particular scene epitomize the severity of Nina's self-harming practices, but it also has the effect of 'stabbing' the spectators, who suddenly become very much aware of the affect of Nina's inner and outer confusion. This renders the film affectively charged and aesthetically disturbing at the same time, ever maintaining tension between the feeling body in pain and the psychological character in turmoil. This draws our attention to the relationship between human subjectivity and embodiment, between horror and eroticism.

Eventually Nina's self-mutilating scratching appears to be merely the beginning of a more fundamentally destructive bodily conversion. This transformation is experienced by Nina herself as gradual physical changes caused by her obsession with achieving perfection. Thus, on the evening before her premiere, spiked, painful black feathers sprout out of her raw shoulder blade, the white in both her eyes turns blood red, and she develops webbed feet as well as bird-like legs. The most drastic bodily transformation takes place during the climax of the Black Swan act, when Nina's arms turn into full-fledged, amazing wings. This event brings the process of her 'becoming-animal' to closure, yet

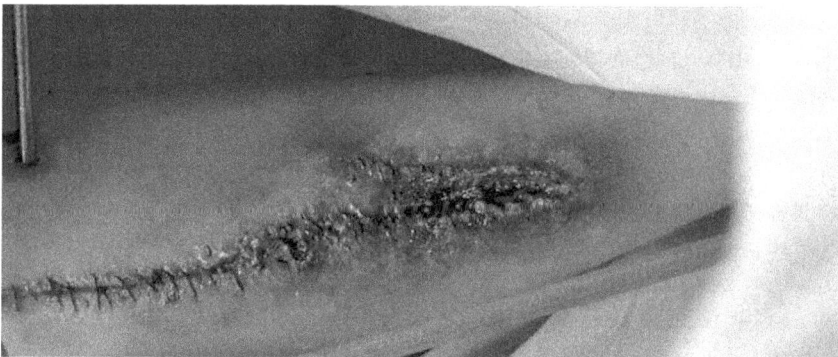

**Figure 5.1.** Film as an open wound. Screen capture, *Black Swan* (2010).

I do not mean this in the Deleuzian sense. In their book *A Thousand Plateaus*, Gilles Deleuze and Felix Guattari discuss the notion of becoming-animal as a form of 'becoming-minoritarian'. It is therefore an important element in what they term 'micropolitics' – politics of desire that are distant from the 'politics of identity' (Deleuze and Guattari 1987: 275–80). True, Nina fulfils her potential by 'becoming-swan'. Yet her transformation is not an example of rhizomatic, productive potentiality, since it finds affirmation in its restricted singularity, instead of in ever-shifting and mutually shaping compositions with others. Or perhaps it could be said that Nina's process of 'becoming-animal' is unsuccessful insofar as it vanishes into a 'black hole' of insanity.

As in *The Wrestler*, the close-up is a salient element in the creation of painful corporeal aesthetics in *Black Swan*. These close-ups have an unsettling emotional effect, because they fill the spectator's field of vision with images of torn skin, resulting in painful engagement with Nina's mutating body. The close-ups in *Black Swan* do not merely show but magnify the marks of decomposition, overwhelming the spectator with raw, visceral aspects of the body. The close-ups almost seem to penetrate deeper into Nina's skin because of their progressive intensity, first showing slight changes in her skin texture, then nastier scrapes and bumps, and finally magnifying rapidly spreading, foul, open sores. The idea behind this painful progressive exposure could be that her skin loses its function of maintaining the integrity of the body and thereby the integrity of the self. We experience this effect so intensely because the progression of close-ups invites us to adopt the mode of seeing-feelingly, transforming our own skin into a kind of resonating membrane. Steven Connor describes this phenomenon as follows: '[In moments like this,] we defend ourselves against penetration . . . by shattering or multiplication . . . the skin can take prophylactic refuge in the very pullulation that it dreads, borrowing a survival from the very kind of life it fears will carry it away piecemeal' (Connor 2004: 244). The emotional effect of *Black Swan* is therefore realized by directly addressing the spectator's skin as a seeing organ beyond the level of narrative comprehension. The film allows embodied pain to emerge indefinitely from underneath aestheticized pain in ways that truly penetrate the spectators' skins as well, making them shiver in horror. As a result, the concept of spiritual self as something separate from the embodied self fades out, prompting different insights that are physically felt during the affective-aesthetic experience of the film.

## Uncanny Personhood

The second theme that is central in *Black Swan* is that of the self and the uncanny double. This is epitomized in the way in which Nina seeks confirmation
of her sense of self by habitually studying her appearance in mirrors or other
reflective surfaces. Indeed, mirrors function as very prominent mise-en-scène
elements in *Black Swan*, by means of which the film expresses the multiplication of Nina's selfhood. Such a multiplication is symptomatic of the severe
dissociative identity disorder from which Nina suffers. In Lacanian thinking,
a mirror functions as a mechanism in the constitution of subjectivity that is
based on a specular (mis)recognition of the self in early infancy (the mirror
stage). By contrast, in *Black Swan*, mirrors function to display Nina's repressed
sexuality, which ultimately finds its expression in her uncanny double. Already
in the first dressing room scene we are shown Nina's impending mental insta-
bility, which will lead to the dissolution of her self. In this scene, the frame is
filled with mirrors of different sizes and forms, creating the distorting effect
of funhouse mirrors. A similar but even more confusing kaleidoscopic effect
occurs in the scene in which Nina returns home after having spent a wild night
on the town with Lily. In this scene, Nina is shot through a sympetalous mirror
that multiplies her reflection and thus directly communicates to the spectator
the stage of her mental breakdown.

Soon Nina's reflection starts living its own life – with dreadful consequences. It appears both inside and outside the mirror, materializing in the
flesh. This has a particularly uncanny effect, as in the scene in which Nina is
measured for her swan costume. First she sees her own reflection multiplied in
the mirrors placed both in front of and behind her. Suddenly, one of the reflections scratches at its shoulder blade, then turns around and gazes forcefully
at Nina. In the rehearsal scene that follows soon after, Nina's reflection stops
mirroring her movements and confronts her directly, and even emerges from
behind her back as if it were about to attack her, until somebody turns out the
lights and the reflection disappears.

The horror effect of these scenes seems to be based on experience of the
uncanny, prompted directly by the corporeal aesthetics of the film. This applies especially to the scenes in which Nina's reflection acquires its own life
outside the mirror as a hallucination in flesh and blood. This means blood in

a literal sense, too, when Nina submerges herself in a bathtub and drops of blood fall into the bath water out of nowhere, suggesting the presence of her uncanny double. A large part of the scene is shot from Nina's point of view under water, and it is from this same perspective that we see the uncanny double suddenly appearing above her. The shock effect of the point-of-view shot conveys what Nina experiences when the uncanny double appears: the feeling of losing hold of one's subjectivity. The most horrific confrontation between Nina and her uncanny double occurs in the scene in which the spectre gloomily appears in the kitchen, masquerading as heavily bleeding 'Beth'. Nina escapes from the menacing intruder into her mother's room, which is filled with her paintings of Nina, only to find that the paintings have turned into moving portraits with monstrous features. Cacophonously, the portraits chant the words 'sweet girl', while Nina rushes to tear them down from the wall. She glances in the mirror and sees the appearance of her bleeding, uncanny double furiously approaching her, but this just turns out to be her concerned mother. The element of blood functions as a powerful indicator of the extent to which Nina's hallucinations have acquired a material form, and it tangibly undermines the spectator's physical comfort, eliciting an immediate and entrenched emotional response. This is perhaps because blood is abject matter, as it is expelled from the inside of the body. Like the hallucination itself, blood transgresses the boundaries between 'inside' and 'outside' as Julia Kristeva (1982) has famously argued. As well, the sight of blood directly affects us because it addresses the spectator's own vulnerability to injury, transmitting pain from the film's (bleeding) body to the spectator's body.

Apart from the uncanny double, her rival, dancer Lily, also reflects Nina's dissociative sense of self. One might argue that Lily could actually be considered Nina's mirror projection instead of an actual character. In other words, Lily could be seen as Nina's mental image onto which she projects repressed aspects of her self, particularly her sexuality and sensuality.[10] There are many hints in the film that seem to suggest this. The first time Nina sees Lily is through a subway window, right after she has studied her own reflection in the very same pane. In the dressing room scene, which introduces this character, the image composition frames Nina and Lily together in the same mirror. At first, Lily is shot in sharp focus in the background, while Nina's face is out of focus in the foreground, after which a racking focus shot shifts from

Lily to Nina. This aesthetic element directs the spectator's attention to the interconnectedness of the two characters. Their interconnectedness is further emphasized in the club scene, in which Nina and Lily dance to music by The Chemical Brothers, with its pounding, energetic, heavy beat and a psychedelic synch line.[11] The strobe flash flickers in sync with the track, alternating between red and green light, which creates an effect that is both visceral and hypnotizing. Once more the mirrors in this scene create distortions, showing multiple versions of Nina's face warping and merging together like in a Francis Bacon painting, while the camera randomly assumes new positions, regularly breaking the 180-degree rule of continuity editing. Rothbart briefly appears on the dance floor to embrace Nina, accompanied by a female voice that hauntingly repeats the words 'sweet girl' while Nina sees a vision of herself masquerading as Odile the Black Swan. Finally we see that Nina is dancing with Lily through the distorting mirrors, but now the mirroring process turns out to be a mirage – a sort of split screen effect – so that in the end she is actually dancing with herself.[12]

The suggestion that Nina and Lily are two sides of the same personality is even stronger in the sequence after the club scene, in which Nina imagines going home with Lily and making love to her. But as soon as Nina has reached orgasm, Lily gets transformed into Nina's uncanny double. In a shot that is filmed from Nina's point of view, this figure contemptuously utters the words 'sweet girl' and then 'suffocates' Nina with a pillow. On the evening before her premiere, in the darkened coulisses of the theatre, Nina experiences a hallucination that is even stranger than the previous ones. In this hallucination Thomas transforms into Rothbart while making love to Lily, who in turn transforms into Nina's uncanny double. Both 'Thomas/Rothbart' and 'Lily/Nina' laugh and stare at Nina challengingly as they approach sexual climax. And in a crucial scene during the actual performance, Nina finds Lily in front of her dressing table mirror, getting herself ready to step in and dance the role of Odile in her place. Turning away from the mirror to face Nina, Lily again transforms into the uncanny double, whom Nina thrusts violently against a wall mirror, so furiously that the mirror breaks. A struggle ensues, during which Nina's uncanny double tries to strangle her, while with a loud cracking noise Nina's neck elongates into an S-shaped swan's neck. The struggle ends with Nina stabbing her uncanny double with a sharp piece of broken mirror – rather fitting, given the film's obsession with mirrors – after which 'she' transforms back into Lily. These scenes could suggest that Lily, as Nina's projection, embodies the sexual aspects of Nina's psyche that she has repressed, possibly because she experiences her sexuality as a (self-)destructive impulse. As a result of this repression, her self has split, and Nina's emotional psyche has taken on a two-part structure that consists of light (white) and dark (black) properties.[13] By stabbing the dark part of her self, Nina in fact internalizes its properties, and this process enables her to dance the role of Odile successfully. This course of events reminds the spectator of the archetypal notion that pain and success go hand in hand ('no pain, no gain'), and it establishes that Nina is dependent on her physical and mental pain in order to be able to perform.

In addition to the literal and metaphorical doubles in the vision (mirrors, hallucinations, screaming portraits, Lily), the use of sound forcefully contributes to the spectator's experience of the uncanny in *Black Swan*. It consists of layered, intertwined mechanical, bestial and human noises, often mixed with the lurid and haunting score by Clint Mansell. The use of sound in *Black Swan* is perhaps best understood in terms of haptic perception, which refers to a 'natural' quality of sound based on its 'material heterogeneity', to use Michel Chion's expression. The sound in *Black Swan* is exceptionally textural, not only when it expresses the growing urgency of Nina's mental dissolution, but also in its affective quality, which has a particularly powerful effect on the spectator. With its sudden, dissonant, steely, creepy, stark, piercing, cutting, rattling, fluttering, hissing, groaning, clanging, ticking, jingling, howling, booming, gasping, scraping, soaring, breaking aural violence and especially with its sinister laughing sounds, the film directly scratches, even wounds the spectator's skin. The sound in *Black Swan* is faint and echoed at first, but it gets louder towards the final stages of Nina's transmutation, so that in the end the film literally screams at the spectator. Especially in the scene with the roaring portraits, the sound makes spectators' skin crawl, confronting them directly with the overwhelming presence of creeping madness, as embodied in the uncanny double. The aesthetic complexity of these scenes compels spectatorial participation in a way that enhances our understanding of madness as originating from a lack of control over one's own perceptions.

As proposed above, a central theme in *Black Swan* is Nina's repressed sexuality, and the film strongly suggests that this is caused by her troubled relationship with her overprotective mother, Erica. In fact, Erica personifies every troubled relationship that Nina otherwise has: she is her idol (Beth), rival (Lily) and mentor (Thomas). But the relationship between Erica and Nina could also be seen as yet another conflict between the self and its double. As a former dancer in the corps de ballet, Erica projects her own unfulfilled hopes and ambitions onto her daughter, but cannot avoid being tormented by her jealousy of Nina's success. In one scene, Nina and Erica sit together sewing ribbons onto Nina's pointe shoes in front of a triptych mirror. Not only their conversation[14] but also the image composition demonstrate the stormy affective dynamics between them. In this scene, Nina is sitting on the left in the foreground of the frame, while her reflection in the mirror is visible in the background on the right side of the image. Erica is positioned exactly opposite, so that in the middle of the image Nina and Erica 'meet' along a diagonal line, as it were. The diagonal parting line in the image bespeaks mother-daughter rivalry, in which Erica seeks personal validation through Nina on the one hand, and perceives her as an 'improved' version of herself on the other. As Mark Fisher points out, this 'deadly ambivalence' contains 'the structure of the double bind which [is] at the basis of schizophrenia: two contradictory demands ("do better than I did", "don't outdo me") are made simultaneously' (Fisher 2011: 58). Thus torn between motherly pride and competitive jealousy, Erica spends her days painting portraits of Nina that fill the walls of her own room. These portraits are naïve paintings characterized by a childlike technique, especially in their unrefined use of the colours pink and green. This is part of Erica's infantilization of Nina, which seems designed to keep Nina in a state of permanent innocence and aspirational immaturity, both as a performer and as a woman.[15] In addition, due to the cultural associations they evoke, these colours communicate emotion and tension between the two characters, and as such, they clearly contribute to the affective quality of the image.

This colour combination is duplicated in the colour scheme of the apartment, which is dominated by a dark shade of green, except for Nina's room, which is mostly pink. Through this juxtaposition, the two colours gain powerful symbolic significance. In Western cultures, green is often associated with toxicity and jealousy, while pink stands for sweetness and all things 'girly'. Throughout the film, Nina is referred to as 'sweet girl' – she often wears pink clothes, and her room is filled with pink, girlish objects such as soft toys and ballerina paraphernalia. Every night, Erica winds up a pink ballerina music box that plays a movement from *Swan Lake,* in order to help Nina fall asleep. This pink instrument has a particular symbolic significance, especially when Nina destroys it. The shattered music box, on top of which the ballerina retains only one leg, is an obvious sign for Nina's psychotic breakdown.[16] But then there is a green armchair in Nina's room, which stands for Erica's poisonous influence on her life. In a scene in which she is masturbating, Nina notices to her horror and shame that Erica has been sleeping in this green armchair all along, and she quickly hides under her pink duvet. Finally, Nina destroys all things pink in her life in a violent rage. First she slams her music box to the ground, then collects all her soft toys and shoves them down the waste shaft. By destroying pink, she destroys the 'prettiness' associated with this colour[17] – a quality often disdained as aesthetically meaningless – in order to achieve 'true' beauty and greatness.

As Rosalind Galt argues, in aesthetics, colour is often excluded from the categories of 'true' beauty, because of the 'inherent inferiority' of colour as a source of emotion and superficial pleasure. More importantly, colour, and especially pink, is considered a property of the feminine, and therefore it is considered insignificant, 'perceived merely as a secondary quality of experience, and thus unworthy of serious consideration' (Galt 2011: 44). In *Black Swan*, it is indeed striking how space is coded as feminine or masculine by means of colour. Apart from Nina and Erica's apartment, the rest of the settings are dominated by black and white 'non-colours', especially Thomas's office and his apartment. Black and white can be considered non-colours, because they are more abstract and detached from nature than those in the colour wheel. Pure black and pure white do not exist in the natural world, and therefore these colours are regarded as aesthetically more significant than others. In *Black Swan* they additionally reflect the Black/White Swan duality throughout the film. By destroying pink, Nina abandons the realm of feminine prettiness, which allows her inner darkness to gain ground. This helps her to develop a sense of emotional urgency that is needed to dance Odile's part – that is, to become her own double – but she is unable to control these emotions so that, finally, they engulf her entirely. The spectator directly feels this derailment of Nina's newfound sense of urgency as a result of the film's nightmarish properties. Especially towards the end of the film, its vigorous affective quality enables the spectator to feel the emotional effect of hallu-cinatory psychosis. This is how the affective intentionality displayed in major parts of *Black Swan* compels spectators to experience its aesthetic system as madness. They are prompted to reflect on the pertinacious complacency of associating artistic creativity with insanity, loss of cognitive control, and abandonment of common human experience.

In his psychoanalytically informed theory of film, Jean-Louis Baudry erro-neously defined cinema as a form of hallucination activated by the 'cinematic apparatus' (Baudry 1976: 121). The definition is erroneous for the simple rea-son that hallucinations are perceptions experienced in a conscious state in the absence of external stimuli, and thus the definition ignores the concrete nature of the cinematic image. Cinema might be more accurately defined as a form of illusion, but this does not necessarily involve a distorted or misinter-preted perception. As Richard Allen points out, in the cinematic experience, although 'we know that what we are seeing is only a film, we nevertheless ex-perience that film as a fully realized world . . . in a manner akin to the experi-ence of a conscious fantasy' (Allen 1995: 4–5). This includes the possibility that cinema could evoke the emotional effect, if not the perceptual experience, of hallucination, without it being the cause of such a phenomenon in reality. Furthermore, this emotional effect is not limited to vision only, but it involves the spectators' *whole* bodies and *all* their senses. As Vivian Sobchack writes: 'Even at the movies our vision and hearing are informed and given meaning by our other modes of sensory access to the world: our capacity not only to see and to hear but also to touch, to smell, to taste and always to proprioceptively feel our weight, dimension, gravity and movement in the world' (Sobchack 2004: 60). The hallucinatory elements of *Black Swan* address the spectators' vision, but also their hearing as well as their sense of touch. In this way, the film evokes a holistic corporeal effect that cannot be defined in visual terms only. Already the first hallucination scene, in which Nina crosses a footbridge, shows how the film style is designed to make the spectator part of her hal-lucinations 'from the inside'. The scene involves ominous sound effects that combine hollow booming sounds with sounds of high heels on a hard floor and Nina's heavy breathing. The depth of field of this scene is enhanced, and the handheld camera alternates between point-of-view and reaction shots of Nina. Finally, there is music that starts as a faint jingle, but abruptly rises to a high pitch as we see that the approaching passerby transforms into Nina's uncanny double, which is accompanied by the sound of distant laughter. In a scene like this, the spectator's fright is caused by the aesthetic elements of cinematography and sound, organized in such a way that a 'faithful' hallucinatory effect is realized. Gradually the hallucinations acquire more tactile qualities, as in a scene in which Nina tears off the skin around her finger to a clearly audible tearing sound, or the scene in which she experiences the delusion of deliberately cutting her finger with a pair of scissors to a sharp cutting sound. According to Michel Chion, the tactile significance of sound is the effect of its 'material heterogeneity', the effect of associating feeling with the sound source. The sonic details that signify the tactility of sound are 'materializing sound indices' that cause the spectator to 'hear feelingly' (Chion 2009: 114). In scenes like these, sound affects by means of touch, the spectator's skin becoming a hearing organ. This is why the scenes described here are painful to experience. They are felt as rough touch to which the spectator's skin responds and starts to crawl. This is even more pronounced in the later scenes in the film, which literally make the spectator shiver. There is the emotional effect of two scenes in, respectively, the costume atelier and the rehearsal studio in which the uncanny double repeatedly emerges from behind Nina's back. Here, spectators may feel the double's appearance directly on their skins as chilly shivering. It is as if the affective quality of these scenes need not be made intelligible to the eye at all. At such moments, one sees with one's skin, which has become a sort of shivering retina. This evokes an uncomfortable sensation that seems to encroach upon the spectator from behind, just like Nina's uncanny double in *Black Swan*.

Eventually, Nina's hallucinations entirely permeate the spectator's experience of *Black Swan* as an emotional event. The emotional effect of the film can only be explained as a state of schizophrenia, as the spectator is positioned inside Nina's embodied mind. Take, for instance, the scene in which Nina's fully materialized uncanny double, wearing Beth's hospital gown covered in blood, appears in a corner of her kitchen. Within the cinematic event, this scene might be experienced as if the double were directly attacking the spectator instead of Nina. At first, only a hardly audible jingle, familiar from earlier hallucination scenes, suggests an unknown presence in the darkened apartment. Then Nina goes to the kitchen to wash her hands, which she imagines are covered in blood. On leaving the room, she turns off the lights at the exact moment when we hear a voice whispering, 'Sweet girl'. This is an internal diegetic sound coming from 'inside' the character's mind. Simultaneously, however, the sound is also heard to come from somewhere in the *real* scene, because at that point the physical space of the apartment and Nina's schizophrenic mind merge. It is interesting to draw a comparison between *Black Swan* and Roman Polanski's *Repulsion* (1965). In that truly classic psychological horror film, the protagonist's apartment can be seen as an analogy for her distorted mind-body, which is utterly beyond her control.[18] Thus, when Nina switches the kitchen lights back on, we suddenly see her uncanny double in the corner, accompanied by an abrupt sound effect that literally makes us jump. A startling acoustic effect of this kind is often experienced as an attack on the integrity of the spectator's body. Its penetrating effect is caused by the intimate relationship between the spectators' physical bodies and the nature of sound as a 'material event' (Altman 1992).[19]

In this scene, Nina flees from the uncanny double into the bathroom, the camera following closely. As indicated before, this camera movement is a central aesthetic element throughout the film, and its function is to blend the spectator's 'touching' and 'touched' experiences of the film. In other words, the spectators sense the hallucinations, and especially Nina's uncanny double, as tangibly present, because the camera not only makes them see the obtrusive nearness of the double's incorporeal presence, but also causes them to feel this sensation on their own skins. Nina reacts to the appearance of the uncanny double by throwing up violently, which lends the scene a disgusting gustatory and olfactory dimension. Lured by strange sobbing sounds, she then enters her mother's room, where she is confronted by the screaming portraits. The portraits yell furiously at her ('Sweet girl', 'It's my turn' and 'Fucking whore'); this is filmed from Nina's point of view to allow the spectator to feel the full impact of this scornful attack. But despite the point-of-view technique, this experience is less a matter of perceptual sharing of Nina's terror than a direct affective engagement of the spectator's body with the aesthetic specificity of the scene. As a result, the spectators experience their own bodies 'under attack' by chaotic sounds, distorted figures and jarring camera movements. Mobile frames, such as the camera riding into a close-up of Nina's terrified face, but also the movement inside the image itself, such as the approaching uncanny double in the mirror, contribute to the effect of whirling violence with which the scene enthrals the spectator. The emotional effect of the scene is full of painful entrapment and isolation, as well as the overwhelming, uncontrollable power of Nina's dark side. The scene's powerful impact is caused by the fact that it touches on the fundamental human fear of being unable to trust one's own senses. The scene conveys the uncanny sense of Nina's lived experience as she suffers from schizophrenia, which nevertheless is also the source of her creativity as a dancer. This paradox highlights the ambivalent emotions – pain and bliss – that characterize her profession. Through the film's aesthetic entrapment, these emotions are tangibly felt by the spectator too.

## Pain and Pleasure

In addition to the disturbing tension between Nina and her uncanny double, there is tension of yet another nature in *Black Swan*, namely between pleasure and pain. Not only do the emotions resulting from these antonyms dominate Nina's inner conflict, they saturate the visual design of the film as well. As a result, the tension between pain and pleasure truly structures the spectator's experience of the film, which is best characterized as sublime. The on-stage scenes in particular are exceptionally astonishing, powerful and overwhelming. What lures the spectator is the beauty of the minimal scenery, achieved by just three drapes with a tree-branch pattern, and a gargantuan full moon in the background, which alternately bathes the scene in red light or white light with a shade of green. Image composition often emphasizes the harmony of the dancers' movements, and the camera circles as if it were one of them. The vulture-inspired, contorted and tattered swan costumes (especially the black one), which were designed by Amy Westcott, create a contrasting impact of delicacy and gothic morbidity. This contrast is emphasized by the pale, angelic makeup of the Swan Queen, and the dark, sinister, sharp lines around the Black Swan's red eyes, as well as her dramatic headpiece. In the Black Swan scenes, the décor is different, aiming at an almost ecclesiastical effect, which further enhances the emotional juxtaposition. And of course there is the Tchaikovsky-inspired music and the dancing itself, especially the climax of the Black Swan variation with 24 fouetté turns,[20] during which Nina's arms sprout glossy black feathers with every rotation. In this scene, Nina dances in a circle, intoxicated with affect, while the camera circulates in the opposite direction. At the end of the phrase, the camera meets her in the middle of the stage, her feather-laden wings fully grown. She finishes the variation with a swan-like pose, arching her back like this majestic animal is wont to do. In the following extreme long shot from the audience's perspective, she is seen without the wings, but her double shadow on the stage wall still shows them. Her performance is an act of transfiguration, which Arthur Danto might describe as 'at once recognizably human and something more than human' (Danto 2005: 37). These are scenes with exceptionally breathtaking aesthetic power, which sublimates the spectator's ordinary level of experience. They have a certain overwhelming grandeur that surpasses 'every standard of sense', as Kant would have it (Kant 1968: 89). Dacher Keltner and Jonathan Haidt write that such awe-inspiring moments in our aesthetic experience are based on an ambivalent valence of the work of art that evokes both 'wonder' and 'power', pleasure and pain. As a result of this ambivalence, the artwork is experienced as 'larger than the self' (Keltner and Haidt 2003: 300). In *Black Swan*, this effect is caused by its beauty and the dynamics of movement on one hand, and the contrasting uncanny, interspecific imagery on the other.

But the awe that one feels for the aesthetic properties of the film is soon blended with painful emotions such as fury, horror and disgust. The close-ups of Nina's face regularly radiate panic, such as when she is about to step onstage. And when she leaves the stage, the lighting rapidly changes colour from green to red, which is accompanied by the sound of laughter. This is suggestive of the turbulence of coexisting negative emotions such as insecurity, jealousy and desperation, the last of which increasingly becomes ore Nina's driving force. This surge of mixed feelings is epitomized in the accelerating sound effects of mocking laughter that accompany the scenes in which Nina witnesses an erotic encounter between her dance partner David (Benjamin Millepied, who also choreographed the ballet scenes) and Lily, or in which she observes the *Pas de quatre* of the four swans. And there is the uncanny moment in the dressing room when Lily turns into Nina's splenetic, uncanny double, and Nina herself into a monstrous, long-necked creature with its vertebrae sticking out. Yet another moment that makes the spectator shiver occurs when blood spurts from

Lily after she has been stabbed with a shard of broken mirror while the whites of Nina's eyes turn red. Bestial sounds such as the flapping of wings and the sound of shredding skin accompany the performance of the Black Swan variation throughout, and the sight of black feathers sprouting from Nina's pale skin is also very disturbing. It is a grotesque sight to watch the painted webbed-foot pattern on Nina's hands creep up her arms like some poison invading her bloodstream. The black feathers that stick out of her white skin suggest impurity, which has its origin in the abject encounter between human and beast, normal and supernatural, good and evil, pain and bliss.[21] Jonathan Haidt, Paul Rozin et al. define this type of repugnance as 'animal reminder disgust' that is rooted in the belief that the body is a 'temple' that houses the soul. However, at the moment of 'animal reminder disgust', one is confronted with death and with the idea that one's spiritual self is inextricably intertwined with one's material being (Haidt, Rozin et al. 1997). And finally, there is the gaping, bloody wound in Nina's abdomen, covered with a virginal white swan costume.[22] With every dance movement this wound grows, both visibly and audibly, until it becomes a void that drains all life out of Nina, who nevertheless sighs in delight. In these scenes, which are alienating (uncanny) and excessive (sublime) at the same time, there is a bestial energy at work that challenges human order and that is located in some dark realm beyond everyday reality.[23]

Thus pain and pleasure, death and delight, excess and estrangement lie at the heart of *Black Swan*. As a cinematic event, the film is therefore best characterized as uncannily sublime, or sublimely uncanny. In his *Philosophical Enquiry*, Edmund Burke describes this kind of experience as 'rapturously terrifying'. This study, from 1757, explores the relationship between strong 'passions' and objects in the world, emphasizing the immediate experience of sublime phenomena. For many philosophers, starting with Aristotle,[24] pain and pleasure occur along a continuum that regulates our passions by directing us to minimize the negative (pain) and to maximize the positive (pleasure). In contrast, for Burke pain and pleasure are no opposite affects but qualitatively different insofar as they are both of a 'positive' nature. Pain and pleasure are 'by no means necessarily dependent on each other for their existence . . . pleasure and pain are [no] mere relations, which can only exist as they are contrasted . . . there are positive pains and pleasures, which do not at all depend upon each other' (Burke 2008: 30–31). This is why the sublime is such an important category for Burke; the sublime is 'an odd mixture [that reveals] the overlap between pain and pleasure' (Phillips 2008: xxi). When a person is faced with majestic natural scenery, for instance, the experience of the sublime overwhelms him or her through the impact of unmanageable fierceness, overwhelming dimensions, magnificence and, in particular, infinity. This experience has the tendency to 'fill the mind with that sort of delightful horror, which is the most genuine effect and truest test of the sublime' (Burke 2008: 67). In works of art, these rapturously terrifying qualities can elicit delightful horror, because works of art do not press too closely when staged by a 'true artist' who is able to impose 'generous deceit' on the spectator. Thus works of art always stay at ample distance. Such 'generous deceit' is, for instance, caused by 'a succession of the same, or others, so quickly, as to make them seem united; as is evident from the common effect of whirling about a lighted torch or piece of wood; which if done with celerity, seems a circle of fire' (Burke 2008: 125).

The overwhelmingly intense 'becoming swan' scene seems to function in a similar way. At first Nina's virtuosity makes it impossible for the spectator to 'know the dancer from the dance'.[25] In this process, the rapid metamorphosis of Nina's arms into wings conveys the thrill of self-surrender in her quest for self-transformation. The scene adopts the strategy of unity within duality – swan and human, dancer and dance. This key aesthetic element is developed faithfully to the rhythm of Tchaikovsky-inspired music. We feel the effect of unity within duality from within, while at the same time we undergo what Elaine Scarry, referring to Simone Weil and Iris Murdoch, terms a 'radical decentring' (Scarry 1999: 111). By its accelerating dynamics of movement, the scene requires us to give up the 'centred position' of our body, so that, confronted by the spectacle, we lose our stability as it were, which is part of the sublime experience. Moreover, the position of the scene within the narrative enhances the intensity of this sublime moment. As Paul Coughlin (2000) argues, the most striking moments in film often depend on the narrative environment surrounding them. The swan scene is doubtlessly the climax in Nina's quest for perfection. But even so, the moment itself reveals the lack of human feeling involved in such a quest, and it is therefore marked by both spiritual and emotional death. The scene evokes a visceral affective response, but also reflective awareness of its artistry, the dominating special effects. The scene is at once mesmerizing and estranging through what Sean Cubitt calls 'triple consciousness'. This renders the spectator 'alert to the mechanisms of illusion, delighted by their effectivity, and entranced by their developments' (Cubitt 2005: 4).[26] Richard Shusterman argues that such delight always requires sentient consciousness, an intentional awareness of experience that is recognized as sublime or extraordinary in some way (Schusterman 2005: 335). Thus as the boundary between human and animal, fantasy and reality becomes blurred in *Black Swan*, the film is sublimely mesmerizing, provoking a disorienting sense of displacement. At the same time, this sensation is placed under siege by the uncanny awareness prompted by a human being doubled by an animal. This potentially directs the spectator's attention to the almost inherent uncanny quality of cinema itself, namely that cinema always involves a phantasmatic doubling of the real world, as Laura Mulvey has argued (Mulvey 2006: 41).[27] But the scene is also an example of what Jeremy Gilbert-Rolfe calls techno-sublime insofar as its computer-generated imagery is not made only by doubling, but also by adding up and layering. Therefore the scene does not 'return' to the presence of the real world, but remains in the presence simulated by the computer (Gilbert-Rolfe 1999: 26–27, 80). It is a moment of cinematic reflection during which the film meditates on its own conditions of existence, on its own status as digitally expanded cinematographic art.

This awareness of the film's mechanisms of illusion may bring the spectator to reflect on the philosophical issues that the film embodies. The insight offered in *Black Swan* has to do with the entangled relationship between the materiality of the body and the immateriality of the soul, the tangibility of the dancer and the ethereality of dance. As phenomenology teaches us, this relationship is not dualistic but conjoined, since the body and the soul are so intimately intertwined that they cannot effectively be separated. This means that even the most transcendent experiences are always grounded in our lived-body, as Vivian Sobchack asserts. She writes about transcendent 'ex-stasis' that 'emerges from our sensual embodiment even as it seems to release us from our bodies' "ontic" constrains and demands' (Sobchack 2008: 197). She argues that in the state of ex-static transcendence the body always reflects its own sensuality, literally enabling us to feel ourselves feeling. In cinema this can be achieved by sublimating 'the experience of transcendent ex-stasis in the *affective materiality* of existence' (Sobchack 2008: 200).

This is precisely what *Black Swan* does. The film addresses the spectators' sensate bodies, bringing them into a state of ex-static pain and pleasure, and enabling them to feel the meaning of the film in and through the flesh. The haunting presence of the camera discussed throughout this chapter functions as a disembodied perceiving subject (immateriality) that is nevertheless felt as a tangibly present object (materiality). As a result, the spectators experience the film, fully aware of their own bodies by virtue of sharing the camera's perceptual field. There is also the amplified sighing sound effect that is heard every time Nina takes a step closer to her darker self; this sound effect exemplifies the power of cinema to generate horror by means of suggesting instead of revealing. As Curtis Harrington has argued, that what takes place off-screen in the imagination of the spectator is the most powerful dramatic tool for building tension and fright. This is horror borne out by the anticipation of the final revelation, not the witnessing of it (Harrington 1952: 195). But even if the source of a sound is invisible (immateriality), its material heterogeneity, signifying its tactile quality, opens it up to the spectator's perception (materiality). The close-ups of wounded, transforming and mutilated skin create a mimetic exchange between the 'skin of film' – to use Laura Marks's expression – and our own spectatorial skin (materiality). This results in something equivalent to the 'commingling skins' through which, in Michel Serres's thinking, soul emerges (immateriality). Serres writes: 'Body and soul are not separate but blend inextricably . . . on the skin. Thus two mingled bodies do not form a separate subject and object. . . . When I touch . . . I feel the soul like a ball passing from one side to the other of the point of contact, the soul quickens when faced with such unpredictability' (Serres 2008: 26).

In his attempt to loosen up Nina emotionally in a private training session, Thomas instructs her to feel his touch and to respond to this touch. In this scene, the camera follows the direction of his touch, lingering on the point where there is contact between them (figure 5.2). The movement of the camera functions as proximity to the touching itself. Thus proximity is brought across to the spectators, so that they literally feel the touching and being touched in the scene. But Thomas and Nina's encounter is not an example of mingled bodies in Serres's sense, because Nina refuses to respond to Thomas's touch. The question could be raised as to whether this scene is 'politically correct' from the perspective of gender equality. Thomas's behaviour can be

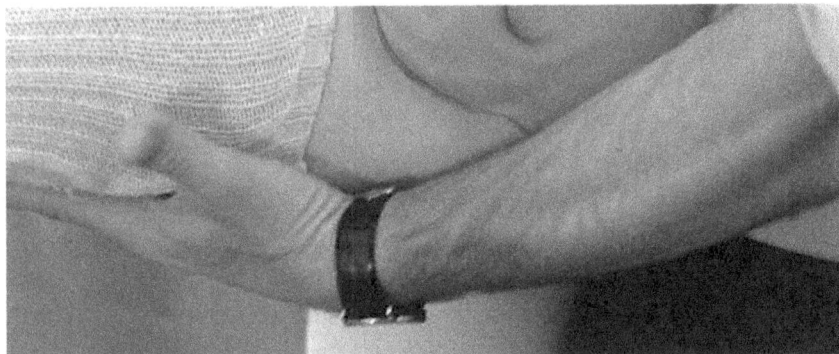

**Figure 5.2.** Touch without contact. Screen capture, *Black Swan* (2010).

interpreted as a moment of erotic intrusion, the moment when a woman who has initially said 'no' is persuaded to say 'yes' by her sheer fascination with the man's virility. Whether or not this is the case here is not my main concern, as the scene's significance is more appropriately found on another level. Thomas temporarily disables Nina's agency by subjecting her to raw choreographic material, so that he can mould her as he pleases, not only physically but also emotionally.

But the scene also makes a statement about the relationship between the toucher and the touched. By refusing to respond to Thomas's touching, Nina renders herself unable to be touched – and as a result, Thomas experiences his powerlessness as a choreographer. In the philosophy of touch, the so-called theoretical model has traditionally been central. In this concept, the subject touches the object in order to gain knowledge of that object. But Thomas's touching Nina is not about knowing; rather, the scene is about the untouchability of one subject (Nina), confronting the touching subject Thomas with his failure to touch. To touch someone who refuses to touch back is to touch without contact, to touch without touching. And when Nina finally responds to touch, it is to Lily's, not Thomas's – albeit Lily's touch is merely Nina's hallucination. The affective materiality of their lovemaking scene is created by alternating reaction shots of Nina's ecstatic face and shots from her point of view. This is combined with shots of her skin transforming with an emphatic cracking sound, as if something were about to burst through it. For Nina, the pleasure of orgasm is combined with the pain of self-transformation. But Nina's response to touch does not mean that she now opens up to the other, given that Lily is a hallucination. She does not share herself with the other – and sharing is at the heart of touching and contact, as Jacques Derrida argues (Derrida 2005: 199).

The lovemaking scene is a moment of counterfeit reciprocity, because Nina does not truly share herself with the other. This inability to share herself leads to her alienation from the world and to imprisonment in her own private world, filled with increasingly frightening confrontations with her uncanny double. Nina's self-absorption and her inability to lose herself is not a form of perfectionism, but a failure to be in contact with the world, to have a 'dancing connection' with the world, as Glen Mazis would have it. Only by inflicting extreme pain on herself does she become able to dance the part of Odile. As Nina is about to step onstage as the Black Swan, the cracking sound that accompanies the sprouting feathers suggests piercing pain, which she nevertheless welcomes with delighted pleasure. However, this is not a kind of transformative pain that would (re)establish her relationship with the world; it is, instead, addictive emotional pain turned inside out. This is perhaps the reason why Nina no longer even seems to feel her pain; she experiences only 'perfection'. It is this insensitivity to pain that allows her to become even more detached from her physical body rhythm in favour of her artistic, 'immaterial' body – albeit one that is sexually passionate and 'carnally' uninhibited – which then leads to ultimate self-destruction.

As on stage Nina prepares to throw herself from the cliff as the White Swan, we witness the bloodstain in her costume growing larger every time she flaps her 'wings'. At the same time, the camera tracks backwards and the image cuts to an extreme long shot, revealing the beauty of the scenery and the movement of the dance in its entirety. In this scene, the stab wound itself is the object of affective materiality, framed as an opening to the immateriality of death. The spectator experiences this as uncannily sublime, enjoying the aesthetic salience of the scene and dreading its affective significance: blinding ambition at the expense of body and soul. The meaningful philosophical comment that *Black Swan* makes is on the relationship between body and soul. It presents itself to the spectator's embodied awareness in such a way that the film becomes both emotionally tangible and subject to intellectual reflection.

Losing insight into the relationship between the body and the world results in loss of the soul; this is what the film embodies in meaning. This is the true tragedy of Nina's ambition. In her struggle for perfection, she becomes her own uncanny creation, her place in the world now occupied by an immaterial hallucination, while she herself falls into a void. The ending is affectively powerful although anti-cathartic, leaving the spectator with a feeling that Nina's uncannily sublime performance was not really worth the sacrifice of her lived-body. Like *Requiem for a Dream* and *The Wrestler*, *Black Swan* cancels out any sense of narrative alleviation, avoiding any conclusion that the suffering in the film is somehow justified by the story it tells. Furthermore, the ending shows that, faced with the material limitations of the body, a strategy whereby personality is split into embodied and disembodied will be unsuccessful. Acknowledgement of this failure potentially allows for something new to emerge, such as a need for an embodied strategy to deal with pain and the possibility of death.

## Notes

Many thanks to Tim Evans and Robert Sinnerbrink for their helpful comments on the earlier version of this chapter.

1. Münsterberg 2002: 180–81
2. Although one could also argue that Nina's artistic progress is energized by her deteriorating mental state. Her personality is split into the white character of Odette and the black character of Odile, which results in her 'killing' her darker double, and thereby incorporating it into herself.
3. Vincent Cassel, who plays Thomas, compares the character to George Balanchine, the founder of the New York City Ballet and 'a control freak, a true artist using sexuality to direct his dancers'. E. Douglas, 2010, 'Vincent Cassel Back for *Eastern Promises 2*', *Comingsoon*. Retrieved 22 July 2012 from http://www.comingsoon.net/news/movienews.php?id=68570.
4. 'I tried to develop something out of Dostoevsky's "The Double", set in the ballet world, and then one day I went to see *Swan Lake*. I had never seen it before, and seeing a black swan and white swan played by the same ballerina, suddenly a light went off in my head because there I had the whole doppelganger thing. And even better than "The Double," it had a really, really strong character divide – one was white, one was black. I had kind of a "Eureka!" moment'. S. Macaulay, 2011, 'Turn Out: Darren Aronofsky's "Black Swan"', *Filmmaker*,

25 February. Retrieved 27 December 2012 from http://filmmakermagazine. com/20334-turn-out-darren-aronofskys-black-swan/.

5.  Mansell explains in an interview how he transcribed the original music by Tchaikovsky into his computer and then 'deconstructed and reconstructed' it as contemporary film score: 'Swan Lake is quite vivid – almost like a silent film in that it is telling you everything that is going on. For a contemporary film score, to do that would have been quite melodramatic, so it was a case of trying to find the tones within it that corresponded with what was going on in the film and then experimenting with those tones.' Because of the use of Tchaikovsky's music, Mansell's score was deemed ineligible for entry into the 2010 Academy Awards for Best Original Score. B. McNulty, 2011, 'Clint Mansell Interview for Black Swan Soundtrack', *The Telegraph,* 20 January. Retrieved 16 January 2014 from http://www.telegraph.co.uk/culture/music/8271034/Clint-Mansell-interview-for-Black-Swan-soundtrack.html.

6.  In contrast, certain contemporary dance techniques, such as the Limón technique, emphasize 'the natural rhythms of fall and recovery and the interplay between weight and weightlessness to provide dancers with an organic approach to movement that easily adapts to a range of choreographic styles'. Retrieved 16 January 2013 from http://limon.org.

7.  The scene is reminiscent of Sara's failed diet attempt in *Requiem for a Dream*, a sign of obsession with attaining perfection, which is also represented as a haunting double in this film: the more youthful Sara 'appearing' on *The Tabby Tibbons Show*.

8.  Although there are other factors that contribute to Nina's 'madness', which are dealt with elsewhere in this chapter. These include the disturbingly infantilizing relationship with her mother (the 'Big Swan'), her guilt about having usurped Beth (the 'Dying Swan'), and her confused sexual feelings towards Lily (the 'Black Swan'). In addition, there is her self-sacrificing masochism, which Aronofsky associates with the pursuit of perfection not only in *Black Swan*, but throughout his entire oeuvre.

9.  Alternatively, one might claim that all Nina's attempts to deny the flesh are aiming at her notion of perfection. Yet this is the perfection of the White Swan, of ethereality beyond embodiment, which denies all innate desires (appetite, sex drive) that are linked to the flesh.

10. In psychoanalysis, this 'return of the repressed' is the process by which repressed elements reappear as unconscious projections, which are perceived in the conscious world as exclusive 'properties' of someone else (Rycroft 1968: 125–26).

11. The track is 'Don't Think' from their 2010 album *Further*.

12. It is very difficult to see what is going on in this 48-second scene unless one watches it frame by frame. In addition to the multiple doublings of Nina into both the Black and White Swans as well as into Lily, the visual elements of the

scene include the Black Swan's red eyes, the moon from the *Swan Lake* set, and butterflies from the wallpaper in Nina's bedroom, symbolizing metamorphosis and transformation.

13. This configuration in fact epitomizes the paranoid-schizoid position as first postulated by Melanie Klein (Rycroft 1968: 111).

14. Erica: I just don't want you to make the same mistake I did . . . as far as my career was concerned.
    Nina: What career?
    Erica: The one I gave up to have you.
    Nina: You were 28 and only in . . . [stops]
    Erica: Only what?
    Nina: Nothing.

15. A position to which Nina often condemns herself by sitting on the floor like a child instead of in a chair.

16. The image has a symbolic significance as well, since it suggests that in order to create something new (to be 'reborn') one first has to destroy oneself. It is a recurring theme in the cinema of Aronofsky.

17. This is also obvious from an exchange between Nina and Erica at the breakfast table, in which they notice the 'pretty' shade of a pink grapefruit.

18. The connection between *Black Swan* and *Repulsion* has been noted by many critics. Mark Fisher writes how in *Black Swan* 'we are always inside Nina's paranoid schizophrenia, just as we are inside the madness of Carole (Catherine Deneuve) in Polanski's *Repulsion*' (Fisher 2011: 59). Many critics see similarities between *Black Swan* and Michael Powell and Emeric Pressburger's *The Red Shoes* (1948) as well, but Aronofsky himself says that he was not influenced by this film at all. Macaulay, 'Turn Out'.

19. Julian Hanich describes these kinds of sound effects as 'scare chords' (Hanich 2010: 136–138).

20. Actually performed by Sarah Lane, a soloist at the prestigious American Ballet Theatre at the time of writing. The Black Swan coda in the 'real' *Swan Lake* choreographed by Marius Petipa actually contains 32 continuous *fouettés rond de jambe en tournant*, a performance that is not seen on stage in Aronofsky's film.

21. On this significance of abjection see Creed 1993.

22. One critic of *The New Yorker* defines this as an image of 'a disappointed vagina'. J. Acocella, 2010, 'Black Swan in Red Shoes', *The New Yorker,* 23 December. Retrieved 13 December 2013 from http://www.newyorker.com/online/blogs/newsdesk/2010/12/black-swan-in-red-shoes.html.

23. From a Žižekian (2000) perspective, it might be claimed that the scene is an example of the Lacanian Sublime, because it renders visible the animalistic substance of being human.

24. In his *Rhetoric*, Aristotle writes: 'We may lay it down that Pleasure is a movement, a movement by which the soul as a whole is consciously brought into its normal state of being; and that Pain is the opposite' (Aristotle 2010: 39).

25. An expression from William Butler Yeats's poem 'Among School Children' (1928).

26. Paul Crowther calls this phenomenon an 'alethetic experience', which occurs when a work of art is so extraordinarily succesful that it makes us reflectively aware of its own status as a 'made thing' (Crowther 1993: 42).

27. And of course *Black Swan* as a whole can be seen as the double of *Swan Lake*, as Mark Fisher argues (Fisher 2011: 61). In a similar vein, one could argue further that the constant doubling in *Black Swan* also thematizes the reflective character of the film as a cinematic work that is self-consciously parasitic on another form of art (ballet), as well as on other films (*Repulsion, The Red Shoes*) and film genres (the dance movie, melodrama, psychological horror).

# Conclusion

Throughout this book I have attempted to show how the relationship between cinema and spectator is to be considered an active process, in which emotion may facilitate philosophical reflection. My emoting with the films by Aronofsky has brought me to the conclusion that *the author* is still a relevant concept in the study of the affective-aesthetic functioning of cinema, because it invites one to imagine the film-spectator relationship as a co-creative process. In their engagement with cinema, spectators often seem to use their intuitive understanding of the process of filmmaking. In their textbook on film analysis, Maria Pramaggiore and Tom Wallis argue that both the aesthetic appreciation and the affective significance that the spectators derive from a film always depend on their understanding of the creative or artistic choices the filmmaker has made (Pramaggiore and Wallis 2011: 10). According to Bruce Isaacs, such understanding is necessary in order to establish a 'measure of intent' in the film, which is crucial in film analysis (Isaacs 2008: 25). In the context of aesthetics, Paul Crowther states that in appreciating art:

> [W]e empathize with that personal vision of the world, or . . . those feelings or intentions which we take to be embodied in a work's formal structure. Here, at the very least, the grounds of our appreciation logically presuppose that we believe the work to be what it seems to be, that is, a product of human artifice, and not a fortuitous natural formation, or the product of animal ingenuity. (Crowther 1993: 22)

Similarly, I have argued that our 'spectatorial desire' to understand the creative choices within a film corresponds both with the 'authorial desire' to create and the film's 'desire to be' (Dufrenne). Many critics of authorship as a critical concept – even Barthes – have retained a certain desire for the author, for instance when talking about the pleasure that the reader/spectator gets from literature/film: 'in a way, I desire the author; I need his figure . . . as he needs mine' (Barthes 1975: 27).

Thus, in the cinematic experience, the spectators seem to identify with the process of making, for lack of a better word, thereby imagining the filmmaker when they search for particular intentional aesthetic clues. In other words, we do not merely desire the author, we desire the authorial process of making as well. Many recent theorists of authorship seem to share this view. Paisley Livingston writes that even if the spectators do not know exactly what went on during the making of the film, their interpretive process requires them to attribute affective attitudes and deeper meaning to the filmmaker's expressive-creative activity (Livingston 1997: 146). Thus, to view and to interpret a film is to take part in a creative process that is functionally aesthetic. Spectator and filmmaker encounter each other in a relationship in which one 'complements' the other. For a film cannot be but an intended object, and the film scholar can only be part of the phenomenon itself – the cinematic event – that he or she seeks to understand. This is why all films always open themselves up to multiple interpretations. There is no recourse to pre-established signification anchored either in the author or in the spectator. This means that there is no guarantee – nor should there be – that the emotional sensations of one spectator will be shared by another.

Needless to say, this approach poses challenges to scholarly validity and rigor, a challenge with which I have often been confronted on the grounds of my affinity for the phenomenological method. Can such an approach, to which direct and individual experience is central, be considered valid and trustworthy? Interestingly, at the time of writing this book there was a vivid debate about scholarly methodologies on the Film-Philosophy discussion list. The debate concerned two different – and allegedly conflicting – approaches to cinema. The one view embraced textual formalism based on the organizational structure of film, and the other favoured impressionistic criticism based on romantic film-philosophy. This book offers itself as a contribution to this debate, starting from the premise that these approaches do not negate each other. As Vivian Sobchack argues, film-phenomenology is 'a mode of empirical and qualitative research that demands focus not only on the cinematic text but also on the cinematic experience' (Sobchack 2011: 192). This includes careful attention to the effects and functioning of cinematic aesthetics, but also to the lived experience or 'impression' of the film. In other words, the process comprises attempts to respond to the film on its own terms, thus reaching an interpretation. Furthermore, as Robert Sinnerbrink points out, the only way to debate whether films can be philosophical is through 'detailed analyses and critical interpretations of the films themselves', by doing 'justice to the aesthetic complexities of film' (Sinnerbrink 2011: 122–23). In my analyses, I have used as central concepts noise, rhythm, grief, masochism and the uncanny sublime, but this was not done in an attempt to force meaning on the films I discussed; on the contrary, I feel as if these concepts were actually *given* to me by the affective-aesthetic system of the films themselves while I was engaging with them. This means that such thematic concepts or even meanings as I encountered in the films do not simply equal subjective impressions based on my personal biography, for instance. Instead, they are instances of the 'vital materiality', to use Jane Bennett's (2010) term, that constitutes the films themselves, and that induces in the spectator affective-aesthetic openness towards the films.

Throughout this book I have tried to demonstrate the way in which Aronofsky's cinema often seems to exploit the discrepancy between the psychological/cognitive and the corporeal/affective. I found that this was epitomized in the troubled relationship between feeling bodies in pain and psychological minds in turmoil. This discrepancy invites an affective/corporeal way of engaging with the aesthetic system of these films, which in turn reveals a philosophical dimension that otherwise might remain hidden in purely formalist approaches. In a co-creative, reciprocal manner, the films pose questions to us that lead to reflection, exploration and interpretation as a way of completing the cinematic experience, so that this ends in 'a consummation and not a cessation' (Csikszentmihalyi 1975: 142). Consummation is a process that seems to go hand-in-hand with aesthetic appreciation of the films. Within film studies I find aesthetic appreciation an underdeveloped topic, something that would merit a separate research project altogether. For the time being, I propose that we admire cinema, and for that matter art in general, because cinema invites us to complete it actively and to expand its influence sensuously, experientially and intellectually. Aesthetic appreciation emerges when spectators actualize the 'vision on the world' that film enacts, in and through their minds, bodies and souls. In other words, appreciation is a performative act, a way of meeting the film halfway.

'Meeting halfway' is Karen Barad's (2006) metaphor for quantum en-tanglement. This is the ontological condition of all individuals in their shared, intra-active, co-creative constitution. From this, individual agencies emerge as ever-changing possibilities of reciprocal becoming. Experiencing the cin-ematic event as a 'halfway meeting' suggests that in order for the affective intentionality of the film and the spectator to converge, both parties must 'exit themselves' to come into contact with each other. The spectators must exit their life-world, while the film exists outside the realm of representation, both becoming co-participants in the sensuous event that is cinema. Thus 'meet-ing halfway' is an apt description for the methodological approach that I have used and developed in this book. By so doing, I have attempted to take into account that understanding cinema does not come from observing films at a distance, but rather from direct, bodily engagement with them, even when this engagement turns out to be conditioned by pain. In addition, I have tried to remain conscious of my own analytic and interpretative process in my read-ing of Aronofsky's films. Consequently I am not claiming that Aronofsky's thoughts and intentions would be similar to my interpretations. Rather, I have attempted to provide an account of how meaning emerges when one engages with film co-creatively, a situation made possible by affective, sensuous fluc-tuation between the spectator's body and the cinematic body.

# Appendix
## Darren Aronofsky Filmography

**1991**

*Supermarket Sweep* (short)
Directed by: Darren Aronofsky
Written by: Darren Aronofsky
Main cast: Seth Gitell, Sean Gullette, Maya Nadkarni, Peter A. Pappas
Country: USA
Language: English

*Fortune Cookie* (short)
Directed by: Darren Aronofsky
Written by: Hubert Selby Jr.
Produced by: Darren Aronofsky, Jody Teora
Director of photography: Lisa Stoll
Main cast: Stanley B. Herman
Country: USA
Language: English

**1993**

*Protozoa* (short)
Directed by: Darren Aronofsky
Written by: Darren Aronofsky
Produced by: Eric Watson
Director of photography: Matthew Libatique
Production designer: Patrick Sherman
Edited by: John Wolfenden
Original score by: Michael Pollack
Main cast: Michael Bonitatis, Lucy Liu, Damon Whitaker
Country: USA
Language: English

## 1994

*No Time* (short)
Directed by: Darren Aronofsky
Written by: Robert Dylan Cohen, Chas Mastin, Billy Portman, Alissa Rosen
Produced by: Nan Helm
Director of photography: Matthew Libatique
Production designer: Warren Alan Young
Edited by: Debrah Light
Original score by: Michael Pollack
Main cast: Robert Dylan Cohen, Chas Mastin, Billy Portman, Alissa Rosen, Andrea Shreeman
Country: USA
Language: English

## 1998

*Pi*
Directed by: Darren Aronofsky
Written by Darren Aronofsky
Produced by: Eric Watson
Director of photography: Matthew Libatique
Production designer: Matthew Maraffi
Edited by: Oren Sarch
Original score by: Clint Mansell
Main cast: Sean Gullette, Mark Margolis, Ben Shenkman
Country: USA
Language: English

## 2000

*Requiem for a Dream*
Directed by: Darren Aronofsky

Written by: Hubert Selby Jr. and Darren Aronofsky
Produced by: Eric Watson and Palmer West
Director of photography: Matthew Libatique
Production designer: James Chinlund
Edited by: Jay Rabinowitz
Costume designer: Laura Jean Shannon
Original score by: Clint Mansell
Main cast: Ellen Burstyn, Jared Leto, Jennifer Connelly, Marlon Wayans
Country: USA
Language: English

## 2006

*The Fountain*
Directed by: Darren Aronofsky
Written by: Darren Aronofsky
Produced by: Eric Watson, Arnon Milchan, Iain Smith
Director of photography: Matthew Libatique
Production designer: James Chinlund
Edited by: Jay Rabinowitz
Costume designer: Renée April
Original score by: Clint Mansell
Main cast: Hugh Jackman, Rachel Weisz, Sean Patrick Thomas
Country: USA, Canada
Language: English, Maya

## 2008

*The Wrestler*
Directed by: Darren Aronofsky
Written by: Robert Siegel
Produced by: Scott Franklin
Director of photography: Maryse Alberti

Production designer: Tim Grimes
Edited by: Andrew Weisblum
Costume designer: Amy Westcott
Original score by: Clint Mansell
Main cast: Mickey Rourke, Marisa Tomei, Evan Rachel Wood
Country: USA, France
Language: English

## 2010

*Black Swan*
Directed by: Darren Aronofsky
Written by: Mark Heyman, John McLaughlin and Andrés Heinz
Produced by: Mike Medavoy, Arnold W. Messer, Brian Oliver
Director of photography; Matthew Libatique
Production designer: Thérèse DePrez
Edited by: Andrew Weisblum
Costume designer: Amy Westcott
Original score by: Clint Mansell
Main cast: Natalie Portman, Vincent Cassel, Mila Kunis, Barbara Hershey, Winona Ryder
Country: USA
Language: English, French

## 2014

*Noah*
Directed by: Darren Aronofsky
Written by: Darren Aronofsky and John Logan
Produced by: Darren Aronofsky, Scott Franklin, Ric Kidney, Mary Parent
Director of photography: Matthew Libatique
Production designer: Mark Friedberg
Edited by: Andrew Weisblum

Costume designer: Michael Wilkinson
Original score by: Clint Mansell
Main cast: Russell Crowe, Jennifer Connelly, Douglas Booth, Logan Lerman,
Emma Watson, Anthony Hopkins, Ray Winstone
Country: USA
Language : English

# Bibliography

Aaron, M. 2007. *Spectatorship: The Power of Looking On*. London: Wallflower Press.

Adamson, G. 2011. 'The Real in the Rococo', in H. Hills (ed.), *Rethinking the Baroque*. Surrey: Ashgate, pp. 143–57.

Albano, C.L. and B.R. Sugar with M. Benson. 2000. *The Complete Idiot's Guide to Pro-Wrestling*. Indianapolis: Alpha Books.

Allen, R. 1995. *Projecting Illusion: Film Spectatorship and the Impression of Reality*. Cambridge: Cambridge University Press.

Altman, R. 1992. 'The Material Heterogeneity of Recorded Sound', in R. Altman (ed.), *Sound Theory, Sound Practice*. London: Routledge, pp. 15–34.

Aristotle. 2010. *Rhetoric*, trans. W.R. Roberts. New York: Cosimo Classics.

Armstrong, I. 2000. *The Radical Aesthetic*. Oxford: Blackwell.

Aronofsky, D. 1998. *Pi: Screenplay and The Guerrilla Diaries*. London: Faber & Faber.

Artaud, A. 2001. 'On Suicide', trans. D. Rattray. In J. Hirschman (ed.), *Artaud Anthology*. San Francisco: City Lights, pp. 56–58.

Barad, K. 2007. *Meeting the Universe Halfway: Quantum Physics and the Entanglement of Matter and Meaning*. Durham, NC: Duke University Press.

Barker, J.M. 2009. *The Tactile Eye: Touch and the Cinematic Experience*. Berkeley: University of California Press.

Barlow, D.H. 2000. 'Unravelling the Mysteries of Anxiety and Its Disorders from the Perspective of Emotion Theory', *American Psychologist* 55(11): 1247–263.

Barthes, R. 1975. *The Pleasure of the Text*, trans. R. Miller. New York: Hill and Wang.

Bartsch, A. 2010. 'Vivid Abstractions: On the Role of Emotion Metaphors in Film Viewers' Search for Deeper Insight and Meaning', *Midwest Studies in Philosophy* 34(1): 240–60.

Baudelaire, C. 2004. *Œuvres complètes*. Paris: Bouquins.

Baudry, J.-L. 1976. 'The Apparatus', trans. J. Andrews and B. Augst, *Camera Obscura* 1: 104–26.

Baumeister, R.F. 1988. 'Masochism ad Escape from Self', *Journal of Sex Research* 25(1): 28–59.

Beauvoir, S. de. 2003. *The Second Sex*, trans. H.M. Parshley. Harmondsworth, UK: Penguin.

Bell, C. 1958. *Art*. New York: Capricorn.

Bending, L. 2000. *The Representation of Bodily Pain in Late Nineteenth-Century English Culture*. Oxford: Oxford University Press.

Bennett, J. [Jane]. 2010. *Vibrant Matter: A Political Ecology of Things*. Durham, NC: Duke University Press.

Bennett, J. [Jill]. 2005. *Empathic Vision: Affect, Trauma, and Contemporary Art*. Stanford: Stanford University Press.

Benthien, C. 2002. *Skin: On the Cultural Border Between Self and the World*, trans. T. Dunlap. New York: Columbia University Press.

Bergman, I. 1960. 'Why I Make Movies', *Horizon* 3(1): 4–9.

Beugnet, M. 2007. *Cinema and Sensation: French Film and the Art of Transgression*. Edinburgh: Edinburgh University Press.

Bianco, J.S. 2004. 'Techno-Cinema', *Comparative Literature Studies* 41(3): 377–403.

Biro, Y. 2008. *Turbulence and Flow in Film: The Rhythmic Design*, trans. P. Salamon, Bloomington: Indiana University Press.

Bordwell, D. and K. Thompson. 2001. *Film Art: An Introduction*, 6th ed. New York: McGraw-Hill.

Brecht, B. 1976. 'A Short Organum for the Theatre', in B.F. Dukore and D.C. Gerould (eds), *Avant-Garde Drama, 1918–1939*. New York: Crowell, pp. 500–532.

Brennan, T. 2004. *The Transmission of Affect*. Ithaca, NY: Cornell University Press.

Bridgers, L. 2005. *Contemporary Varieties of Religious Experience*. Lanham, MD: Rowman and Littlefield.

Brooks, X. 2001. 'Requiem for a Dream', *Sight & Sound* 11(2): 48–49.

Buckland, W. 2012. 'Solipsistic Film Criticism: Review of *The Language and Style of Film Criticism*', *New Review of Film and Television Studies* 10(2): 288–98.

Bukatman, S. 'Disobedient Machines: Animation and Autonomy', in R. Hoffmann and I.B. White (eds), *Beyond the Finite: The Sublime in Art and Science*. Oxford: Oxford University Press, pp. 128–48.

Burke, E. 2008. *A Philosophical Enquiry*. Oxford: Oxford University Press.

Burnett, Ron. 2004. *How Images Think*. Cambridge: MIT Press.

Calhoun, C. and R.C. Solomon, 1984. 'Introduction', in C. Calhoun and R.C. Solomon (eds), *What Is an Emotion?* New York: Oxford University Press, pp. 3–40.

Chion, M. 2009. *Film: A Sound Art*, trans. C. Corbman. New York: Columbia University Press.

Code, L. 1995. *Rhetorical Spaces*. London: Routledge.

Connor, S. 2004. *The Book of Skin*. London: Reaktion Books.

Coughlin, P. 2000. 'Sublime Moments', *Senses of Cinema* 11. Retrieved 9 January 2013 from http://www.sensesofcinema.com/2000/11/sublime/.

Coward, R. 1984. *Female Desire: Women's Sexuality Today*. London: Paladin.

Creed, B. 1993. 'Horror and the Monstrous-Feminine: An Imaginary Abjection', *Screen* 27(1): 44–71.

Crowther, P. 1993. *Art and Embodiment: From Aesthetics to Self-Consciousness*. Oxford: Oxford University Press.

Csikszentmihalyi, M. 1975. *Beyond Boredom and Anxiety*. San Francisco: Jossey-Bass.

Cubitt, S. 2005. *The Cinema Effect*. Cambridge: MIT Press.

Daniel, E.V. 1994. 'The Individual in Terror', in T.S. Csordas (ed), *Embodiment and Experience: The Existential Ground of Culture and Self*. Cambridge: Cambridge University Press, pp. 229–47.

Danto, A.C. 2005. *Unnatural Wonders: Essays from the Gap between Art & Life*. New York: Columbia University Press.

D'Aquili, E.G. and A.B. Newberg. 1999. *The Mystical Mind: Probing the Biology of Religious Experience*. Minneapolis: Fortress Press.

Deleuze, G. and F. Guattari. 1987. *A Thousand Plateaus: Capitalism and Schizophrenia*, trans. B. Massumi. Minneapolis: University of Minnesota Press.

Deleuze, G. 1977. 'On Music', trans. T.S. Murphy. Retrieved 9 January 2013 from http://www.scribd.com/doc/7277240/Deleuze-On-Music.

———. 1989. *Cinema 2: The Time-Image*, trans. H. Tomlinson and R. Galeta. London: Athlone Press.

Derrida, J. 2005. *On Touching—Jean-Luc Nancy*, trans. C. Irizarry. Stanford: Stanford University Press.

Dewey, J. 1958. *Art as Experience*. New York: Capricorn Books.

———. 1981. *Experience and Nature*. Carbondale: Southern Illinois University Press.

Dijkhuizen, J.F. van. 2009. 'Religious Meanings of Pain in Early Modern England', in J.F. van Dijckhuizen and K.E.A. Enenkel (eds), *The Sense of Suffering: Constructions of Physical Pain in Early Modern Culture*. Leiden: Brill, pp. 189–220.

Dijkhuizen, J.F. van and K. Enenkel. 2009. 'Constructions of Physical Pain in Early Modern Culture', in J.F. van Dijckhuizen and K.E.A. Enenkel (eds), *The Sense of Suffering: Constructions of Physical Pain in Early Modern Culture*. Leiden: Brill, pp. 1–17.

Doane, M.A. 1980. 'The Voice in Cinema: The Articulation of Body and Space', *Yale French Studies* 60: 67–79.

Donnelly, K. 2005. *The Spectre of Sound: Music in Film and Television*. London: British Film Institute.

Dufrenne, M. 1973. *The Phenomenology of Aesthetic Experience*, trans. E.S. Casey. Evaston, IL: Northwestern University Press

———. 1987. *In the Presence of the Sensuous: Essays in Aesthetics*. Atlantic Highlands, NJ: Humanities Press.

Dulac, G. 1978. 'The Essence of the Cinema: The Visual Idea', in P.A. Sitney (ed.), *The Avant-Garde Film: A Reader of Theory and Criticism*. New York: New York University Press, pp. 36–42.

Eisenstein, S.M. 1957. *Film Form: Essays in Film Theory*, trans. J. Leyda. New York, Meridian Books.

———. 1969. *The Film Sense*, trans. J. Leyda. Orlando, FL: Harcourt.

Elsaesser, T. 2012. *The Persistence of Hollywood*. New York: Routledge.

Elster, J. 1999. *Strong Feelings: Emotion, Addiction, and Human Behaviour*. Cambridge: MIT Press.

Epstein, J. 1993a. 'Magnification', in R. Abel (ed.), *French Film Theory and Criticism 1907–1939*. Princeton: Princeton University Press, pp. 235–41.

———. 1993b. 'The Senses', in R. Abel (ed.), *French Film Theory and Criticism 1907–1939*. Princeton: Princeton University Press, pp. 241–46.

———. 2012. *Critical Essays and New Translations*. Chicago: The University of Chicago Press.

Esch, K. 2006. '"I Don't See Any Method at All": The Problem of Actorly Transformation', *Journal of Film and Video* 58(1/2): 95–107.

Fisher, M. and A. Jacobs. 2011. 'Debating *Black Swan*: Gender and Horror', *Film Quarterly* 65(1): 58–62.

Fisher, P. 2002. *The Vehement Passions*. Princeton: Princeton University Press.

Foucault, M. 1977. 'What is an Author?' in D.F. Bouchard (ed.), *Language, Counter-memory, Practice*. Ithaca, NY: Cornell University Press, pp. 113–38.

———. 1996. 'Sex, Power, and the Politics of Identity', in S. Lotringer (ed.), *Foucault Live: Collected Interviews 1961–1984*. New York: Semiotext(e), pp. 382–90.

Frampton, D. 2006. *Filmosophy: A Manifesto for a Radically New Way of Understanding Cinema*. London: Wallflower Press.

Freeland, C.A. 1999. 'The Sublime in Cinema', in C. Plantinga and G.M. Smith (eds), *Passionate Views: Film, Cognition, and Emotion*. Baltimore: Johns Hopkins University Press, pp. 65–83.

———. 2001. 'Explaining the Uncanny in *The Double Life of Véronique*', *Film and Philosophy* 6 (Special Issue on Horror): 34–50.

Freud, S. 1957. 'Mourning and Melancholia', in *Standard Edition* vol. 14, pp. 237–58.

Funt, D. 1968. *Diderot and the Aesthetics of the Enlightenment*. Geneva: Librairie Droz.

Galt, R. 2011. *Pretty: Film and the Decorative Image*. New York: Columbia University Press.

Gilbert-Rolfe, J. 1999. *Beauty and the Contemporary Sublime*. New York: Allworth Press.

Girard, R. 2005. 'From Ritual to Science', in N. Abbas (ed.), *Mapping Michel Serres*. Ann Arbor: University of Michigan Press, pp. 10–23.

Girgus, S. 2010. *Levinas and the Cinema of Redemption: Time, Ethics, and the Feminine*. New York: Columbia University Press.

Glucklich, A. 2000. *Sacred Pain: Hurting the Body for the Sake of the Soul*. Oxford: Oxford University Press.

Goddard, M., B. Halligan and P. Hegarty. 2012. 'Introduction', in M. Goddard, B. Halligan and P. Hegarly (eds), *Reverberations: The Philosophy, Aesthetics and Politics of Noise*. London: Continuum, pp. 1–11.

Gunning, T. 1990. 'The Cinema of Attractions: Early Cinema, Its Spectator, and the Avant-Garde', in T. Elsaesser (ed.), *Early Cinema: Space Frame Narrative*. London: British Film Institute, pp. 56–62.

Gustafson, D. 1989. 'Grief', *Noûs* 23: 457–79.

Haidt, J. et al. 1997. 'Body, Psyche and Culture: The Relationship between Disgust and Morality', *Psychology and Developing Societies* 2: 107–31.

Hallam, J. with M. Marshment. 2000. *Realism and Popular Cinema*. Manchester: Manchester University Press.

Hanich, J. 2010. *Cinematic Emotion in Horror Films and Thrillers: The Aesthetic Paradox of Pleasurable Fear*. London: Routledge.

Haraway, D.J. 1991. *Simians, Cyborgs and Women: The Reinvention of Nature*. New York: Routledge.

Harbord, J. 2007. *The Evolution of Film: Rethinking Film Studies*. Cambridge: Polity Press.

Harrington, C. 1952. 'Ghoulies and Ghosties', *The Quarterly of Film Radio and Television* 7(2): 191–202.

Hart, L. 1998. *Between the Body and the Flesh: Performing Sadomasochism*. New York: Columbia University Press.

Hill, J. 1986. *Sex, Class and Realism: British Cinema 1956–1963*. London: British Film Institute.

Himber, J. 1994. 'Blood Rituals: Self-Cutting in Female Psychiatric Inpatients', *Psychotherapy* 31(4): 620–31.

Hogan, P.C. 2011. *Affective Narratology: The Emotional Structure of Stories*. Lincoln: University of Nebraska Press.

Holler, L. 2002. *Erotic Morality: The Role of Touch in Moral Agency*. New Brunswick, NJ: Rutgers University Press.

Hume, D. 2007. 'Of Tragedy', in *The Philosophical Works of David Hume*, vol. 3. Boston: Elibron: 237–47.

Ihde, D. 1979. *Experimental Phenomenology: An Introduction*. New York: Paragon Books.

Isaacs, B. 2008. *Toward a New Film Aesthetics*. New York: Continuum.

Jackson, J. 1994. 'Chronic Pain and the Tension between the Body as Subject and Object', in T.J. Csordas (ed.), *Embodiment and Experience: The Existential Ground of Culture and Self*. Cambridge: Cambridge University Press, pp. 201–28.

James, W. 1976. *Essays in Radical Empiricism*, ed. F. Bowers. Cambridge: Harvard University Press.

————. 1997. *The Varieties of Religious Experience*: New York: Touchstone.

Kalha, H. 2005. 'Pehmeä lasku kovaan pornoon', in K. Nikunen, S. Paasonen and L. Saarenmaa (eds), *Jokapäiväinen pornomme: Media, seksuaalisuus ja populaarikulttuuri*. Tampere: Vastapaino, pp. 30–58.

Kant, I. 1968. *Critique of Judgment*, trans. J.H. Bernard. New York: Hafner.

Keller, P.E. and E. Schubert. 2011. 'Cognitive and Affective Judgements of Syncopated Musical Themes', *Advances in Cognitive Psychology* 4: 142–56.

Keltner, D. and J. Haidt. 2003. 'Approaching Awe: A Moral, Spiritual, and Aesthetic Emotion', *Cognition & Emotion* 17(2): 297–314.

Kemp, R. 2009. 'The Lived-Body of Drug Addiction', *Existential Analysis* 20(1): 120–32.

Kierkegaard, S. 1964. *The Concept of Dread*, trans. Walter Lowrie. Princeton: Princeton University Press.

Kipnis, L. 1992. '(Male) Desire and (Female) Disgust: Reading *Hustler*', in L. Grossberg, C. Nelson and P. Treichler (eds), Cultural Studies. London: Routledge, pp. 373–91.

———. 1999. *Bound and Gagged: Pornography and the Politics of Fantasy in America*. Durham, NC: Duke University Press.

Kolk, B.A. van der. 1994. 'The Body Keeps the Score: Memory and the Evolving Psycho-biology of Posttraumatic Stress', *Harvard Review of Psychiatry* 1(5): 253–65.

Kracauer, S. 1997. *The Theory of Film: The Redemption of Physical Reality*. Princeton: Princeton University Press.

Kristeva, J. 1982. *Powers of Horror: An Essay on Abjection*, trans. L.S. Roudiez. New York: Columbia University Press.

Kulezic-Wilson, D. 2008a. 'A Musical Approach to Filmmaking: Hip-Hop and Techno Composing Techniques and Models of Structuring in Darren Aronofsky's *Pi*', *Music and the Moving Image* 1(1): 19–34.

———. 2008b. 'Sound Design is the New Score', *Music and the Moving Image* 2(2): 127–31.

Kuntzel, T. 1980. 'The Film Work 2', trans. Nancy Huston, *Camera Obscura* 5: 6–69.

Laine, T. 2011. *Feeling Cinema: Emotional Dynamics in Film Studies*. New York: Continuum.

Langer, S. 1976. *Philosophy in a New Key*. Cambridge: Harvard University Press.

Leder, D. 1990. *The Absent Body*. Chicago: The University of Chicago Press.

Lefebvre, H. 1991. *The Production of Space*, trans. D. Nicholson-Smith. London: Blackwell Publishing.

Levinas, E. 1981. *Otherwise than Being, or Beyond Essence*, trans. A. Lingis. The Hague: Martinus Nijhoff Publishers.

Lindner, E.G. 2002. 'Healing the Cycles of Humiliation: How to Attend to the Emotional Aspects of "Unsolvable" Conflicts and the Use of Humiliation "Entrepreneurship"', *Peace and Conflict: Journal of Peace Psychology* 8(20): 125–38.

Livingston, P. 1997. 'Cinematic Authorship', in R. Allen and M. Smith (eds), *Film Theory and Philosophy*. Oxford: Oxford University Press, pp. 132–48.

Lord, C.M. 2009. 'Angels with Nanotech Wings: Magic, Medicine and Technology in Aronofsky's *The Fountain*, Gibson's *Neuromancer* and Slonczewski's *Brain Plague*', *Nebula* 6(4): 162–74.

Lucas, P. 2011. *Ethics and Self-knowledge: Respect for Self-interpreting Agents*. Dordrecht: Springer.

Malins, P. 2005. 'Body-Space Assemblages and Folds: Theorizing the Relationship between Injecting Drug User Bodies and Urban Space', *Journal of Media and Cultural Studies* 18(4): 483–95.

Marks, L.U. 1999. *The Skin of the Film: Intercultural Cinema, Embodiment, and the Senses*. Durham, NC: Duke University Press.

————. 2002. *Touch: Sensuous Theory and Multisensory Media.* Minneapolis: University of Minnesota Press.

————. 2010. 'A Noisy Brush with the Infinite', Noise not Noise Conference, Western Front, Vancouver, 26 March 2010.

Martin, A., B. Mousoulis and F.A. Villella. 2002. 'Editorial', *Senses of Cinema* 21. Retrieved 9 January from http://sensesofcinema.com/2002/editorial/21index/.

Mazer, S. 1998. *Professional Wrestling: Sport and Spectacle.* Jackson: University Press of Mississippi.

Mazis, G.A. 2002. *Earthbodies: Rediscovering Our Planetary Senses.* Albany: State University of New York Press.

McLane, J. 1996. 'The Voice on the Skin: Self-Mutilation and Merleau-Ponty's Theory of Language', *Hypatia* 1(4): 107–18.

McLuhan, M. 2005. *Understanding Media: The Extension of Man,* 2nd ed. London: Routledge Classics.

Merleau-Ponty, M. 1968. *The Visible and the Invisible,* trans. A. Lingis. Evanston, IL: Northwestern University Press.

————. 2002. *Phenomenology of Perception,* trans. C. Smith. London: Routledge.

Metz, C. 1982. *Psychoanalysis and Cinema: The Imaginary Signifier,* trans. C. Britton et al. London: Macmillan Press.

Mey, J.L. 2000. 'The Computer as Prosthesis: Reflections on the Use of a Metaphor', *Hermes: Journal of Linguistics* 24: 15–29.

Moreno, C.M. 2009. 'Body Politics and Spaces of Drug Addiction in Darren Aronofsky's *Requiem for a Dream', GeoJournal* 74: 219–26.

Mulvey, L. 1975. 'Visual Pleasure and Narrative Cinema', *Screen* 16(3): 6–18.

————. 2006. *Death 24 x a Second: Stillness and the Moving Image.* London: Reaktion Books.

Münsterberg, H. 2002. *Hugo Münsterberg on Film: The Photoplay: A Psychological Study.* London: Routledge.

Nevitt, L. 2010. 'Popular Entertainment and the Spectacle of Bleeding', *Popular Entertainment Studies* 1(2): 78–92.

Nietzsche, F. 1999. *The Birth of Tragedy,* trans. S, Speirs. Cambridge: Cambridge University Press.

Noudelmann, F. 2012. *The Philosopher's Touch: Sartre, Nietzsche, and Barthes at the Piano,* trans. Brian J. Reilly. New York: Columbia University Press.

Nussbaum, M.C. 2001. *Upheavals of Thought: The Intelligence of Emotions.* Cambridge: Cambridge University Press.

Paasonen, Susanna. 2011. *Carnal Resonance: Affect and Online Pornography.* Cambridge: MIT Press.

Palmer, Tim. 2006. *Brutal Intimacy: Analyzing Contemporary French Cinema.* Middletown, CT: Wesleyan University Press.

Pearlman, K. 2009. *Cutting Rhythms: Shaping the Film Edit.* Waltham, MA: Focal Press.

Peters, D. 2012. 'Touch: Real, Apparent, and Absent: On Bodily Expression in Electronic Music', in D. Peters, G. Eckel and A. Dorschel (eds), *Bodily Expression in Electronic Music: Perspectives on Reclaiming Performativity*. London: Routledge, pp. 17–34.

Phillips, A. 2008. 'Introduction', in E. Burke, *A Philosophical Enquiry*. Oxford: Oxford University Press.

Pillow, K. 2003. *Sublime Understanding: Aesthetic Reflection in Kant and Hegel*. Cambridge: MIT Press.

Pisters, P. 2010. 'Numbers and Fractals: Neuroaesthetics and the Scientific Subject', in P. Gaffney (ed.), The Force of the Virtual: Deleuze, Science, and Philosophy. Minneapolis: University of Minnesota Press, pp. 229–51.

Poole, R. 1972. *Towards Deep Subjectivity*. New York: Harper and Row.

Pramaggiore, M. and T. Wallis. 2011. *Film: A Critical Introduction*, 3rd ed. London: Laurence King.

Price, B. 2010. 'Pain and the Limits of Representation', in B. Price and J.D. Rhodes (eds), *On Michael Haneke*. Detroit: Wayne State University Press, pp. 35–48.

Prinz, J.J. 2004. *Gut Reactions: A Perceptual Theory of Emotion*. Oxford: Oxford University Press.

Putnam, F.W. 1989. 'Pierre Janet and Modern Views of Dissociation', *Journal of Traumatic Stress* 2(4): 413–29.

Quirk, T. 2011. *Bergson and American Culture: The Worlds of Willa Cather and Wallace Stevens*. Chapel Hill: University of North Carolina Press,

Riley, D. 2012. *Time Lived, Without Its Flow*. London: Capsule.

Rosen, G. 1975. 'Nostalgia: A "Forgotten" Psychological Disorder', *Psychological Medicine* 5: 340–54.

Rycroft, C. 1972. *A Critical Dictionary of Psychoanalysis*. London: Penguin.

Sartre, J.-P. 1992. *Being and Nothingness: A Phenomenological Essay on Ontology*, trans. H.E. Barnes. New York: Washington Square Press.

———. 1993. *The Emotions: Outline of a Theory*, trans. B. Frechtman. New York: Citadel Press.

———. 2012. *Saint Genet: Actor and Martyr*, trans. B. Frechtman. Minneapolis: University of Minnesota Press.

Sass, L.A. 1992. *Madness and Modernism: Insanity in the Light of Modern Art, Literature and Thought*. Cambridge: Harvard University Press.

Saxton, L. 2010. 'Ethics, Spectatorship, and the Spectacle of Suffering', in L. Downing and L. Saxton, *Film and Ethics: Foreclosed Encounters*. London: Routledge, pp. 62–75.

Scarry, E. 1985. *The Body in Pain: The Making and Unmaking of the World*. Oxford: Oxford University Press.

———. 1999. *On Beauty and Being Just*. Princeton: Princeton University Press.

Schoenfeldt, M. 2009. 'The Art of Pain Management in Early Modern England', in J.F. van Dijckhuizen and K.E.A. Enenkel (eds), *The Sense of Suffering: Constructions of Physical Pain in Early Modern Culture*. Leiden: Brill, pp. 19–38.

Schusterman, R. 2005. 'Somaesthetics and Burke's Sublime', *British Journal of Aesthetics* 45(4): 323–341.

———. 2008. *Body Consciousness: A Philosophy of Mindfulness and Somaesthetics*. Cambridge: Cambridge University Press.

Serres, M. 1995. *Genesis*, trans. G. James and J. Nielson. Ann Arbor: The University of Michigan Press.

———. 2000. *The Birth of Physics*, trans. J. Hawkes. Manchester: Clinamen Press.

———. 2007. *The Parasite*, trans. L.R. Schehr. Minneapolis: University of Minnesota Press.

———. 2008. *The Five Senses: A Philosophy of Mingled Bodies*, trans. M. Sankey and P. Cowley. London: Continuum.

Shaviro, S. 1993. *The Cinematic Body*. Minneapolis: Minnesota University Press.

Sinnerbrink, R. 2011a. 'Re-enfranchising Film: Towards a Romantic Film-Philosophy', in H. Carel and G. Tuck (eds), *New Takes in Film-Philosophy*. London: Palgrave Macmillan, pp. 25–47.

———. 2011b. *New Philosophies of Film: Thinking Images*. New York: Continuum.

Sliwinski, S. 2004. 'A Painful Labour: Responsibility and Photography', *Visual Studies* 19(2): 150–61.

Smith, J. 1999. 'Movie Music as Moving Music: Emotion, Cognition, and the Film Score', in C. Plantinga and G.M. Smith (eds), *Passionate Views: Film, Cognition, and Emotion*. Baltimore: Johns Hopkins University Press, pp. 146–67.

Smith, M. 1995. *Engaging Characters: Fiction, Emotion, and the Cinema*. Oxford: Clarendon Press.

Sobchack, V. 2004. *Carnal Thoughts: Embodiment and Moving Image Culture*. Berkeley: University of California Press.

———. 2008. 'Embodying Transcendence: On the Literal, the Material, and the Cinematic Sublime', *Material Religion* 4(2): 194–203.

———. 2011. 'Fleshing Out the Image: Phenomenology, Pedagogy, and Derek Jarman's *Blue*', in H. Carel and G. Tuck (eds), *New Takes in Film-Philosophy*. London: Palgrave Macmillan, pp. 191–206.

———. 2012. 'Being on the Screen: A Phenomenology of Cinematic Flesh, or the Actor's Four Bodies' In J. Sternagel, D. Levitt and D. Merch (eds), *Acting and Performance in Moving Image Culture: Bodies, Screens, Renderings*. Bielefeld: Transcript.

Solomon, R.C. 2007. *True to Our Feelings: What Our Emotions Are Really Telling Us*. Oxford: Oxford University Press.

Sousa, R. de. 1980. 'The Rationality of Emotions', in A. Oksenberg Rorty (ed.), *Explaining Emotions*. Berkeley: University of California Press, pp. 127–52.

Stadler, Jane. 2012. *Pulling Focus: Intersubjective Experience, Narrative Film, and Ethics.* New York: Continuum.

Stocker, M. with E. Hegeman. 1996. *Valuing Emotions.* Cambridge: Cambridge University Press.

Suyemoto, K.L. and M.L. Macdonald. 1995. 'Self-Cutting in Female Adolescents', *Psychotherapy* 31(1): 162–71.

Tan, E.S. and N.H. Frijda. 1999. 'Sentiment in Film Viewing', in C. Plantinga and G.M. Smith (eds), *Passionate Views: Film, Cognition, and Emotion.* Baltimore: Johns Hopkins University Press, pp. 48–64.

Tanner, L.E. 2007. '"Looking Back from the Grave": Sensory Perception and the Anticipation of Absence in Marilynne Robinson's *Gilead*', *Contemporary Literature* 48(2): 227–52.

Thompson, L. 2011. 'In Praise of Speed: The Value of Velocity in Contemporary Cinema', *Dandelion* 2(1): 1–15.

Thompson, M. 2012. 'Music for Cyborgs: The Affect and Ethics of Noise Music' in M. Goddard, B. Halligan and P. Hegarly (eds), *Reverberations: The Philosophy, Aesthetics and Politics of Noise.* London: Continuum, pp. 207–18.

Vaneigem, R. 1967. *The Revolution of Everyday Life: Impossible Participation or Power as the Sum of Constraints.* Retrieved 9 January 2013 from http://library.nothingness.org/articles/SI/en/display/36.

Van Leeuwen, T. 1985. 'Rhythmic Structure of the Film Text', in T.A. van Dijk (ed), *Discourse and Communication: New Approaches to the Analysis of Mass Media Discourse and Communication.* Berlin: Walter de Gruyter, pp. 216–32.

Walsh, K. 2010. 'Why Does Mickey Rourke Give Pleasure?' *Critical Inquiry* 37(1): 131–62.

White, K. 2012. 'Considering Sound: Reflecting on the Language, Meaning and Entailments of Noise', in M. Goddard, B. Halligan and P. Hegarly (eds), *Reverberations: The Philosophy, Aesthetics and Politics of Noise.* London: Continuum, pp. 233–43.

Williams, L. 1989. *Hard Core: Power, Pleasure, and the Frenzy of the Visible.* Berkeley: University of California Press.

———. 1991. 'Body Genres', *Film Quarterly* 44(4): 2–13.

———. 2001. 'Cinema and the Sex Act', *Cineaste* 27(1): 10–25.

Wilson, G.T. 1987. 'Cognitive Processes in Addiction', *British Journal of Addiction* 82: 343–53.

Wolff, J. 2008. *The Aesthetics of Uncertainty.* New York: Columbia University Press.

Woods, A. 2012. 'Mathematics, Masculinity, Madness', in G. Araoz and I. Travis (eds), *Madness in Context: Historical, Poetic, and Artistic Perspectives.* Oxford: Interdisciplinary Press, pp. 1–11.

Young, J. 2006. 'Death and Transfiguration: Kant, Schopenhauer and Heidegger on the Sublime', *Inquiry: An Interdisciplinary Journal of Philosophy* 48(2): 131–44.

Yumibe, J. 2012. *Moving Color: Early Film, Mass Culture, Modernism.* New Brunswick, NJ: Rutgers University Press.

Zeiler, K. 2010. 'The Phenomenological Analysis of Bodily Self-Awareness in the Experience of Pain and Pleasure: On Dys-appearance and Eu-appearance', *Medical Health Care and Philosophy* 15: 333–42.

Žižek, S. 2000. *The Art of the Ridiculous Sublime: On David Lynch's* Lost Highway. Seattle: University of Washington Press.

# Index

Lightning Source UK Ltd.
Milton Keynes UK
UKHW02f2105050118
315614UK00005B/366/P